Socially Responsible Investing

FOR

DUMMIES®

By Ann C. Logue

WILEY

Wiley Publishing, Inc.

Socially Responsible Investing For Dummies®

Published by
Wiley Publishing, Inc.
111 River St.
Hoboken, NJ 07030-5774
www.wiley.com

About the Author

Ann C. Logue is the author of *Hedge Funds For Dummies* (Wiley, 2006) and *Day Trading For Dummies* (Wiley, 2007). She has written for Alpha, Barron's, MSN Money, Newsweek Japan, and Wealth Manager. She is a lecturer at the Liautaud Graduate School of Business at the University of Illinois at Chicago. Her current career follows 12 years of experience as an investment analyst. She has a BA from Northwestern University and an MBA from the University of Chicago, and she holds the Chartered Financial Analyst designation.

Dedication

Once again, to Rik and Andrew, for their love and support.

Acknowledgments

So many friends and strangers alike helped me with this book. Among them were Nazim Ali of the Islamic Finance Project at Harvard University, Snehal Bhagat, Cody Craynor at the Church of Jesus Christ of Latter-day Saints, Jeffrey Dekro of Jewish Funds for Justice, Peyton Fleming at Ceres, Michael Saleh Gassner, Nitesh Gor of Dharma Investments, Robert Gough of the National Association of Socially Responsible Organizations, Aviya Kushner, Rik Lantz, Eric Lee, David Loundy at Devon Bank, Bruce MacDonald of Accion International, Ann McKenzie, Nell Minow of The Corporate Library, Mark Orloswki at Sustainable Endowments, Brad Pokorny of the Baha'i International Community, Nicole Rea, Lynne Meredith Schreiber, and Morgan Simon of the Responsible Endowments Coalition. Their insights and ideas made it much better.

As for the mechanics of putting together the book, Natalie Harris, Alissa Schwipps, Vicki Adang, Patricia Hathaway, and Stacy Kennedy of Wiley were great to work with. Finally, my agent, Marilyn Allen, made it all happen again.

Thanks, everyone!

Publisher's Acknowledgments

We're proud of this book; please send us your comments through our Dummies online registration form located at www.dummies.com/register/.

Some of the people who helped bring this book to market include the following:

Acquisitions, Editorial, and Media Development

Project Editors: Natalie Faye Harris, Alissa Schwipps

Acquisitions Editor: Stacy Kennedy

Senior Copy Editor: Victoria M. Adang

Assistant Editor: Erin Calligan Mooney

General Reviewer: Patricia Hathaway

Editorial Manager: Christine Meloy Beck

Editorial Assistants: Jennette ElNaggar, David Lutton, Joe Niesen

Cover Photos: © lmasses.com/corbis

Cartoons: Rich Tennant (www.the5thwave.com)

Composition Services

Project Coordinator: Patrick Redmond

Layout and Graphics: Reuben W. Davis, Sarah Philippart

Proofreaders: Amanda Graham, Bonnie Mikkelson

Indexer: Potomac Indexing, LLC

Publishing and Editorial for Consumer Dummies

Diane Graves Steele, Vice President and Publisher, Consumer Dummies

Kristin Ferguson-Wagstaffe, Product Development Director, Consumer Dummies

Ensley Eikenburg, Associate Publisher, Travel

Kelly Regan, Editorial Director, Travel

Publishing for Technology Dummies

Andy Cummings, Vice President and Publisher, Dummies Technology/General User

Composition Services

Gerry Fahey, Vice President of Production Services

Debbie Stailey, Director of Composition Services

Contents at a Glance

Table of Contents

Introduction

Doing well while doing good. That's the goal — and the cliché — of socially responsible investing. Investing can help you reach major personal goals: retirement, college education for your children, charitable donations. *Socially responsible* investing allows you to take care of your finances while being true to your values. It can encourage companies and governments to operate cleanly and ethically, and it can help improve the community where you live. It's becoming popular because investing is one way to take action to make the world better.

Done incorrectly, socially responsible investing is nothing but window dressing. It sometimes emphasizes feeling good over making money or making a difference in the world. That's unfortunate. Savvy socially responsible investors, which include major university endowments and pension funds, understand that socially responsible investing isn't separate from good investing. You don't need to compromise your finances or your goals when you invest socially.

Socially Responsible Investing For Dummies tells you what you need to know to invest better. I start out with facts on why and how social investing works. I tell you how to do research so you can determine whether an investment is a good one for you in terms of financial potential and your personal needs. I explain how to use your investment clout to influence a company's performance for the better. I cover the different ways that investors define social responsibility to help you clarify your own goals. And I lay out the different types of investments that you can use to put your plan into action. I also include some information on how to find brokers, financial planners, and mutual fund companies that can help you with your decisions.

This book is designed to get you started. You may want more information on different types of investments and investment techniques, or you may want to research a particular type of social investing in greater depth than I cover here. That's fine. I have plenty of references in the book to help you figure out where to go next.

About This Book

Let me tell you what this book is not: It's not a textbook, nor is it a religious tract. If you want to know more about the theory and mechanics of the market, you can find lots of great texts in a college bookstore. If it's important to your mortal soul to do precisely the right thing, see your clergy person for guidance. I went to business school, not the seminary!

This book is designed to be simple. It assumes that you don't know much about investing, but that you're a smart person who wants to find out more about doing it right. And so it has straightforward explanations of what you need to know to understand how investing can be socially responsible, how to identify your concerns and do research to address them, and what the alternatives are for your portfolio.

If you want to read some textbooks or religious works, I list a few in the appendix.

Conventions Used in This Book

I put important words that I define in *italic* font. I often **bold** the key words of bulleted or numbered lists to bring the important ideas to your attention. And I place all Web addresses in `monofont` for easy access.

I cover investment research in this book, and I introduce you to some technical terms that will come up in the investment world. You don't need to know all this information to be a successful social investor, but I think it's helpful to show the array of possibilities to help you identify what may suit you. Sometimes I throw in references to deeper academic investment theories. To alert you to these topics, I often place them under a Technical Stuff icon (see the section "Icons Used in This Book").

During printing of this book, some of the Web addresses may have broken across two lines of text. If you come across such an address, rest assured that I haven't put in any extra characters (such as hyphens) to indicate the break. When using a broken Web address, type in exactly what you see on the page, pretending that the line break doesn't exist.

What You're Not to Read

I include *sidebars* (the gray boxes containing a heading and a couple of paragraphs) in the book that you don't really need to read to follow the chapter text. With that stated, though, I do encourage you to go back and read through the material when you have time. Many of the sidebars contain examples that help you get an even better idea of how some of the investment concepts work!

You can also skip the text marked with a Technical Stuff icon, but see the preceding section for an explanation of why you may not want to skim over this material.

Foolish Assumptions

The format of my summa opus requires me to make some assumptions about you, the reader:

- You need to know a lot about social investing in a short period of time.

- You may be starting a college fund for a new baby, planning for your retirement, or trying to decide how best to manage a windfall.

- Maybe you've volunteered for your church's finance committee or were elected to your union's pension board, and you want to make smart decisions that reflect the organization's values.

- You may be an experienced investor who wants to use your accumulated funds and market savvy to change the world, or at least your neighborhood.

- You have money to invest, even just a little to start with, and you want to generate a good return as well as goodwill.

Although some readers may have investing experience, I'm assuming that most are new to the concepts. Maybe you've been afraid to invest because you worry that doing so will contribute to the world's worst problems.

No matter your situation or motives, my goal is to give you enough information so you can ask smart questions, do careful research, and handle your money so you can meet *your* goals.

I'm also assuming that the world will continue to change constantly and the social issues that matter to you will change, too. That's why much of this book emphasizes research. As new issues emerge, you'll be prepared to find investments that will — and will not — work for you. I'm assuming that you want to take responsibility for your money and for your place in the world.

How This Book Is Organized

Socially Responsible Investing For Dummies is sorted into parts so you can find what you need to know quickly. The following sections break down the book's structure.

Part I: Getting Started in Social Investing

The first part describes what socially responsible investing is, how it works, and how to do research to determine whether an investment is socially responsible. It also includes information about the performance of socially responsible businesses and of investors who apply this philosophy to show you that it does make a difference.

Part II: Issues to Invest In

Not all socially responsible investors are alike. Some care about the environment. Some care about the community where they live. Some want to follow the precepts of their religion. Some simply want corporate executives to live up to their fiduciary responsibilities. In this part, I describe the different ways that people think about social investing to help you determine what's most important to you. That way, you can better direct your investments.

Part III: Putting Your Socially Responsible Choices into Action

This part is all about the different asset classes that you can invest in. Some will help you meet specific social and investment goals; others can be socially responsible if used appropriately. You can find information about how to buy and sell, where to look, and what to watch out for, whether you're buying commercial real estate or a mutual fund.

The information here can help you make better portfolio decisions, even if you're not fully committed to being socially responsible or don't have a lot of money to invest right now. Given how often circumstances change and new investment products come to market, you can use the material in this part to adjust your portfolio as needed.

Part IV: The Part of Tens

In this *For Dummies*-only part, you get to enjoy some top-ten lists. I present ten tips for social investors, ten traps that they sometimes fall into (but that you, I'm sure, will not), and ten success stories of change that happened in part due to the work of social and activist investors. I also include an appendix full of references so you can get more information if you desire.

Icons Used in This Book

You'll see four icons scattered around the margins of the text. Each icon points to information you should know or may find interesting about social investing. They go as follows:

This icon notes something you should keep in mind about social investing. It may refer to something I've already covered in the book, or it may highlight something you need to know for future investing decisions!

Tip information tells you how to invest a little better, a little smarter, a little more efficiently. The information can help you make better decisions about how an investment is socially responsible or ask better questions of people who are offering you investment opportunities.

I include nothing in this book that can cause death or bodily harm, as far as I can figure out, but plenty of things in the world of investing can cause you to lose big money or, worse, your sanity. These points help you avoid big problems.

I put the boring (but sometimes helpful) academic stuff here. By reading this material, you get the detailed information behind the investment theories, or you can get some interesting trivia or background information.

Where to Go from Here

Are you ready to open up the book and get going? Allow me to give you some ideas. You may want to start with Chapter 1 if you know nothing about socially responsible investing so you can get a good sense of what I'm talking about. If you need help convincing someone else that social investing works, look at Chapters 2 and 3. If you want to find out how to do research and put it into action, check out Chapters 4 and 5. If you need to figure out what issues you want to emphasize, look at Chapters 6 through 11. Those chapters get you started.

If you're already on board with the idea of social investing and want to turn your values into action, go straight to Part III. Chapters 12 through 16 cover investing alternatives from bank accounts to hedge funds. In Chapter 17, you can get the lowdown about microfinance and venture philanthropy, where the returns may be lower but the global payoffs larger.

Part I
Getting Started in Social Investing

The 5th Wave   By Rich Tennant

Defining your investment risk with the:
TOAST RETRIEVING RISK TOLERANCE TEST

LOW RISK | Waits for toast to pop up even though it's burning.

MODERATE RISK | Goes after toast with wooden toast prongs.

HIGH RISK | Goes after toast with all metal butter knife.

ULTRA HIGH RISK | Goes after toast with metal butter knife wearing a wet swim suit and a stainless steel colander on head.

In this part . . .

Social investors want to make money and make a difference in the world while staying true to their beliefs. The process is similar to regular investing, but it does have a few differences. Instead of doing research only on a company's growth prospects, a social investor looks for additional information on what the business is doing to get that growth. Instead of waiting for management to deliver results, the social investor may push the managers for changes. In this part, you discover the basics of investing, social style.

Chapter 1

Investing the Socially Responsible Way

In This Chapter
▶ Getting a good return on your money
▶ Evaluating research
▶ Deciding to invest responsibly
▶ Using your money to influence change
▶ Making smart investments

*W*henever I mentioned to people that I was writing *Socially Responsible Investing For Dummies,* they'd get excited. "Wow!" they'd say. "I'd love to know more about how to do good through investing." And that's probably what you had in mind when you picked up this book.

Very quickly, though, I realized that each of these people defined "doing good through investing" a little bit differently. Some people want to change the world; they want to be part of new technologies and new ideas that could make our society better in the years to come. Some want to avoid businesses that produce products that they disapprove of. And some want to make sure that they aren't undermining their charitable activities with their investments.

Socially responsible investing can help you put your money to work financing activities that you support. It can also help you avoid businesses that you'd rather not deal with. Done right, your performance should be no different than if you invested without regard to social responsibility; it helps that more companies are trying to be responsible with their businesses. As the number of social investors grows, maybe even more companies will change how they operate.

This book is a guide to figuring out whether an investment is responsible. If you can do that, you can be a responsible investor all your life, no matter how your finances and social priorities change.

Social Investing DOES Give a Good Return

Have a laundry list of things that bother you about the world? Think companies should treat workers and suppliers better, meet relevant government regulations without prompting, and make better products? Well, you may be able to ease some of your troubles through a socially responsible investing approach. Even better, you may be encouraging more companies to do the right thing. And contrary to popular belief, this sort of investing *does* pay off.

A lot of people who work in financial services think that social investing is nice if you don't care about return. They'll suggest that you instead follow a standard, nonjudgmental investment strategy, and then give the extra profits to charity.

Some social investors say they're happy giving up a little bit of return if they feel good about where their money is. To use the fancy terms of economic theory, this is a *utilitarian argument:* These investors get "utility" from their investment in addition to the money that they make, so they're just as happy as an investor who gets all return and no utility.

I really wish I could tell you that both of these arguments are wrong and that social investors make more money than others. But what I know is that both of those arguments are wrong because the evidence is that social investors can make as much money as others — and get their added utility, too. The keys to success seem to be carefully selecting asset classes and using activist techniques to boost returns. This book contains plenty of examples in support of successful social investing.

Many financial theorists believe that markets are efficient. They say that any investment is as likely as another to outperform the market; you could throw a dart at the pages of the *Wall Street Journal* to pick stocks that would be no better or no worse than any a fancy professional would pick. There are some problems with the idea of market efficiency, but it's true enough that it explains why a social portfolio is likely to be no better or no worse than any other.

Liberal bias? Think again!

Some people think of social investing as some sort of pinko plot to undermine capitalism. They see it as the province of people with more money than sense — and not a lot of either.

Like all stereotypes, a few people do fit this profile. However, the vast majority of social and activist investors come to their practice in hopes of making more money. They are the owners, so they're in charge. That means their investments work for them. He who has the gold should be able to make the rules, as the cliché says.

Activist investing is pure capitalism. It uses the power of capital ownership to make change.

Social investors look for investments that reflect their values, and they use their clout to create change. That's what they have in common. Where they differ is on those values. Some social investors care about the environment; others are concerned about social and political issues, religious restrictions, or corporate governance. Many have values that cross categories; finding those commonalities allows investors to come together to make a difference in the world.

Yes, Responsible Behavior Does Help Businesses

Following socially responsible principles can help many organizations thrive. Can it get them the proverbial win-win, where it does better for shareholders by doing better by society as a whole? There's a whole lot of research on that very topic.

In general, companies can do well by doing good; just how good they have to be and how well they can do is subject to a bit of debate. (But debate is good! That's what makes markets, as the traders like to say.) A review of some recent studies, which I cover in the following sections, shows the benefits and limitations of this style of management and investing. This information can help you clarify what you're trying to do when you invest socially.

Effects of charitable contributions

Elsewhere in this chapter, I mention the pure capitalist notion that companies should be run to maximize profits. If investors want to change the world, the thought goes, they should do that on their own with their investment profits, rather than expect companies to do it for them.

Ah, but charity helps business. In 2006, Baruch Lev and Christine Petrovits of New York University and Suresh Radhakrishnan of the University of Texas at Dallas found that companies that made charitable donations had larger revenue growth than companies that did not ("Is Doing Good Good for You? Yes, Charitable Contributions Enhance Revenue Growth," July 2006). This effect was strongest for consumer companies. Most notably, the researchers did not find that revenue growth led to greater charitable donations. The effect was only one way.

Identifying the 100 most sustainable companies

Each year, a group of the world's movers and shakers meets in Davos, Switzerland, for the World Economic Forum. They get together to have cocktails and run the world. Well, okay, maybe they don't quite run the world, but the CEOs, politicians, and academics who attend the conference carry a lot of influence back home.

Each year at the conference, a new list of the 100 most sustainable corporations in the world is released (www.global100.org). Each of these companies is listed in the Morgan Stanley Capital International (MSCI) World Index, which tracks markets all over the world. These companies are scored on their environmental, social, and governance performance, and then ranked. The 100 at the top are pulled out and announced with great fanfare. Historically, stock in these Global 100 companies has outperformed the MSCI.

It's not a perfect list for all social investors because it doesn't take into account what a company's business is. Hence, defense contractors and alcoholic beverage manufacturers, which would be loathsome to some investors, make the list.

Others have argued that the methodology lets the analysts pick stocks with better performance to make the index look good. Still, it's impressive to see so many companies worldwide trying to improve their overall performance in order to be one of the rarified 100.

Weighing social performance against financial performance

Research by Joshua Margolis of Harvard and Hillary Anger Elfenbein of Berkeley ("Doing Well by Doing Good? Don't Count on It," *Harvard Business Review*, January 2008) found a very weak relationship between corporate social performance and corporate financial performance. Companies that behaved slightly better than average performed slightly better than average, but not by so much that the researchers could wholeheartedly recommend social investing.

On the other hand, they found that social investing doesn't cost companies anything, so as a social investor, you don't have to give up profits to invest in companies whose managers are committed to good behavior.

What's going on? It could be that companies that have surplus funds can engage in good works. It could also be that it simply takes everyone a long time to find out just how bad the few bad apples really are.

Corporate misdeeds are costly, but only after people find out about them. Enron was on several lists of best-run companies until it turned out that much of what was going on was fraudulent. (And hence, socially responsible investors need corporate transparency, which is covered a little bit later in this chapter and a lot in Chapters 4 and 7.)

The Moskowitz Prize for social investing research

Each year, the Center for Responsible Business at the University of California at Berkeley offers the Moskowitz Prize, a $5,000 award for the best research paper on a social investing subject. And each year, the result is at least one paper that pushes forward the frontiers of social investing. (You can see the complete list at `www.haas.berkeley.edu/responsiblebusiness/MoskowitzResearchProgram.html`.) Among the findings of the prize winners:

✔ The stocks of companies named to the annual *Fortune* magazine list of the best companies to work for tend to beat the market, indicating that treating employees well helps companies perform better.

✔ The California Public Employees Retirement System (also known as CalPERS) generated $3.1 billion in wealth for its beneficiaries between 1992 and 2005 from its shareholder activist activities. (You can read more about CalPERS's strategies in Chapter 3.)

✔ Using measures of the amounts of corruption tolerated in different countries, companies based in places that tolerate more business corruption trade at lower stock market multiples than companies based in places where corruption is rare.

That's nice evidence that doing well does right by shareholders!

Let's Make a Deal: Exchanging Money for Everyone's Benefit

The financial markets operate with one goal: to bring together buyers and sellers. That's what all the hours of business news on television, the chatter on investing radio shows, the commentary on Internet sites, and the pages of *The Wall Street Journal* are covering: Who are the buyers, and what do they want right now? Who are the sellers, and what do they want right now? And given what both sides want, what should the price be?

It doesn't matter if it's real estate, the stock market, oil prices, or new cars. The market functions when it brings together the needs of the buyers and the sellers at a price that both will accept.

Economists like to talk about a *market clearing price,* which is the price where the buyer and the seller are willing to make a deal. The buyer won't go any higher, and the seller won't go any lower.

From the perspective of social investing, the sellers of stock and bonds — the people who need money — may want to make themselves attractive to as many prospective investors as possible. Thus, they may clean up their acts! The people who have money to buy stocks and bonds may have nonfinancial goals; all else being equal, they may prefer to finance companies that match their social interests as well as their economic goals. That's how social investing creates change.

Companies and governments need financing

Here's the thing: Organizations need to raise money. Small businesses need funds to get started. Big businesses need funds for acquisitions. Governments need money to build roads and schools. Hospitals need money for new facilities. All of these organizations need to borrow money or find shareowners to join with them. The more potential sources of funding they can approach, the easier it will be to fund the project and the lower the cost will be.

So businesses and others who need money have an incentive to be the kind of borrowers or partners that investors want. If investors want companies that have a strong board of directors, then maybe these companies need to have one. If investors prefer companies that pay workers in developing countries fair wages, then maybe the companies should do just that.

Naturally, investors prefer to deal with companies that make good on their financial promises, and social investing may help with that. A company that doesn't pay bribes may not get hit with big tax penalties, for example. A company that finds ways to reduce the carbon emitted in shipping goods may save a lot of money that goes straight to the bottom line.

Individuals and institutions need investments

Who has money to invest? Anyone saving for retirement, to start with, and that's pretty much everyone (or at least it should be!). Many people are also saving money for other goals, such as college education for their children or grandchildren, or to have money to support a charity after their death. Some people are saving for a new car, and others are saving up to take a two-year missionary trip with their church.

Bigger investors need to get a return on their money. The Bill and Melinda Gates Foundation and Harvard University have billions to put to work to help them meet their goals, whether distributing polio vaccines or expanding undergraduate financial aid programs. The better return those funds can earn, the more people they can help. Pension funds may have millions or even billions of dollars in benefits obligations to meet, and a good investment return will help them pay up at a lower upfront cost. Trust fund managers want to make sure they have enough money to meet the growing needs of future generations of a rich family.

At some nonprofit organizations, the investment manager brings in more money a year than the folks in the fundraising office.

Whether large or small, investors set aside money that they don't need now in the hopes of having more money for future needs. Many of those investors care about social issues, and it's not just those with the 10 to 12 percent of funds that are invested socially. Many other investors would be willing to invest along social criteria if they could find more investment opportunities that matched their interests.

Who Invests Responsibly, and Why?

Social investing is big business. Geoffrey Heal, professor of public policy and business economics at Columbia University, estimates that 10 to 12 percent of all professionally managed investments in the United States come with social restrictions of some sort. That's a lot of money! These restrictions can be anything from a refusal to invest in the so-called "sin" industries (alcohol, gambling, pornography, and tobacco companies) to a comprehensive style looking at the environment, society, and corporate governance.

Investors who like this style look at how employees are paid and whether they can become owners in the company. They look at the company's mission statement, and then evaluate how well it's put into practice. They want to know: Does this company understand its business, and is its business making friends rather than enemies?

Who are these investors? Some are religiously observant and want to avoid anything that may interfere with their spiritual journey. Some simply think it's about time that company managers listened to the people who own the joint. And some would just like a mutual fund option in their 401(k) plan that doesn't make them nervous.

The leaders in social investing are the leading institutional investors (I cover these in detail in Chapter 3):

✔ Pension funds

✔ Charitable foundations

✔ Institutional endowments

The role of institutions is important for two reasons:

✔ First, these investors care deeply about performance. Most pension funds are required by federal law to consider investment performance first. They can consider other factors, such as social criteria, only as long as the performance is met. Pension funds for religious orders and labor unions often want to consider social criteria, so money managers have figured out how to accommodate the performance have-to-have and the values nice-to-have factors. Foundation and endowment managers have a fiduciary responsibility to the philanthropists who donated the money in the first place. Because these investors have to worry about performance, all investors can benefit from their experience with social investing.

The U.S. law regulating pension management is the Employee Retirement Income Security Act of 1974, known as ERISA (rhymes with "Alyssa"). Among other things, it affects the choices of funds in your 401(k) plan. When the Feds get involved, companies pay attention.

✔ In a changing world, investing can be a tool for making a difference. The simple reason to invest socially is to maintain a clear conscience, but many social investors believe they can also get better performance through responsible investments (this is beyond the pension fund requirement that performance be as good as it would be without the social component):

• If investors look for companies that are trying to reduce their effect on the environment, they may find companies that are saving money and generating more profits.

- If they search out businesses that pay workers well, they may find some that create more consumers to grow the overall economy.

- If they avoid companies with bloated executive pay packages and cronies on the board of directors, they may avoid scandals and a string of bad financial results.

Contributing to the community

Not all social investors want to change the world. They don't care about sin stocks or business practices in far-off lands. They just want their corner of the globe to be in better shape. They'd like to see new employers creating jobs and paying taxes in their hometown. They'd like to see nicer, safer neighborhoods for people to live in. Maybe they just want to keep their money with a bank that isn't likely to be taken over by some major mega-global financial institution.

If this describes your investing outlook, you can find many different opportunities. If you have substantial assets and an appetite for risk, you can provide start-up funds to small businesses in the area. If you're looking for a safe, conservative investment, you may want to purchase a certificate of deposit with a federally insured *Community Development Financial Institution*, which is a bank that provides services to local residents. I cover this style of investing and places to park your money in Chapter 6.

In between those extremes are stock, bond, and real estate investments that may make your town a better place to live, work, and play.

Monitoring a company's managers

Many investors don't care so much what business a company is in; they're more concerned that the business is truly run for the shareholders (this is called *corporate governance*). That means management has to be paid for performance, no more and no less. The members of the board of directors should concentrate on providing management oversight and accurate reports to shareholders rather than enhancing their social status. Shareholders should be able to vote democratically and present proposals for management to consider.

Some governance investors look for companies that have great internal practices and a demonstrated history of service to shareholders. Others seek out companies where the management and board have terrible conflicts of interest, performance is lousy, and governance is a mere afterthought. They use their power as owners to force the company to change its ways, improving investment results.

And some governance investors combine tactics. They may be interested in companies that are located in their own community, but if the company doesn't perform well, the investors are in there with all of their activist tools to press the company managers to do better. Someone may have inherited shares in a company that can't be sold under the terms of a trust agreement, but that doesn't mean she has to accept the firm's environmental practices. She can use her power as an owner to push for a board and management that are more responsive to her needs. I cover governance issues in more detail in Chapter 7.

Not all governance activists care about the public good. Some are more notorious than noble. However, they're doing nothing more than exercising their rights as owners of the company.

Hugging those trees

Global warming is hot stuff, and it's not the only issue involving investment and the environment. The way that companies make goods, ship them, sell them, and then handle the waste has a huge effect on the planet — and on the bottom line.

The buzzword is *sustainability,* which is a company's ability to maintain its profits over the very long haul. If a company relies on petroleum, for example, its ability to sustain the business is entirely dependent on the supply and the price of oil. If the company figures out ways to reduce total fuel consumption and use more alternative fuels, it will have an easier time staying in business and generating long-term profits for shareholders. Sustainability is the topic of Chapter 8.

Maybe you're an investor who is excited about environmental investing because of the potential for revolutionary new technologies. Maybe alternative fuels could be the next television, plastics recycling the next instant photography, or greenhouse gas reduction the next Internet. When you're on the ground floor of new technologies, you take a lot of risk, but you have the opportunity for big profits. Where there's a chance of good growth from major change, there will be investors ready to support it.

Not only do investors want to make money, but so do entrepreneurs. People with great ideas are likely to come forward if they see that they can get financing for them.

Investing internationally and socially

The modern corporation operates all over the world. Its managers don't pay too much attention to borders unless there are taxes involved to get across them. Investors do pay attention to the countries where companies operate, though. Companies that operate in many countries can choose how much they pay workers and how they operate their facilities. (Wages too high in one country? Move the work somewhere with a lower standard of living.) They also have to deal with governments everywhere they operate, and some national leaders are downright unsavory people.

An international social investor wants to support businesses that do the right thing, even if there aren't laws forcing proper behavior. This can range from paying better-than-market rates to refusing to pay bribes to government officials. In many countries, corporations have the money and the power to improve conditions, and social investors want to be a part of that. Chapter 9 shows you how.

Reminders from religion

Some investors have religious practices that set forth rigid restrictions. These people must avoid certain investments if they want to live according to their faith. Others aren't necessarily risking their salvation, but they'd prefer that their investments line up with their beliefs. If they don't smoke, for example, they may not want to be involved with companies that grow, distribute, or sell tobacco. If they're opposed to war, they may not want to invest in defense contractors. If they aren't allowed to receive interest, they won't be buying bonds. Turn to Chapter 10 for an overview of how religious beliefs influence investment choices.

New mutual funds and financial services have been cropping up to meet the needs of religious investors. These range from index funds that exclude offending companies to new ways to finance home purchases — new ways from an American perspective, at least.

Finally, some of the most active investors are affiliated with religious schools, charities, and other institutions. They are quick to use the power of their material resources to push for positive change. If you're interested in activist investing, you'll see groups such as the Interfaith Center for Corporate Responsibility (www.iccr.org) working to get company managers to pay attention to their interests. It's the owner's prerogative, after all.

If your religion has strict rules about money and finance, you should talk to your clergy to make sure your investing program follows them.

Choosing, Monitoring, and Influencing Your Investments

After social investors identify their investment criteria, they have to invest the same way that any other investor would: by reading financial statements, looking up news reports, and maybe even visiting the company.

Easier said than done, right? Not to worry. I give you plenty of help in finding the right investment vehicle that also aligns with your criteria.

Ensuring socially responsible choices

Your criteria may exclude certain investments, whether they're industries, such as alcohol, or investment classes, such as bonds. Other social strategies may actually expand your investment universe. After you identify the issues that are important to you, you may find investments that fit that you may not have known about.

Social criteria aren't enough, though. You have to combine those with information about the investment's financial condition and outlook. No investment will do well just because you want it to. Chapter 4 tells you how to research investments.

Social investors tend to fall in love with a company's mission, and then assume it will be a great investment. It doesn't work that way.

Keeping abreast of changes

The beauty of social investing is that it forces companies to make changes. But the marketplace is so dynamic that companies change all the time anyway. To be a successful social investor, you have to stay on top of the news (see Chapter 4 for more on this). You want to know if your investment is making financial progress and if it still fits your style.

Some companies that fit when you first put money into them won't always stay aligned with your goals: Maybe you don't invest in companies involved in gambling, and the company just acquired a hotel and casino operation.

Some companies that didn't fit your criteria may be a good match for you now because the management responded to shareholder pressure. The positive change may be rewarded with your investment.

The specific issues that matter to social investors change all the time. International investors have to change their lists of companies and tactics as new world hot spots develop. Thirty years ago, many people wouldn't invest in companies that did business in South Africa. Today, the concern for many investors is companies that do business in Sudan. What will the concern be in 30 years? Who knows, but an investor clinging to old notions of good and bad will miss opportunities that an up-to-date investor will seize.

Making a careful selection of assets

To be successful as a social investor, you have to do more than just find good companies to invest in. You need to find a mixture of investments that reflects your risk and return parameters. If you only invest in stocks, you may take too much risk and lose too much money in those years when the stock market is down. If you put your money in a federally insured bank CD, even if the bank specializes in community lending, you'll have a responsible investment that barely beats inflation and probably won't help you meet your goals.

The good news is that there's a huge range of investments to help you diversify your risk and improve your returns without compromising your investment goals. The chapters in Part III have information on everything from life insurance to hedge funds. You can invest in real estate, venture capital, and exchange-traded funds without compromising your social beliefs. And that diversification across assets will help you get a better return at the same time.

Using shareholder activism

Shareholders are part owners of a company. *Bondholders* are lenders, and lenders set a lot of terms for behavior. The money gives them power. The CEO won't necessarily take your call if you own 100 shares and the company has several million of them outstanding, but you can be an activist nonetheless. This book gives you some ideas for how smaller investors can research issues, find out who the big investors are, and put the power of their purses to work.

As a stockholder, you have the right to vote on some corporate issues, including the members of the board of directors and certain compensation packages. Although no one shareholder usually has enough votes to count, many shareholders together can combine their votes and put pressure on a company's management to make changes, or else they may have to deal with new directors who may not be as accommodating.

Companies also accept proposals for shareholders to vote on. You can ask for a report on environmental policies or for the closing of operations in a world trouble spot or for more equitable pay for workers. Even if these resolutions don't pass (and, in truth, they rarely do), the mere fact that they're proposed can sometimes get a management group to think about addressing the issue later. Chapter 5 explains how shareholder activism works.

Andrew Carnegie and "The Gospel of Wealth"

Andrew Carnegie was on the scene long before Bill Gates and Warren Buffett. Adjusted for inflation, Carnegie was worth about $300 billion, which made him far richer than either of his early 21st-century counterparts. He was a Scottish immigrant who arrived in Western Pennsylvania in 1848 at the age of 13. He went to work almost immediately, and at a series of successively better jobs, he proved himself to be clever and hardworking. He saved as much money as he could and invested it in railroad, oil, and steel companies, which were the high-tech industries of their day. Carnegie developed a reputation for being tight with money and ruthless in business. He didn't pay his workers well because he believed that they'd squander their money. His deputy, Henry Clay Frick, hired security guards who shot and killed striking workers at Carnegie's Homestead Steel Works.

And yet, although he may not have been a model employer, Carnegie believed he had an obligation to give his money back to society. He became one of the greatest philanthropists in history, funding libraries around the United States, sponsoring paleontological expeditions, establishing a university in Pittsburgh (now Carnegie-Mellon University), and creating many other institutions all over the world that still thrive today, including Carnegie Hall in New York City and the Carnegie Corporation, a $3 billion charitable foundation.

In 1889, Carnegie wrote an essay about his views of philanthropy, entitled "The Gospel of Wealth." In it, he says that capitalism makes society better for everyone, but that it also creates disproportionate wealth for a few. Those few have an obligation to spend it on philanthropy while they're alive rather than spend it on themselves, give it to their children, or leave it to charity only after they die. "Under its sway we shall have an ideal state, in which the surplus wealth of the few will become, in the best sense the property of the many," he wrote. "Thus is the problem of Rich and Poor to be solved."

Carnegie's practices have influenced those who have come after him, even if they choose to pay their workers well and negotiate rather than open fire. You can read "The Gospel of Wealth" online at www.swarthmore.edu/SocSci/rbannis1/AIH19th/Carnegie.html.

Chapter 2

The Socially Responsible Enterprise: Understanding and Monitoring Performance

*W*hether it's a business or a school district, organizations need financing to grow, and they often have to rely on outside investors to help them. That means they need to operate in ways that make investors comfortable and ensure a good return on the investment. A business that plays fair and respects all of its stakeholders — employees, customers, vendors, and the community — not just its shareholders, is likely to do well in the long run. And that's the point of social investing.

This chapter looks at the research and approaches covering how responsible organizations perform. Social responsibility doesn't seem to cost shareholders anything in the way of performance, a concern of some people interested in responsible investing. In fact, socially responsible businesses may have an edge in attracting low-cost capital, recruiting great talent, satisfying customers, and operating with less interference from government regulators.

In this chapter, I also help you understand how responsible organizations operate and what information they share with investors. Knowing this information helps you justify your social investing activities (like you need any help with that, because you're reading this book). I also introduce and give you some insight into the research and analysis steps covered in more detail in Chapters 4 and 5.

Looking at How a Company Makes Its Money

The hardest thing for any company to do is to come up with a product or service that people are willing to pay for. Companies have to do that (and, it is hoped, do that responsibly) to stay in business. Because it's the first step for business success, it should also be the first step for an investor who cares about social change.

Those goods or services that people are willing to pay for lead to a return for shareholders, and that's a company's reason for being. Social investors are investors first! Many of the things that companies can do that are socially responsible are also good for the shareholders, and a lot of other things don't matter one way or the other, so the company can make the right choice and keep shareholders happy.

In academic theory, a firm has no purpose other than to maximize shareholder value. In practice, many companies can maximize shareholder value while also behaving responsibly.

Businesspeople like to talk about their *business models,* which are nothing more than the explanations of how a company makes its money. It's the way that a company captures the value that it offers to customers. Is its model to be the lowest-cost provider? If so, the company will approach business differently than one offering luxury goods. For that matter, a company that wants to be a low-cost provider through volume discounting will have a different business model than one that wants to be a low-cost provider by making it easier for customers to do things for themselves.

A company's business model influences the social choices that a company can make because it affects how it can spend money while keeping shareholders happy. If customers demand the absolute lowest prices, then management may have less leeway to spend money on responsible initiatives and still keep its customers — and shareholders — happy.

On the other hand, Wal-Mart (NYSE: WMT), which uses this low-price business model, found that it could keep prices low if it reduced energy costs not only in its stores, but also in every step of its supply chain by helping its suppliers reduce their costs and by managing its transportation better. Hence, the company was able to deliver on its business model while improving the environment.

The business model is set out in three parts: the mission, strategy, and tactics. A few companies set these out for you in a nice brochure, but most make you figure out what's what. In the following sections, I explain how business models work, as well as how a company's product may influence your decision to invest in the company. Then I take a look at how a company gets its products and services into customers' hands.

Mission, strategy, and tactics

Many companies have *mission statements* to describe what they hope to do. The statements are usually just two or three lines long and describe the company's business and operating philosophy at the very highest level: "We will be the premier widget company, exceeding customer expectations. We recognize that employees are our number-one asset and that everyone in the organization is responsible for our sterling reputation."

But even though many mission statements rely on clichés to telegraph complex ideas, they still give an indication of what the company's priorities are: Is it the product or the service? Does the company emphasize low prices or high quality? Does it make an explicit statement of responsibility toward customers, the community, or employees? Is the mission high-minded, such as creating a healthy world, or is it practical, such as to be the market leader? It's the starting point for all decisions down the line.

Not all companies have an explicit mission statement, but it's possible to get a sense of a company's mission from its different shareholder reports and marketing materials.

The *strategy* is the plan for putting the mission statement into action. It looks into the future. It isn't updated frequently, but it does change as needed to reflect changes in the company's operating environment. If the company's mission is to offer low prices to customers, then the strategy may be to buy in volume, sell direct rather than through retail stores, or operate with very low overhead. A company with a mission of offering cutting-edge technology may have a strategy of doing intensive research to develop completely new products, or it may choose to find new technologies through acquisitions or licensing arrangements.

Tactics are the methods the company uses to meet its strategy. If the strategy is to do intensive research, then the tactics may include such matters as recruiting scientists, choosing promising areas for further study, and applying for patents whenever appropriate. Because the tactics are the specific steps used to run the business, managers may change them frequently to meet the needs of the ever-changing marketplace.

An organization that really wants to be socially responsible needs to behave well in its mission, its strategy, and its tactics. Ultimately, though, the tactics are most important because they are responsibility in practice. Tactics are where the rubber meets the road.

More than one company has written a highfalutin' mission strategy and used a business model that could be socially responsible. Day to day, though, the managers used tactics that generated immediate results with no thought to long-term effects or social missions. Why? Because they were paid for those immediate results, with no questions asked about how they got them.

Sometimes mission statements are marketing tactics rather than true guidelines for corporate behavior. Don't invest based on a mission statement. Do your research to see if the management walks the talk in its strategy and tactics.

Those goods and services that make the money

Many social investors look at the revenue line first. Does the company make alcohol? Pork sausage? Pornography? Weapons? If so, then the investment may not be acceptable under their investment guidelines, and no other factor can change that — not the company's governance, its treatment of employees, or its environmental practices.

If the company passes that top-line cut, though, you've got some more work to do if you care about what a company produces. Are the products good ones that add value to society? Does the company management manage the product portfolio responsibly? Is the company working on new products that could have a profound change on society? Are the fastest growing markets ones that you want to support as a shareholder?

Evaluating existing products

Assuming that a particular company passes that first cut for you, you have to do a bit more research. Even if the company's line of business doesn't rule it out, other factors related to the product could, including how the product can be used and how it's disposed of. For example, toymaker Mattel (NYSE: MAT) had a serious problem on its hands in 2007, when many of its toys tested with higher lead levels than were allowed. Consumers were upset, needless to say, and the stock price fell. Investors wanted to be confident that the company was going to make good products that didn't harm the children who played with them.

Some companies sell products that are inherently dangerous (such as tobacco), while others sell products that may be dangerous if used by the wrong person, such as sporting equipment. Likewise, some companies make products that may be appropriate for some users but not others, such as R-rated movies. Not all of these dangers translate into business risks. As an investor, you're free to invest in anything you want; some decisions may give you comfort but not additional profits.

Building the better mousetrap

For some companies, the path to changing the world is through a better product. Bill Gates's vision was to put a computer on every desktop, and his company, Microsoft (Nasdaq: MSFT), changed the way we work, play, and communicate. Not everyone loves Microsoft, but its products made the world a very different place. Let's face it, if companies are run for shareholders, then a socially responsible corporation is designed to harness shareholder greed to make the world different.

Greed may not be good, but it's not always bad, either. You're investing money because you want to have more money in the future. It may be for things that are important to you, ranging from college for your children to a comfortable retirement or bequests to charities that you care about, but still, you want more money. So do businesses.

Many businesses come about because a visionary entrepreneur sees the opportunity to make a lot of money by developing a product that changes the way the world works. Some are good, some are bad. A bottled water company simply takes something that's more or less free from the tap, puts it into plastic packaging, hauls it to stores in trucks that burn fossil fuels, and charges more money per gallon for it than gasoline costs. It's a sweet business model — it takes a lot of vision to realize that there's a way to charge people $1.49 for something that used to be free — but it's not exactly socially or environmentally responsible.

Companies produce what consumers want to buy. Bottled water may not be the most responsible product on the market, but if people stopped buying it, the companies that package it would find new products to sell. If they didn't, other companies would see the open space in store refrigerators, and they'd figure out something new to bring to market.

Some people have the vision to see that there are huge profits to be made from a car that runs on something other than fossil fuels. There are profits to be made growing food without pesticides, and profits to be made developing low-cost computers for people in developing countries. You don't necessarily have to invest in start-up companies to have a stake in innovative new products, because successful large companies are often working on the Next Big Thing too.

Getting the products to market

After a company has a product to sell, it has to figure out a way to do just that: Sell it. This involves a combination of packaging, advertising, promotion, and distribution; like all things socially responsible, getting the product from the factory to the shop and into the customers' hands can be done in responsible, neutral, or irresponsible ways.

Packaging and distribution are closely related matters of sustainability and cost control. Packaging can be designed with reused and recycled materials and then be easy to reuse or recycle, or it can be made from all new materials and in as big a quantity as possible. Likewise, the choice of distribution method and location also has environmental and cost effects; the more efficiently companies can get goods from place to place, the fewer resources will be consumed. You can find out more about packaging and distribution issues in Chapter 8.

But then, who buys those packaged goods after they end up on the shelf? Some investors don't care, because it's not part of their investing style. But some do. They may not feel comfortable investing in companies that market to teenagers with R-rated catalogs, that sell expensive products to people who can't afford them, or that push goods too aggressively toward children.

It's probably easier to find out about a company's marketing practices than almost any other aspect of its business, because the goal of marketing is to grab attention. If you don't feel comfortable with the product or how a company sells it, you don't have to buy the stock. This is one of those operating areas where a change may not add to shareholder value. In fact, changing an effective (although tacky) marketing strategy can take value away.

Why Businesses Need Investors

Why even take on investors in the first place? You can probably think of companies that are owned by the founder or that have a small number of investors and never issued shares of stock or borrowed a dime from anyone.

And all of these companies are small. That's the sad truth.

At some point, most business owners have to make a choice: stay small and make a good living for the owner, or get a lot bigger (and quite possibly make an even better living for the owner).

Do you want a big piece of a small pie or a small piece of a big pie? That's the nut of the expansion question (and if we're talking nuts, I suppose we're talking about a pecan pie).

Expansion can be risky, but risk generates the potential for return. The owner can give others a share of the business in exchange for the money to help it grow larger, or he can take on debt to fund the growth, choosing to deal with lenders instead of additional owners.

Think of financing an expansion this way: Suppose you want to buy a house. You can save up money for years and then pay cash for it; you can find a partner to go into it with you — maybe your parents will give you some of the money, or maybe you find a friend and you split the purchase of a two-flat; or you can go to the bank and take out a mortgage. If you find a partner or take out a loan (or both), you can probably buy a larger place and enjoy it for more years than if you save up your money until you have enough to buy the place yourself. Of course, if you borrow money or share the purchase with someone else, you add some risk. Miss a payment and the bank will foreclose. Get into a fight with your partner, and you may both have to sell to someone else to get out of the deal.

Businesses want to keep investors happy, because they want the funds that will help them get larger. A larger business means more opportunities for the managers to make money and gain experience, and it means more opportunities for the founding owners to make big bucks.

Companies that want to grow need money. Some companies generate enough money from their business to finance all the expansion they could possibly take on, but most companies reach a point where they need to issue stock or borrow money to build a new factory, make an acquisition, or get great new products out to market. To get that money, the firm has to persuade someone else that it deserves it. Incorporating social principles into the company's culture can help a business attract capital and meet investor expectations for return.

Attracting capital

Research shows that about 11 percent of assets under professional management follows social criteria. Many social investors are large institutions, such as pensions or charitable endowments, which control millions or even billions of dollars (you can read more about these investors in Chapter 3). With so much money at stake, an organization that wants to expand ignores the concerns of social investors at its own peril.

Some social investors look at governance factors, like the makeup of the board of directors (you can find out more about that in Chapter 7); others may have strict criteria dictated by their religious faith (see Chapter 10 for some of those restrictions). The more investors that a company or investment project can attract, the easier time it will have raising money — and the lower the cost of fundraising will be.

In order to expand, many business managers find that they have to listen to investors' concerns and make changes accordingly. Whether it's releasing more accounting data, adding strict requirements for contractors operating in developing nations, or getting out of a product line that generates a great deal of pollution, social policies can help businesses expand by attracting new sources of funds.

Meeting investor expectations

At heart, companies are to be run for shareholders. In theory, shareholders just want to make as much money as possible. However, some investors will take a lower return as long as their goals are being met. They'd rather make a little less money in a company that suits their nonfinancial preferences than go for the gusto in a business that doesn't match their personal mores. A savvy corporate treasurer may find that following social principles may help the company borrow money at a lower rate, pay a lower dividend, or manage with less attention to the stock price. That can save the company a lot of money, which can go to executive bonuses (ahem) or to fund future growth.

When you do your research, you figure out if the company is responsible for the right reasons — or if it's truly responsible at all.

One tool that many companies use for figuring out what projects to take on is the *net present value rule*. A company forecasts the revenue and expenses of the proposed project (which could be as big as an acquisition or as small as a new marketing campaign), and then it finds the present value of these by using the rate of return that shareholders expect to make (which is usually based on historic returns or analyst estimates). If the net present value is positive, then the project is likely to be a good one.

Following social principles can help generate more positive net present value projects in two ways.

- First, it may attract new revenues or reduce certain operating costs, which will increase the forecasted cash generated from the proposed project.

- Second, it may lead to a lower cost of financing for the company because investors will have a lower required rate of return, and that leads to a higher net present value.

Balancing What's at Stake: Shareholders versus Stakeholders

A business can't be socially responsible unless it can make the business case for being so. That's not impossible, because many companies have done just that over the years. But it's not always easy.

Legally, corporations are managed for the benefit of their shareholders, who own the company. The owners expect the managers to make money for them! In the United States, corporate managers have a fiduciary responsibility to maximize shareholder value while complying with other laws (Chapter 3 covers fiduciary responsibility in more detail). Some managers have interpreted that to mean that even the teensiest bit of philanthropy is wrong, wrong, wrong because it hurts shareholders. But over the long term, making money for shareholders involves behaving responsibly to others who have a stake in the business.

The following sections cover the differing interests of shareholders and others so you can understand the situation that managers are in as they try to do the right thing. I also talk about a philosophy that can bridge the gap between the shareholders and everyone else, the so-called *triple bottom line*.

Maximizing shareholder value

The key responsibility of a company is to maximize wealth for its owners, the shareholders. That's a main tenet of financial theory, and it's held up in courts as well. A company's management has a fiduciary responsibility to serve shareholders.

This isn't as mercenary as it may seem to someone who's not a shareholder. Usually, what makes shareholders happy makes everyone else happy, too: good products or services that customers gladly pay for, with good employees who are paid well for running the company efficiently. But there are some potential pitfalls.

Potential problems

Sometimes management's desire to get paid well while keeping those pesky shareholders off its back leads to cut corners and even outright fraud, destroying the business.

There's another problem with simply maximizing shareholder value. Some shareholders care only about the short term. They just want a big profit now, and they don't really care about what happens a month or a year or a decade from now.

Most investors are big institutional investors, such as pension plans or mutual fund companies, and the managers of those funds have to show high performance or the money will go to someone else. They need to beat the market right now, this month, this quarter. Sure, the money in the fund may not be needed for a long time, but that doesn't mean the money manager has the luxury of thinking long term.

In 2002, the last year for which the New York Stock Exchange has data, 21.5 percent of U.S. stocks were held by pension funds and 49.8 percent by such other institutional investors as foundations, endowments, and mutual funds. Another way to think about that is that 71.3 percent of stocks are held by institutions that live and die by quarterly performance, which forces a lot of managers into a short-term perspective. Ouch!

Customer service

Much of what maximizes value over the long term can be costly now, and that doesn't maximize value for the shareholder with the short-term perspective. Think about customer service. It's expensive to keep customers happy. You have to take back defective products, answer a lot of questions, and have a happy staff that smiles a lot. Keeping those customers happy keeps them coming back over the long term.

Customer service is an ongoing expense that creates long-term value. A company can boost its profits in the short run by cutting back on customer service, which may make the short-term shareholders happy, but all the annoyed customers will go elsewhere, harming long-term shareholders.

The key debate about socially responsible behavior by corporations is whether it's good or bad for shareholder wealth. Is it a big expense that detracts from the ongoing mission of making money, or is it an investment that may take a little from profits now but make the company stronger for years to come? Investments in good governance, clean technology, or sustainable economic development may take years to pay off, even if the payoff will be spectacular. Not all shareholders are patient enough to wait, and some may push the company to give up the project.

Remembering stakeholder value

Stakeholders are not shareholders. They're all the other people that contribute to the success or failure of the corporation: employees, vendors, customers, members of the community where the company has facilities, and regulators, among others. In the short run, corporations can maximize shareholder value without even thinking about the other stakeholders, but it can't do so in the long run. A company that wants to maximize shareholder value for years to come needs to think about its stakeholders — how it will recruit workers, retain employees, and work with the community at large.

Companies are supposed to maximize shareholder value because the shareholders are the owners. They put up the money for the company to operate, and they expect a return. However, companies use more than just shareholder capital to make the business possible. They need other inputs for their operations. And some of the key inputs belong to no one but affect everyone: air, water, soil.

Externality is the term economists use to describe the effects that a business has on things that are outside of the price of the goods or services that it sells. For example, if a business is polluting the water, there's a cost to the world, but it's not included in the price of the product. That's a negative externality. Externalities can be positive, too; maybe the company sponsors the local symphony as a way of marketing to its target customers, but all music lovers benefit from the donation.

Uniting shareholders and stakeholders with the triple bottom line

Because a company's management team has the responsibility to maximize shareholder value, it can't pursue any projects that benefit stakeholders unless it can show that these would ultimately pay off for the shareholders. A company that plans to stay in business for a long time needs to keep other stakeholders happy.

The *triple bottom line,* popularized by a book of the same name (written by Andrew W. Savitz and Karl Weber and published by Jossey-Bass), asks companies to account for how their operations and strategies affect people, the planet, and — of course — profits. The goal is to get companies thinking about how they will generate profits over the long haul by protecting important inputs.

A key maxim in business is that you get what you measure, because that's how managers set their priorities. That's why an accounting system that looks at externalities as well as plain old profit is more likely to generate good results for society as a whole.

A U.K. organization, AccountAbility (www.accountability21.net), has drawn up standards similar to Generally Accepted Accounting Principles (GAAP; the rules that govern accounting in the United States) to help companies report their social and sustainable activities. About 200 companies use them now, and the hope is that more will soon adopt the standards to help investors and others understand the effects of business activities.

Remembering the people

Companies involve all sorts of people: employees, customers, contractors, and residents in the communities surrounding their facilities. The people part of the triple bottom line recognizes that companies are accountable to the people they touch. The needs of the people may vary from place to place and time to time, but paying attention to how they are treated — and keeping track — will lead the company to do the right thing for its stakeholders and shareholders alike.

One reason to pay attention to people? People talk. And sometimes, they sue, which costs the company money. An organization's reputation is built on how it treats the people whom it deals with, no matter who they are or what they do.

Protecting the planet

The planet measure of the triple bottom line looks at how a company's activities affect the environment, from the very moment a product is a gleam in an industrial designer's eye until it's dead and buried — or not — in a landfill somewhere.

A company's environmental responsibility derives from how a product is sourced, manufactured, and moved to market, but it's also affected by what the company does at headquarters and how it works with its contractors. (No fair claiming to be clean while outsourcing your manufacturing to a contractor in a country with no environmental laws, and then flying in a big old carbon-spewing airplane to check up on things!)

The planetary measures on the triple bottom line can be controversial because the science around air, water, soil, and climate evolves as researchers discover more about the world around us. No matter how strong the effects of carbon on climate change, polluted air isn't good for anyone. Businesses (and their customers and shareholders) need natural resources to survive, so they need to use them with care.

Don't forget profit!

The bottom line is that a business has to make a profit to stay in business, and the triple bottom line philosophy recognizes that. Without profits, the business will close, and that harms the employees who need jobs, the customers who need what the company provides, the government that relies on it for taxes, and the shareholders who need a rate of return to meet their goals. The company has to show a profit, or the enthusiasm for its social activities will die off faster than a polar bear on a melting iceberg.

Ideally, the short-term profits will allow the company to afford its investments in people and planet, while those sustainability investments will pay off in long-term profits for the smart, socially responsible shareholders.

Heading Off Principal-Agent Problems

Socially responsible investors want to invest in companies that reflect their values. As owners, they want the managers who work for them to behave in responsible ways.

But managers are human beings, and as human beings, they may want to do what's best for themselves, not necessarily for the people they work for (not all are this way). Most corporate managers want to maximize their own compensation and career opportunities. Although that's to be expected, raises for employees may well mean reduced profits for the shareholders.

Then throw into the mix that some investors have a short-term perspective (a problem outlined earlier in this chapter), while others want the company to be around for the ages.

There's a term for these conflicts of interest between managers and different types of investors. It's the *principal-agent problem*, with the investors (or owners) being the *principals* and the managers being the *agents*. It's hardly insurmountable, but it requires that management be transparent about what it's doing so the shareholders have enough information to make decisions. It also requires that shareholders pay attention so they can influence what the management team is doing before problems develop. The following sections provide information on what you, the potential shareholder, can look for in terms of what you are and are not likely to find out about a business.

Transparency: How clearly you can understand the business

Managers often have very good reasons for not telling everyone everything about what they're doing. Suppose a company that you invest in is about to announce an amazing new technology that would reduce energy costs and improve water quality in developing nations. Well, gosh, wouldn't they want everyone to know? Wouldn't you, as a part owner of this company, want to know exactly what the technology is, and when it will be rolled out, and at what price, and what profit level, and what goals for market share? Sure you would.

And so would every one of the company's competitors. They, too, would want to know all about this technology, how profitable it is, and how much it will cost so they'll be ready to strike back!

Hey, it's tough out there. Businesses all over the world are fighting each other every day for customers, for great employees, and for slight advantages that add up over time.

As a shareholder, you don't have the right to information about the tiniest details of the business, because the business can't compete without keeping some information confidential. However, you have the absolute right to basic information about the company's finances. More on that in the next section.

Monitoring your holdings

Much of this book is about how to do research on different companies and investments to find out how well they match your investment criteria.

Now, all investing requires some work. You have to

- Figure out your risk parameters and your desired return
- Set appropriate goals
- Find suitable investments
- Track your returns to see if you need to make changes

Social investing adds one more layer: tracking how an investment is meeting your personal goals as well as your financial ones. (Many a business has announced an exciting new initiative, and then switched course midstream.) As an owner, you take on the cost of making sure that the business you invest in meets your priorities.

In a perfect world, the managers tell you everything you need to know. But where is this perfect world? Most managers report only what they have to, usually as mandated by such government regulators as the U.S. Securities and Exchange Commission, and not always in a format that's easy for regular folks to read. Because the managers don't perfectly represent the interests of all the shareholders, at least a few of them have to do their own research to see how management is doing.

Of course, that's why you're reading this book! Much of it is about how to determine whether an investment suits you. So keep reading!

Getting owners and managers on the same side

Owners and managers don't have to be locked in bitter combat. Just as the business can do well for shareholders while still respecting the interests of other stakeholders, so can it make shareholders wealthy while still rewarding managers for their hard work. The way to do that is by making owners out of the managers. This may call for a little shareholder activism (see Chapter 5 for more information).

Many companies give employees an ownership stake in the company. That way, the employees benefit when the shareholders do. Companies can do this several ways:

- **Giving stock as compensation:** Some companies give all employees a few shares of stock when they join the company or after several years of service. The stock may come in the form of a bonus, or it may be part of the ordinary compensation package.

- **Retirement plan matching:** If the company offers employees a voluntary retirement plan, such as a 401(k), it may match some or all of the employee contributions with company stock.

- **Stock purchase plan:** As an employee benefit, many firms allow workers to buy stock without commission, often at a discount to the market price.

- **Employee Stock Ownership Plan:** Often called an *ESOP* (pronounced *eee-sop*), an Employee Stock Ownership Plan allows the employees as a group to purchase all or part of the company. This often occurs when a division of a larger company is being spun out as a separate company or when a business is doing a major restructuring.

✔ **Granting employee stock options:** A stock option gives an employee the right, but not the obligation, to buy shares of stock in the future at a price agreed to today. For example, a company may give employees the right to buy stock three years from now at $5 per share. If the price is above $5, then the employee can exercise the option and sell the shares on the market for a nice profit. That gives the employees an incentive to get the stock price up above the exercise price. Stock options are cheap for companies to offer, too.

Check out Chapter 11 for more details on these employee stock plans.

Stock options can make managers rich, but they don't always benefit share-holders. Companies have been known to give too many options away, to set the price so low that holders will always make money, or even to reset the price so employees can exercise the option at a profit even if the stock price went down on their watch. Although options can ally managers with owners, it's more effective to give employees actual shares if reducing conflicts of interest is the goal.

Operating the Organization: Better Performance from a Clean Approach

Investors do well when their investments do well. Social investors hope to do good, too. But does good behavior help a company to do well? In many cases, yes. Following social principles can help a company stand apart in a crowded market. It can attract new customers, retain strong employees, and avoid the hassles of regulation while also keeping its investors happy.

In this section, I cover just a few of the ways that a clean approach to operations helps the company perform better (and better operating performance should lead to better investment performance).

Courting customers

Think of just about any product you can buy. Do competitors offer alternatives? Can you find a suitable substitute? Can you do without it? If the answer to even one of those questions is yes, then the company has to fight for your business.

Many companies find that customers want to do business with ethical companies that treat their employees well and work to minimize *externalities* (the effects that a business has on things that are outside of the price of the goods or services it sells). Customers who are trying to be more conscious of the effects of their purchasing decisions appreciate businesses that help them out by offering goods and services that are good for society and the environment, or at least not as bad as those offered by other companies. Thus, following socially responsible tenets can help a company attract and retain customers.

And attracting and retaining customers is key to business success! The hardest thing for any company to do is come up with a product or service that people want to spend money for. When you think of all the choices you have, any company that you deal with should be trying to keep you happy. (Not all do, of course. But that's probably because the management figures that you have few other options or that it's cheaper to get a new customer than to satisfy a current one. It happens.)

Because customers, like investors, care about how their money ties to their values, they're more likely to do business with companies that support their values. Whether it's developing environmentally friendly packaging, divesting from a war zone, or dropping advertisements from violent television shows, many businesses find that a social perspective brings dollars in the door.

If customers don't like how a business operates, they'll take their money elsewhere. At an extreme, they'll organize a *boycott,* in which they not only avoid a company's products, but they also encourage everyone they know to do so, too. The negative publicity from a well-publicized boycott often generates enough pressure to get the company to make changes. And in some cases, the bad public relations linger long after the business has improved its standards.

Attracting employees

Companies are only as good as the people who work for them. That's why most businesses struggle to attract and retain good employees. While there may be ups and downs in employment as the economy zigs and zags, the long-run outlook is good for skilled workers: As the U.S. population ages, more workers will retire, leaving fewer folks to mind the store.

Many people want to work for an employer with integrity, one that doesn't cut corners on compliance matters, customer service, or care for the environment. When the *baby busters* (the smaller demographic group following the baby boom) have their pick of employers, companies will have to compete for their talent, and workplace culture will be one of those measures.

No matter how competitive the job market is, organizations want employees whom they can count on. Many a business has been damaged by the actions of one or two rogue workers who take money, arrange kickbacks, or selectively overlook wrongdoing to get a deal done. A business that has an ethical workplace culture is likely to avoid such problems, if only because the workers it is most likely to attract are least likely to behave badly.

Reducing regulatory hassles

Free markets? Unfettered capitalism? Not hardly. No matter where in the world a business operates, it has government overseers. A whole range of national, regional, and local agencies keeps an eye on what companies operating in their little corner of the world do. The agencies want to make sure that the company meets whatever laws apply: employment conditions, worker and product safety, environmental regulations, accounting integrity, taxation.

Regulators can create hassles for a company. When a regulatory agency suspects a problem, it can send investigators and use subpoenas to get information about the situation. Even if it finds nothing wrong, complying will cost the company money and take time away from the business at hand. And if the agency does find a problem, it can slap the company with fines and sanctions that don't exactly enhance shareholder returns. At a minimum, mention of the investigation in the media will bring unwanted publicity to the company.

If a company doesn't behave well, new regulations can be passed to try to get change, creating a new layer of costs and headaches. (At an extreme, the Sarbanes-Oxley Act of 2002, which overhauled the U.S. financial reporting system and cost companies millions of dollars to meet its requirements, was passed in response to the behavior of just a handful of people at a handful of companies, like Enron and WorldCom. Ouch!)

Regulation isn't going away, because there are always going to be a few companies that don't play nice with everyone else. Given that it's a reality, the best way for a company to avoid the pain of regulation is to do right in the first place. Sure, there will still be pages of forms to wade through and lists of requirements to check off, but there will be less interference from the agencies for those businesses that get it right the first time. Companies that meet many social investing criteria are more likely to follow the rules and less likely to run into trouble with the Feds.

Opening international markets

It's a big global world out there, and businesses that have a reputation for good behavior have an easier time with global expansion. Sure, a corrupt company has a big advantage in a few locations, but those aren't exactly the most desirable markets to be in. Instead, a company that's looking for joint venture partners, overseas distributors, or plain old customers is better off if it has a good reputation back home and a culture that supports such transparent business practices as cooperation with regulators and disclosure of payments in order to head off bribery.

A global brand is an enormous asset, one that forms the competitive advantage that investors and managers alike crave. One way to build that brand is to adhere to high standards, no matter where the business operates. That prevents problems at home and abroad.

Investors at home care about a company's actions overseas. Many a corporation with a household-name product has found itself in hot water with customers when investigators discover that it operates sweatshops, pollutes the environment, or does business with countries with human rights violations on the other side of the globe.

Accounting for tax advantages

Taxes pay for schools and roads, but no one really enjoys paying their share. Many businesses can reduce their pain come April 15 through clean, socially responsible operations. How? Well, national, regional, and local governments offer tax breaks that savvy social businesses can claim.

For example, many economically disadvantaged regions want to attract employers. One way they can do this is by offering tax breaks to companies that agree to add a certain amount of business or hire a set number of workers in the local economy. Many investors seek out companies that are committed to economic development, which you can read about in Chapter 6; social investors who prefer investments in real estate, which is covered in Chapter 15, will almost always look at the tax benefits related to economic development projects.

Charitable donations are deductible from income taxes, and one way that many companies give back to their local communities and build their brands is by supporting philanthropic activities. It's another twofer: a benefit to society and a benefit to the business, and what social investor doesn't like that?

Finally, spending to support the workforce is almost always deductible, and it's almost always associated with the kind of company that a social investor likes. Healthcare, retirement benefits, and safe workplaces all cost money, but those expenses lead to tax savings (not to mention lower workforce turnover and higher productivity). You can read more about how companies support their employees in Chapter 11.

Chapter 3

Understanding Why Institutions Invest the Way They Do

*I*f you're simply trying to do better with your life and your investments, you may be tempted to skip this chapter. Do you care about what big, rich, professional investors are involved with? Probably not. But if you're interested in social and activist investing, then you may want to pay attention to what the people with the mega millions are doing.

For example, if you would like your employer to offer a socially responsible mutual fund as one of the choices in its 401(k) plan, or you want your college to consider greenhouse gas emissions when choosing investments, you need to know how to make your case! This chapter covers the constraints that pensions, foundations, and endowments have so you can better understand how to influence their choices.

And if you're not interested in this chapter, that's okay. It won't be on the final exam.

Pensions, foundations, and endowments dominate most stock market trading, and they lead many of the big shareholder activism projects. But they aren't faceless institutions. The folks who manage these funds are accountable to many others, including average people (who may be beneficiaries, donors, or employee representatives) simply trying to live better lives and make better investments. They may be managing your retirement, supporting charities that you care about, and financing your education.

Getting Familiar with the Rules

It may seem that Wall Street is populated with gun-slinging capitalists who do whatever they want, but it's not. Many corners of the investment business are highly regulated, and that can affect if and how investors choose to be responsible.

Because pensions are required by law to maximize investment performance, much of the research on how to make social investing profitable has come from these rich and rarified corridors. Money managers who want to collect fees for managing these large pots of money work to find ways to help these institutions meet their social and financial obligations. Their efforts, in turn, have helped improve the performance of other social investments, such as mutual funds. However, there are rules that must be followed.

The U.S. government guarantees employee pensions in the event that the sponsoring employer goes bankrupt. In exchange, the government places strict rules on how pension plans are invested to ensure that those plans remain solvent. That's why pension plans have to put social responsibility behind performance. Still, many manage to invest responsibly, and their experiences have influenced the entire field.

These rules can affect how your retirement money is invested. But you may find yourself in a position where you have to follow them. Maybe your union elects you to the board of the pension trust. Maybe you join a nonprofit organization's board of directors and have to make decisions about what to do with the endowment. Or maybe you take a job with a not-for-profit hospital or university and find that your budget is constrained because of endowment restrictions. If you know a bit about the rules and why they exist, you can ask better questions and make better decisions.

The fiduciary fix

A *fiduciary* has legal responsibility for investing for the beneficiary's benefit and no one else's. Someone acting as a fiduciary can't invest for his personal gain, nor can he make decisions that may benefit anyone other than the beneficiaries.

Fiduciary decisions are different from business decisions. A fiduciary decision involves how to invest in the plan, but a business decision is whether to offer the pension plan in the first place. After the plan is in place, all fiduciary requirements have to be met.

In general, fiduciaries must

- ✔ Act solely in the interests of the investment program's beneficiaries for the purpose of providing benefits to them
- ✔ Carry out their duties prudently
- ✔ Follow the investment documents
- ✔ Diversify investments
- ✔ Pay only reasonable expenses

Covering corporate pensions

A *pension* is a retirement plan offered by an employer. In the United States, pensions fall into two main categories:

- ✔ **Defined benefit:** In a defined benefit plan, the employer agrees to pay retirees a set percentage of their salaries when they retire. The employer is responsible for investing the money appropriately.
- ✔ **Defined contribution:** In a defined contribution plan, the employer agrees to set aside some amount of the worker's pay (often as a match for whatever money the worker agrees to contribute); usually, the worker can choose to invest the money in a variety of mutual funds or other investments. (A 401(k) plan is one of the most common defined contribution plans.) The return isn't guaranteed.

The organization setting up and managing the pension has plenty of rules to follow to ensure that workers receive the money they've been promised. Those rules affect social investing practices. It's not easy for a pension to be socially responsible, but it's not impossible as long as the legal requirements are met first (which I explain in the following sections).

The following sections help you understand why your pension is invested as it is and why your 401(k) includes the choices that it does. Knowing this information can also help you make your case for change, because change has to be within these constraints.

Participation in many retirement plans is optional, but you shouldn't opt out if the fund doesn't offer an investment choice that matches your mores. You can often save far more money within a retirement plan than outside of it because of the tax advantages and employer matching funds. That employer contribution is free money! All you have to do to get it is join the plan. In most cases, you can do more good by investing in the retirement plan. For example, you can donate some of the money that you otherwise would pay in taxes to organizations that you care about, instead of opting out of the retirement plan in favor of a social investment that doesn't have tax benefits or an employer contribution.

Introducing ERISA

ERISA is a pretty word, isn't it? Doesn't it seem like it would be a unique name for a baby girl? It stands for the *Employee Retirement Income Security Act* of 1974, and it's a powerful law. It explains what a private company offering a pension plan must do to keep the plan legal; in exchange, the IRS gives employers a tax deduction for contributions to many types of plans, and the U.S. government will insure pension benefits in the event of a corporate bankruptcy.

Under ERISA, a company offering a pension plan must

✔ Have a written plan explaining how the pension is set up and operated

✔ Create a separate trust fund to hold plan assets outside of the corporation

✔ Develop a record-keeping system to track funds

✔ Prepare documents giving information to employees and to the government

Employees, who are the pension's *beneficiaries* (people who receive the investment's income), often have their own ideas about how the money should be invested. Some of these ideas would seem to benefit them, too, but that doesn't mean the ideas can be included in the pension's investment policy.

"Wouldn't it be great if our pension were only invested in unionized companies?" the employees might say. And yes, it would be great, if (and only if) stock in those companies offered comparable investment returns to nonunionized companies. However, the risk-and-return decision has to come first. The pension has to be invested in order to generate the return required to meet the payment obligations to the plan beneficiaries (for defined benefit plans).

Now, that doesn't mean that the pension has to invest in any old company that meets the risk-return criteria. It simply means that the fund managers have to look at return first. If they come up with a list of five companies that meet their financial criteria, they can choose to invest in only the three that also meet social criteria. But if no socially suitable investments are available, the money must be put into the most financially appropriate investments.

If you want your employer to add a socially responsible mutual fund to its 401(k) plan, you'll have a better case if you offer the names of funds that have competitive performance. A great place to research mutual funds is Morningstar, www.morningstar.com. There's also a company called SocialK (www.socialk.com) that offers a socially responsible 401(k) program that companies can adopt.

Quashing an ERISA myth

There's a common myth that pensions aren't allowed to pursue socially responsible investments under ERISA, but that's not true. In 1998, the U.S. Department of Labor, which enforces ERISA and other pension regulations, issued an advisory opinion to Calvert Group, a money management firm following a socially responsible style, about whether such a fund is appropriate under the law. The department ruled that it is, as long as the risk-and-return profile is better than or equal to that of a similar investment with no social criteria. You can see the opinion, in all its glorious legalese, at `www.dol.gov/ebsa/programs/ori/advisory98/98-04a.htm`.

Some social screens may not increase investment return but can reduce the costs of investing, and holding down costs is a major concern for fiduciaries under ERISA. For example, companies with good governance may not always have a better return, but it's easier for investors to analyze and monitor them. That's one way a fiduciary can justify a socially responsible investment.

Fiduciaries: Looking out for the pension's best interests

Remember when you were a kid and your parents wouldn't let you do something that you really wanted to do? They'd say, "I'm only doing this for your own good, and someday you'll thank me." Your mom or dad was doing exactly what fiduciaries have to do sometimes.

A fiduciary's loyalty to the beneficiaries is based on providing plan benefits, not other matters that may be of interest to the beneficiaries. (Check out the earlier section, "The fiduciary fix," for more details on fiduciaries.) It's not always clear how a fiduciary's decisions today best benefit the plan participants in the long run. The fiduciaries act for the beneficiaries' own good, and someday, during retirement, those beneficiaries will thank them. (Just like you may now be grateful to your parents, or you may be in therapy to heal the damage they did.)

For example, suppose the employer's biggest customer is about to be taken over by a competitor, and the plan owns shares in that company. Employees may want the plan's fiduciaries to vote against the takeover. After all, if it goes through, it may hurt their business and cost them their jobs. That would be bad for the beneficiaries! But if the acquisition increases the share price, then the plan should vote for it because it would be good for the beneficiaries from the perspective of their pension benefits, which the fiduciaries must put first.

As for how the business will compete after the acquisition? That's an issue for the company's managers, not for its pension fund officers.

Fiduciaries aren't just for ERISA plans. Anyone you hire to help you with your investment planning may be a fiduciary. What you need to know is, are their fiduciary responsibilities to you or to the firm that employs them? That's a key question to ask!

Being prudent about managing money

ERISA creates another standard, that of a *prudent expert*. It's an extension of state laws that require people managing money for others to be *prudent persons*. And just who is a prudent person? It's a person who acts with discretion and intelligence to seek a reasonable investment return. It's an unfortunate "you'll know it when you see it" standard.

Under the prudent person rule, fiduciaries are expected to avoid speculative investments. The prudent expert standard is higher; it assumes that this person of discretion and intelligence has been trained in investing and stays up-to-date on the state of the financial markets. So a prudent expert can invest in speculative investments if they make sense relative to the entire pension portfolio.

If you're invited to serve on an employee pension committee at your workplace, or if you're elected to serve on your labor union's pension board of trustees, you'll be held to a prudent person standard (unless, of course, you have a degree in finance and work in the financial markets). But you'll be expected to use that status to hire prudent experts to help manage the fund's investments.

Managing state and local pensions

A state or municipal employee pension doesn't have to meet ERISA standards. Why? Because the federal government can't interfere with the business of running a state as long as the state laws are in accordance with the U.S. Constitution. But this doesn't mean that these pensions can do whatever they want to, even if it looks like they can under the law.

ERISA was passed so that if a corporation goes bankrupt, the U.S. government will take over the pension liabilities. However, if a state or local pension goes bankrupt, who takes over the liabilities? You, the taxpayer, do. So if you're a taxpayer with an interest in social investing, it's good to understand the financial issues and vote accordingly. But vote with your head before your heart.

Here's the thing: The good citizens of a state may want the pension money invested in ways that suit their political and economic goals. "Wouldn't it be great if our state employee pension invested in companies that were based right here? Think what that would do for our economy!" they say.

But not every state is a booming economic machine, and not every company is a worthwhile investment. In some places, billions of dollars invested in local businesses would quickly lead to poor investment performance, and then the taxpayers would be on the hook for making up the shortfall.

Some social investment styles can add value to the pension fund. For example, maybe a company has a history of lax environmental standards that have created huge liabilities. Avoiding that stock may help increase investment returns.

The citizens aren't the only ones with an agenda. Sometimes politicians want the state and local pension funds to be invested in ways that suit their pet projects. Maybe they want big investments in agriculture or in residential real estate in their district or in alternative energy. They may make announcements in hopes of garnering votes without considering the long-term tax consequences of sloppy social investment policies. If these ideas don't make financial sense, then the pension beneficiaries will suffer and so, ultimately, will the taxpayers.

When it comes to pension investing, the rule should always be beneficiaries first, social criteria next.

Checking out charitable foundations

A *charitable foundation* is a pool of money that's invested for philanthropic purposes. Some foundations support a specific organization, while others give away grants to a range of worthy causes. You can usually deduct contributions to charitable foundations from your income tax, and the foundation doesn't pay any tax on its investment performance.

Under U.S. tax law, a foundation has to give away at least 5 percent of its net assets for appropriate charitable purposes each year. Some foundations are tiny, and others are huge. The Bill and Melinda Gates Foundation, the largest in the United States, has $37.3 billion in assets as of March 31, 2008, and pays out about $2 billion each year.

Charitable foundations have a lot of freedom in their investment strategy because they don't have the same amount of oversight as that of an ERISA fund. Some foundations view responsible investing as part of their mission. Others prefer to invest for higher returns, with or without concern for the responsibility of the investments, to maximize the amount of money they can spend on their missions. A foundation's trustees have a fiduciary responsibility to the foundation's beneficiaries, which means that they have to consider investment performance.

The Internal Revenue Service expects foundations to spend their money on bona fide charitable purposes. The operation of a foundation is covered by state laws governing trusts, which require boards of trustees made up of *prudent persons* (those people who use diligence and care; see the "Being prudent about managing money" section earlier in this chapter). Any charges against a foundation for a breach of fiduciary responsibility are brought under the law of the state where it's based, not under federal law.

Most states have adopted the Uniform Trust Code, which standardizes the management of trusts and foundations and the requirements of their trustees — namely, that they be loyal to the trust's beneficiaries. You can see the model law at www.law.upenn.edu/bll/archives/ulc/uta/2005final.htm.

The foundation investment trustees are not only legally accountable to the fund's beneficiaries, but they're also morally accountable to those who donate money. If the board isn't making smart investment decisions, the foundation may find that its ability to raise funds is limited. Donors want their money to be put to good use, after all, and that means generating enough investment return to serve the foundation's beneficiaries for years to come. Often, major donors are invited to serve on the board of trustees as a way of creating accountability. And often, when a board is suspected of violating its fiduciary responsibilities, it's the donors who cause the fuss.

Appreciating endowments

Endowments are like foundations in that they're designed to support a philanthropic institution; donations to them are deductible from income taxes; and the income they earn isn't taxed. But they have one key difference: An *endowment* is designed to support the institution in *perpetuity* (that is, to go on forever). Whether the beneficiary is a university, a museum, or a synagogue, and whether the endowment is in the thousands or billions, not one penny of it has to be spent in any given year.

The biggest American endowments support universities. Harvard, for example, has $34 billion and is the second-largest charitable fund in the United States, behind the Bill and Melinda Gates Foundation (Mr. Gates, of course, isn't a Harvard alumnus because he dropped out after starting Microsoft in his dorm room. He's a contributor to his not-quite alma mater, though.)

Setting endowment spending rules

Universities tend to spend 3 to 5 percent of their endowments each year, even though they don't have to. Still, a lot of graduates leave with big student loan burdens. That's because many endowment funds are earmarked for specific purposes, ranging from research in ancient Chinese literature and medieval music concert series to scholarships for students from particular congressional districts. The endowment trustees have to honor the donors' wishes when they determine how much money to spend each year.

By law, endowments don't need to spend any of their money; the funds are there for the perpetual support of the institution. If it doesn't need the money this year, then it doesn't have to spend anything. Nevertheless, some people believe that an endowment has a responsibility to spend its money.

However, many endowments do spend large amounts of their capital every year on the institutions that they support. Therefore, they have to consider their spending in their investment policy; it's more important than any social criteria in place.

Although foundations and endowments don't have the same spending requirements, endowments, like foundations, are accountable to people who give money to the fund and to those who receive it. Some donors may not like their money going to stocks in countries with repressive political regimes, but others would be really unhappy to find out that fewer scholarships could be given or less cancer research could be performed because the trustees made the nature of the investments more important than the financial considerations.

Protesting for change on campus

Unlike endowments at other institutions, colleges and universities have faculty and students who follow the news, study issues carefully, and are happy to protest when they don't like what they see. In fact, many faculty members view endowment issues as an opportunity to help students learn more about current events, ethics, and finance at the same time.

Protesting endowment investments is a time-honored tradition on many campuses, whether or not the trustees like it. Because the world changes so quickly, a social investing policy that made sense a few years before may not fit anymore. As the issues change from sweatshops to the Sudan and a new crop of students arrives on campus, there's new pressure.

There's even an organization to help students stay focused and run effective campaigns. The Responsible Endowments Coalition, www.endowmentethics.org, is a clearinghouse for student and faculty activities promoting social investing on their campuses. The site includes information on key issues, advice on how to work with administration and trustees, and sample proposals for new investing policies.

On some campuses, students have worked with alumni to start alternative foundations that invest according to socially responsible guidelines. Donors can give money to the fund rather than to the endowment. Each year, the alternative fund sends money to campus for current operating needs.

Tools for Institutions with a Social Mission

An individual who wants to follow a social investment strategy is responsible only for herself, but an institution has to be careful that it doesn't short-change stakeholders. This means an institution's fiduciaries need to be more diligent about researching and selecting the right investments.

It's not enough for the trustees of a pension to do a Web search on Islamic mutual funds, for example; it requires some study to show that the fund has a plan for generating income to meet agreed-to spending requirements while avoiding fixed-income securities.

But social investors have more tools than just investment selection. Institutional investors who had to balance performance with their missions pioneered techniques for improving their social position without compromising other aspects of their business. These techniques can help you, whether you care about a pension or an endowment or if you're trying to do better on your own.

There's no reason that a social investing program should shortchange anyone, but it has to be carefully thought out first.

Using consultants

Because the trustees of pensions, foundations, and endowments need to show that they're meeting all of their fiduciary responsibilities, they usually hire consultants to audit financial results, analyze investment performance, and recommend changes based on performance, contributions, and expected spending needs. Some consultants specialize in social investing and can work with the trustees to design an investment policy and find suitable investments while still meeting all financial objectives.

Consulting fees are paid by the plan beneficiaries, because the money comes out of their return. Fiduciaries must ensure that the beneficiaries' money is spent properly — that the fees go to the consultant offering the best services, rather than to the one who has the best baseball tickets or other client perks.

Maintaining transparency

Investors tend to prefer companies that are *transparent,* which means that they

- ✔ Publish financial reports in more detail than is required by the Securities and Exchange Commission
- ✔ Give regular updates on the progress of the business
- ✔ Have managers who are willing to answer investors' questions

However, the same pension, foundation, and endowment investors who want transparency from the companies that they invest in aren't always willing to give it to their own stakeholders. The double standard is alive and well.

I'd argue that maintaining transparency is an important first step in social investing, one that costs nothing. True, some investing strategies are proprietary, but beneficiaries deserve information about the asset classes used and the general investing principles followed.

Joining coalitions

In addition to choosing investments that fit the social mission, a pension, foundation, or endowment can generate change by finding other like-minded institutions to join it in pressuring companies to improve their performance.

CalPERS is an example of how creating a coalition works (see the nearby sidebar for more details). CalPERS, the pension system for employees of the state of California, identifies troubled companies, and then it finds other investors and asks them to join its campaign. Those investors meet as a group with the company's management to explain their case, and they agree that they'll vote for board members who support them. CalPERS is able to force laggard companies to make changes because they can get other investors to go along with their ideas. (It doesn't hurt that CalPERS has shown great performance from this technique.)

The CalPERS Story

The largest state pension in the United States is the California Public Employees Retirement System, also known as CalPERS. It has $242.2 billion to invest on behalf of 1.5 million beneficiaries, and much of that money is invested with clear social goals in mind. The fund has a long track record of success, so it's often viewed as a model for what a public pension should be. Much (but not all) of CalPERS's money is invested along social lines, making its success even more notable.

Under its current investment strategy, CalPERS allocates some of its portfolio to investments in the state of California and some to emerging environmental technologies. It invests much of its money internationally, but only in countries with political stability, basic democratic institutions, and enforced labor laws, among other standards.

Where CalPERS has earned the most renown in the activist investment world is with its corporate governance investment strategy. Each year, the fund identifies several companies in its portfolio that are underperforming their industry groups and that have terrible corporate governance practices. For example, one of the companies on the 2008 list is The Cheesecake Factory, a restaurant chain based in California. For the five years ending February 2008, the stock underperformed the average restaurant company by 140.5 percent. That's real money that could go to real California pensioners!

Being in CalPERS's home state doesn't give a company a pass on performance. When a company makes the target list, CalPERS staffers get together with their peers at other pension funds, charitable foundations, and mutual fund companies, and then press the company for major changes in management compensation, the board of directors, and disclosure practices. Companies that make the list are often forced to change, and on average, they end up outperforming the S&P 500 index the year after they make the list.

Voting proxies

A *proxy* is the form that investors use to vote for members of the board of directors, executive compensation packages, and other proposals that a company presents. Under ERISA, a proxy belongs to the fund's beneficiaries and must be voted in their best interests. That's a good policy for fiduciaries who aren't beholden to ERISA, too. It's a way of showing a company's management that the investors are paying attention and either support what they're doing or want change. (Chapters 4 and 5 have more information on proxies.)

Chapter 4

How to Research Responsible Investments

Social investing means different things to different people. A Muslim has a different investment universe than a tree hugger. Furthermore, companies change over time, so a definitive list of acceptable investments would be out of date in a matter of months.

This is why a socially responsible investor has to be a *fundamental analyst,* too. What's that? A person who does careful research into the financials and the business to figure out how a company makes its money, whether that source of profits will continue, and how the company fits into an investment portfolio. Social investors need to figure out what to look for, and then find it, before making an investment. And that's what this chapter is all about.

Most of the information here is most useful for analyzing public stocks, but it can be applied to other investments, too. Accounting terms, board of director responsibilities, and monitoring ongoing events come into play for almost any investment you come across.

Reading and Understanding an Annual Report (10K)

The *annual report* is the key to understanding what a public company does to earn money. In most cases, it's the first place to look for information to help you determine whether to make an investment.

Every year, publicly traded corporations have to file an annual report with the Securities and Exchange Commission. The required form is called *10K*, and it is a veritable treasure trove of information about a company. The problem? It's not very pretty. It's usually printed in plain type on plain paper, with nary a chart, graph, or photo to break up the text and numbers.

But that's the annual report you should be reading. Many companies also publish a glossy, four-color annual report that contains some, but by no means all, of the information in the 10K. Some annual reports are gorgeous; there are even competitions for annual reports that judge their photography and design. The 10K is beautiful only to those who take the time to read it and find the rich information within.

Every quarter, the SEC requires companies to file an update on their progress on form *10Q.* These reports are similar to the annual report, although without as much detail; they're important for tracking changes in the business over the year. I cover these in more detail later in the chapter.

The 10K report starts out with an overview of what the company does to make money. The company's management describes the business, its history, and its strategy. The report gives a lot of data about products, business locations, and employees. The key business risks are described, as well as any outstanding legal issues and related matters that employees need to know about.

Next, you get to the meat: management's discussion and analysis of financial conditions and operating results; signatures and certifications; the financial statements, including the income statement, balance sheet, and statement of cash flows; and the footnotes to the financial statements. I describe all of these in the following sections.

Want to find a 10K report to help you follow along as you read the next sections? Go to the U.S. Securities and Exchange Commission's EDGAR database (www. sec.gov/edgar.shtml), which includes all filings of all public companies in the United States. You can search for a company that interests you and find its 10K report. Any company will work because the basic format is standard.

Management's discussion and analysis

The *management's discussion and analysis* of financial conditions and results of operations, usually shortened to the much more concise abbreviation *MD&A,* is the executive spin on what happened. It's not a marketing document, though, so you can expect to see bad news. What it tells you is where the company made its money and what the outlook is for its different business lines.

The MD&A starts with a repeat of some of the business description listed earlier in the 10K. Then it describes how the company's profitability changed line by line from one year to the next — maybe not in as much detail as you'd like, but it's better than you trying to guess! It may break revenues down into different business lines and geographic areas, describe such extraordinary circumstances as natural disasters or lawsuits that affected operations, and discuss areas where the management plans to invest and expand.

After reading the MD&A, you may be finished with your analysis — the company may not be what you had hoped it would be when you started your analysis. Or maybe you're intrigued. If you are, then it's time to look at the certifications.

Signatures and certifications

Financial reports are prepared by company management, but publicly traded companies have to have their financial reports audited by an outside firm. The audit firm issues two statements that are included in the 10K report. The first is the certification of the accounting results, and the second is the report on internal controls.

How many days are in a year?

"Thirty days hath September, April, June, and November; of 28 hath but one; and all the rest have 31." Unless you happen to be an accountant. Accountants would prefer that a year be composed of 12 months that have 30 days each, for a total of 360 days. Of course, the world isn't run by accountants.

Companies have different practices for setting the ending dates of months, quarters, and years. Some go by the calendar, some by the last business day of the month, and some by the last Friday of the month. After a few reporting periods, the company may be off by a week, and that has to be tacked on somewhere. Companies disclose their calendar practices in the management's discussion and analysis and in the footnotes to the financial statements. Sometimes the difference in performance between two companies in the same industry may be that one company had 51 weeks in its accounting year, while another had 53. Also watch out for sudden changes in calendar practices, which may indicate that the company is stretching to make its estimates.

Certification of financial results

The first certificate is a letter from the accounting firm describing what it did in the audit and what it found. A typical letter is printed below in italics; my explanation of what the different sections mean follows each paragraph in plain old regular text.

SocialCo
Report of Independent Registered Public Accounting Firm

To the Board of Directors
SocialCo, Inc.

We have audited the accompanying consolidated balance sheets of SocialCo, Inc. (the "Company") as of December 31, 2006, and December 30, 2007, and the related consolidated statements of operations, shareholders' equity and comprehensive income, and cash flows for each of the three years in the period ended December 31, 2007. These financial statements are the responsibility of the Company's management. Our responsibility is to express an opinion on these financial statements based on our audits.

Here, the auditors are making clear that management is responsible for the numbers presented. If it turns out that a handful of executives made up the results, well then, don't blame the auditors.

We conducted our audits in accordance with the standards of the Public Company Accounting Oversight Board (United States). Those standards require that we plan and perform the audit to obtain reasonable assurance about whether the financial statements are free of material misstatement. An audit includes examining, on a test basis, evidence supporting the amounts and disclosures in the financial statements. An audit also includes assessing the accounting principles used and significant estimates made by management, as well as evaluating the overall financial statement presentation. We believe that our audits provide a reasonable basis for our opinion.

The *Public Company Accounting Oversight Board,* often referred to by the acronym *PCAOB* (some people pronounce it *peek-a-boo,* but most simply say each letter), is an organization created by the Sarbanes-Oxley Act of 2002 to create standards for audits. Here, the accounting firm is explaining that it followed the guidance of the PCAOB. You'll never see an audit firm say that it didn't!

In our opinion, the financial statements referred to above present fairly, in all material respects, the consolidated financial position of SocialCo, Inc. at December 31, 2006, and December 31, 2007, and the consolidated results of their operations and their cash flows for each of the three years in the period ended December 31, 2007, in conformity with U.S. generally accepted accounting principles.

At last, the key paragraph! The audit firm is willing to say that the financial statements are a fair representation of the firm's financial position. That means it's an *unqualified opinion* — there are no exceptions or catches to the statement. Most companies will have a similar statement in their annual reports, but every now and again, an audit firm will issue a *qualified opinion*. It will say that the financial results are fair representations except for whatever issues the auditors uncovered. Investing in a company with a qualified auditor opinion is riskier than investing in one without, but an unqualified opinion like this one doesn't signify a safe investment.

> *We also have audited, in accordance with the standards of the Public Company Accounting Oversight Board, the effectiveness of SocialCo, Inc.'s internal control over financial reporting as of December 31, 2007, based on criteria established in Internal Control–Integrated Framework issued by the Committee of Sponsoring Organizations of the Treadway Commission and our report dated February 29, 2008, expressed an unqualified opinion thereon.*
>
> *Giant Accounting Firm LLP*
> *February 29, 2008*

Here, the audit firm discusses the *financial controls* of the company, which it must test to ensure that the company is able to create accurate financial statements. Financial controls cover such things as whether people lose access to the computer system when they quit or who approves any adjustments to sales figures, and they show up in more detail in the next certification you see, discussing financial controls.

Certification of financial controls

The Sarbanes-Oxley Act of 2002 was passed in response to some nasty corporate frauds, and it requires companies to prove that their financial systems work. The idea is to make it harder for management to blame low-level employees or their own ignorance if a problem crops up. Here's an example of a certification of financial controls, with the standard language in italics and an explanation in regular type.

> *SocialCo, Inc.*
> *Report of Independent Registered Public Accounting Firm on Internal Control over Financial Reporting*
>
> *To the Board of Directors*
> *SocialCo, Inc.*
>
> *We have audited SocialCo, Inc.'s internal control over financial reporting as of December 31, 2007, based on criteria established in Internal Control–Integrated Framework issued by the Committee of Sponsoring Organizations of the Treadway Commission (the COSO criteria). SocialCo, Inc.'s management is responsible for maintaining effective internal control over financial reporting,*

and for its assessment of the effectiveness of internal control over financial reporting included in the accompanying Management's Report on Internal Control over Financial Reporting. Our responsibility is to express an opinion on the company's internal control over financial reporting based on our audit.

The *Committee of Sponsoring Organizations,* or *COSO,* is a group of accounting and financial trade groups, such as the American Institute of Certified Public Accountants. It's been around since 1985 and gained power after the Sarbanes-Oxley Act was passed when accounting firms and corporate executives started paying attention to the need for effective accounting systems.

We conducted our audit in accordance with the standards of the Public Company Accounting Oversight Board. Those standards require that we plan and perform the audit to obtain reasonable assurance about whether effective internal control over financial reporting was maintained in all material respects. Our audit included obtaining an understanding of internal control over financial reporting, assessing the risk that a material weakness exists, testing and evaluating the design and operating effectiveness of internal control based on the assessed risk, and performing such other procedures as we considered necessary in the circumstances. We believe that our audit provides a reasonable basis for our opinion.

Here, the accounting firm describes a bit of what it did to determine whether the company's accounting process comes up with accurate numbers.

A company's internal control over financial reporting is a process designed to provide reasonable assurance regarding the reliability of financial reporting and the preparation of financial statements for external purposes in accordance with generally accepted accounting principles. A company's internal control over financial reporting includes those policies and procedures that (1) pertain to the maintenance of records that, in reasonable detail, accurately and fairly reflect the transactions and dispositions of the assets of the company; (2) provide reasonable assurance that transactions are recorded as necessary to permit preparation of financial statements in accordance with generally accepted accounting principles, and that receipts and expenditures of the company are being made only in accordance with authorizations of management and directors of the company; and (3) provide reasonable assurance regarding prevention or timely detection of unauthorized acquisition, use, or disposition of the company's assets that could have a material effect on the financial statements.

Here's a description of what internal controls do. In simpler terms, having good internal controls means that the company has some assurance that the numbers being tracked are accurate.

Because of its inherent limitations, internal control over financial reporting may not prevent or detect misstatements. Also, projections of any evaluation of effectiveness to future periods are subject to the risk that controls may become inadequate because of changes in conditions, or that the degree of compliance with the policies or procedures may deteriorate.

The auditors want you to know that even with good internal controls, the company can still have fraud.

In our opinion, SocialCo, Inc. maintained, in all material respects, effective internal control over financial reporting as of December 31, 2007, based on the COSO criteria.

But, with all that being said, the auditor is certifying that the company has good financial controls. Now, not all companies do; the standards for internal controls are complex, so it's not unheard of for a good company to miss a few. You may arrive at this paragraph and see a qualified statement, explaining that the company has good controls except for a new acquisition, except for one or two international operations, or except for a new accounting system that's been installed but not yet tested.

We have also audited, in accordance with the standards of the Public Company Accounting Oversight Board (United States), the consolidated balance sheets of SocialCo, Inc. as of December 31, 2006, and December 31, 2007, and the related consolidated statements of operations, shareholders' equity and comprehensive income, and cash flows for each of the three fiscal years in the period ended December 31, 2007, of SocialCo, Inc. and our report dated December 31, 2007, expressed an unqualified opinion thereon.

And that audit, of course, is the subject of the statement above.

Giant Accounting Firm LLP
February 29, 2008

Income statements

The *income statement* tells how much money the company brought in from sales of its goods and services, and how much money it had to spend to get those sales. Here's a sample income statement:

SocialCo Income Statement

Dollars in thousands except per share
Years ending December 31

	2007	*2006*
Sales	$6,591,773	$5,607,376
Cost of goods sold	4,295,170	3,647,734
Gross profit	2,296,603	1,959,642
Selling, general, and administrative costs	1,999,152	1,640,633
Operating income	297,451	319,009
Interest expense	(4,208)	(32)
Interest and other income	11,324	20,736
Pretax income	304,567	339,713
Income taxes	121,827	135,885
Net income	$182,740	$203,828
Shares outstanding	140,088	139,828
Earnings per share	$1.30	$1.46

Here's what you should note while examining the income statement:

✔ *Sales,* also called *revenue* or *turnover,* is the money that came in from selling the company's goods and services. The MD&A, described earlier in the chapter, usually has a detailed breakout. In most cases, you want to see sales go up each year.

✔ *Cost of goods sold,* sometimes abbreviated as *COGS,* are any expenses that can be directly tied to a particular sale. It includes the cost of inventory, sales commissions, and promotional advertising, such as coupons that can be redeemed for a specific product. It should stay more or less constant, or go down, as a percentage of sales.

✔ *Gross profit,* sometimes called *gross margin,* is the difference between sales and cost of goods. It's how much money is left over to cover the costs of operating and financing the company. You calculate it as a percentage by dividing gross profit by sales. The result is a useful number for tracking how the profits from sales change over time.

The hardest thing for any company to do is come up with something that people will pay money to have. The next hardest thing is to come up with something that people will pay enough money for that the business costs will be covered. A business's success hinges on its ability to generate sales and manage cost of goods sold.

✔ *Selling, general, and administrative costs,* sometimes called *SG&A* or *operating expenses,* are the costs of running the business that can't be directly tied to any particular sales. These include the costs of the headquarters staff, accounting and legal services, insurance, and other expenses. These costs should grow more slowly than sales.

✔ *Operating income* is gross profit less SG&A. It shows how much money the company has to cover its financing, both debt and equity. It's sometimes called *EBIT*, for *earnings before interest and taxes;* yes, people really say *eee-bit.*

✔ *Interest expense* is the money that the company has to pay to anyone whom it owes money to: bondholders, banks, suppliers. It should be a small percentage of operating income; if the company misses payments to anyone who has loaned it money, it may be forced into bankruptcy.

✔ *Interest and other income* is the money that a company makes on its cash balances. Some companies have a lot of cash, so they put it on deposit or buy short-term bonds and generate interest from those. Companies often provide financing to customers, and that generates interest income, too.

✔ The *income tax* line isn't the amount of taxes that the company actually pays. Instead, it's the liability that the company is expected to have, given current tax rates. The taxes actually paid are reported in the footnotes to the financial statements (I describe footnotes later in the chapter).

✔ *Net income* is how much of the profit is left over for shareholders after interest and taxes are considered. It's usually divided by the number of *shares outstanding* to generate *earnings per share,* which is compared to the stock price as a way of measuring how cheap a stock is. The higher the price per share is relative to earnings per share, the more expensive the stock is.

After you look at the annual report and financial statements for a company that you're interested in investing in, check out the annual report of its largest competitor, even if you would never consider buying shares in that company. The comparison will give you a sense of what your company is doing right, where it has room to improve, and where it's vulnerable.

Balance sheets

The *balance sheet* tells you what a company owns and what it owes. It has to balance, by definition, because every transaction has to have an offsetting transaction somewhere else. That's a useful check for the company's bookkeepers when they're looking for errors. By the time the balance sheet gets published for your perusal, everything adds up nicely. The only question for you is, how strong is it? By that, what are the company's assets, and how are they financed? What follows is a sample balance sheet for the fictitious SocialCo Inc., and the following sections tell you what you need to know while reviewing it.

SocialCo Balance Sheet

Dollars in thousands
Years ending December 31

Assets	2007	2006
Cash and equivalents	$2,310	$62,317
Short-term investments	165,054	193,847
Accounts receivable	105,209	82,137
Inventory	288,112	203,727
Prepaid expenses	40,402	33,804
Deferred income taxes	66,899	48,149
Total current assets	$667,986	$623,981
Property, plant, and equipment (net)	$1,666,559	$1,236,133
Goodwill	668,850	113,494
Intangible assets (net)	97,683	34,767
Deferred income taxes	104,877	29,412
Other assets	7,173	5,209
Total long-term assets	$2,545,142	$1,419,015
Total assets	$3,213,128	$2,042,996

Liabilities and Shareholders Equity	2007	2006
Current installments of long-term debt and leases	$24,781	$49
Accounts payable	225,728	121,857
Accrued payroll and benefits	181,290	153,014
Dividends payable	25,060	—
Other current liabilities	327,657	234,850
Total current liabilities	$784,516	$509,770
Long-term debt and capital leases	$736,087	$8,606
Deferred lease liabilities	152,552	120,421
Other long-term liabilities	81,169	56
Total long-term liabilities	$969,808	$129,083
Total liabilities	$1,754,324	$638,853
Par value of common stock	$1,233	$1,148
Additional paid-in capital	1,231,612	1,146,724
Treasury stock	(199,961)	(99,964)
Retained earnings	425,920	356,235
Total shareholders equity	$1,458,804	$1,404,143
Total liabilities and shareholders equity	$3,213,128	$2,042,996

Assets

The first part of the balance sheet is the firm's *assets,* which are all the things that it owns, listed in order from short term to long term. The first group, known as *current assets,* are those that are cash or that can be turned into cash quickly. These include

- ✔ Cash and equivalents (such as bank CDs) are listed first, followed by short-term investments, such as Treasury notes, that can be converted to cash in short order. Some cash is good; too much means there's a risk of management doing something stupid with it.

- ✔ *Accounts receivable* is money owed to the firm by customers. Many firms sell items long before customers pay for them. For example, you use electricity, the electric company sends you a bill, and then you have a few weeks to pay it. The billing starts when you flip the switch the first day of the new billing period, but payment may not be received until almost two months later. Some customers are deadbeats; if receivables increase faster than sales, there may be a problem.

- ✔ *Inventory* is those goods held for sale. They may be items in stores right now, items still being assembled, or components that will be assembled. It is hoped that all of these things will be sold and turned into cash, but it may not happen right away or at the price the company hopes to achieve. No matter what it cost to produce VHS tapes, who wants to pay full price for them today? Inventory should grow at about the same rate as sales.

- ✔ *Prepaid expenses* show up when the company pays its bills in advance. Maybe its landlord offers management a deal if it pays its rent for the year all at once, or maybe the utility company has allowed the company to lock in rates in exchange for an advance payment.

- ✔ I mention in the section on the income statement that the tax expense on that document isn't necessarily the amount of taxes that the company paid. In some cases, the company has paid more than the income statement shows. If the overpayment will be resolved soon, say if the company can apply it to its income tax bill next quarter, then it's a deferred tax asset treated as a prepaid expense.

After the current assets, the company reports the longer-term ones. These are items that are more permanent in nature:

- ✔ *Property, plant, and equipment,* sometimes shown under the abbreviation *PP&E,* includes land, buildings, and machinery ranging from giant cranes to desktop printers. Each year, the company has to expense a portion of the value of buildings and equipment to show how they are wearing out;

this is known as *depreciation*. The balance sheet shows the value after depreciation. Land isn't depreciated, but it's shown at the price paid, which may not be the current value. Because of how the accounting for PP&E works, the value may not tell you much about the company.

✔ *Goodwill* is a funny number. It's the difference between the price that a company pays for an acquisition and the net value of the acquired business's balance sheet. It's supposed to represent the added value of brand names, customer relationships, and other business niceties. It rarely tells you much about the company.

✔ *Intangible assets* are patents, trademarks, customer lists, and other items that are important to the business's success. But here's the thing: In most cases, intangibles only show up on the balance sheet when they've been acquired, because that's the only easy way to assign a value to them.

Coca-Cola's (NYSE: KO) secret formula has no value for accounting purposes. The only way an accountant could give it value would be for the company to try to sell it; then the buyer would be able to record the price paid as an intangible asset. Whether your beverage of choice is Coke or Pepsi (NYSE: PEP), it's clear that that secret blend of ingredients is worth a heck of a lot more than the zero value that Coke has to use. That's the problem with intangible assets.

✔ *Deferred income taxes* sometimes make an appearance as a long-term asset. These are taxes paid over and above what was reported on the income statement. Long-term deferred income tax assets may never be recovered. On the other hand, many companies pay less in taxes than is shown on the income statement. That creates a deferred tax liability that may never be paid. Check the footnotes to find out how much money a company actually pays in taxes.

Liabilities

The *liabilities* section of the balance sheet tells what the company owes. As with the assets section, it's arranged in order from current — due in less than a year — to noncurrent. Here's what you may see:

✔ *Current installments of long-term debt and leases* are payments that are due in a year. For example, you may have a 30-year mortgage, but each time you make a payment, you pay down a little bit of the principal. It's your very own current installment on a long-term debt. Compare this to the cash balance to get a sense of how easy it will be for the company to make the payment.

✔ *Accounts payable* are bills that the company owes. If the company doesn't pay its bills, then it has more cash, but at some point, the electric company comes in and turns off the lights if the bills aren't paid. Anytime a supplier sends a bill, an account payable is created, and it stays on the balance sheet until the bill is paid. Some payables are good, but if the amount grows much faster than sales, the company may not be paying its bills.

✔ Most employees are paid every two weeks or once a month, even though they come to work every day. Until payday, a liability for *accrued payroll and benefits* shows up on the balance sheet.

✔ *Dividends payable* shows dividends that have been declared to share-holders but not yet paid. Not all companies pay dividends, so not all companies will have this line on their balance sheets.

The difference between current assets and current liabilities is called *working capital.* It's a measure of cash that has to be invested in the business on an ongoing basis to support sales.

✔ *Long-term debt* represents money owed to bondholders, banks, and other creditors. It all has to be paid back, but it's not necessarily bad for the company to owe money as long as it generates enough cash each year to pay on schedule.

✔ *Deferred leases* are long-term contracts with landlords or equipment holders. Accounting rules handle leases differently from debt, but in practice, they're the same: If you don't pay your mortgage, the bank will have you evicted. If you don't pay your rent, the landlord will do the same.

Shareholders equity

The difference between assets and liabilities is the *shareholders equity.* It's what the shareholders get to keep after all the bills are paid, at least according to the values recorded on the balance sheet. The total value matters more to you than any of the line items, but here's the play-by-play so you know what's happening:

✔ *Par value* is a minimum value of the shares. Many companies set the par value of the shares at just a penny; some don't even bother with a par value.

✔ *Additional paid-in capital* is the value of the shares over and above the par value at the time they were issued. It's an historical number.

✔ *Treasury stock* is the value of any shares that the company bought back in the open market. It represents a reduction in equity.

✔ *Retained earnings* are the total value of profits that the company earned on the income statement, minus the amount of any dividends paid.

Statement of cash flows

The *statement of cash flows* is one of the most mysterious of the financial statements, but it's also really important. It tells you how much of a company's sales bring in cash, and how much of a company's expenditures send out cash.

Many customers make purchases with no money upfront, which affects the cash flow. For example, many appliance retailers allow customers to wait six months before making a payment, with no interest charged in between. That's because a lot of people have to buy an appliance on short notice to replace one that stopped working, and demanding payment upfront may be the difference between getting a sale and losing it to a competitor. The retailer can book the sale to revenue when it takes place, but it won't collect the cash for 180 days. And that can be a problem if the company needs the money in the meantime.

The statement of cash flows is broken down into three sections:

- *Cash from operating activities,* which shows how much money was generated from the company's basic business

- *Cash from investing activities,* which shows spending on property, plant, and equipment

- *Cash from financing activities,* which explains how the company raises money or returns it to shareholders

Following is an example of cash flows from financing activities. The following sections tell you what you should look for on the statement of cash flows.

SocialCo Statement of Cash Flows

Dollars in thousands
Years ending December 31

	2007	*2006*
Cash flows from operating activities		
Net income	$182,740	$203,828
Depreciation and amortization	186,390	156,223
Deferred income taxes	(27,203)	(15,521)
Accounts receivable	(5,179)	(17,720)
Inventories	(51,055)	(32,200)
Prepaid expenses	1,345	(7,849)
Accounts payable	42,064	18,509
Accrued payroll and benefits	1,845	26,033
Other current liabilities	22,893	129,886
Other adjustments	44,763	(8,525)
Net cash from operations	$398,603	$452,664
Cash flows from investing activities		
Property, plant, and equipment	$(529,682)	$(340,202)
Acquisitions of assets	(618,396)	(13,024)
Purchase of available-for-sale securities	(277,283)	(555,095)
Sale of available-for-sale securities	475,625	362,209
Net cash from investing activities	$(949,736)	$(546,112)

Cash flows from financing activities

Dividends paid	$(96,742)	$(358,075)
Common stock issued	54,383	222,030
Purchase of treasury stock	(99,997)	(99,964)
Tax benefits from employee stock options	9,839	52,008
Proceeds from long-term borrowings	(93,357)	(5,680)
Payments on long-term debt and leases	717,000	—
	$491,126	$(189,681)
Net change in cash and equivalents	$(60,007)	$(283,129)
Cash and equivalents, beginning of the year	$62,317	$345,446
Cash and equivalents, end of the year	$2,310	$62,317

Cash flows from operating activities

The difference between making the sale and collecting the cash shows up on the statement of cash flows. It starts with net income, and then adds and subtracts different values to show how much net income was turned into cash. It also explains the changes in values on the balance sheet from one year to the next.

The first item to be added back to net income is *depreciation and amortization,* the gradual write-down of the company's buildings, equipment, and intangible assets. This is an accounting charge that doesn't use up any cash.

The next set of numbers shows the changes in current assets and current liabilities. If a company were able to get out of paying cash by drawing on a prepaid expense account or letting its accounts payables build, then there is an *addition to cash* on the statement of cash flows. If the company spent cash, say to buy more inventory, then there is a *subtraction to cash.* There will also be a subtraction to cash if the company booked a lot of sales on credit, because it will take a while for the customers to pay for their purchases.

The bottom line for this section is *net cash from operations,* and it tells you if the company's business is bringing in cash or using it up. Over the long run, this number has to be positive or the company can't stay in business. When a company is expanding, it may have negative cash from operations as it spends on inventory and extends credit to more customers. When a company is running into trouble, it may also have negative cash from operations, so check to see where your business is.

Cash flows from investing activities

In order to grow, businesses have to invest. They have to spend money on the equipment that employees need to get their jobs done. They may need to add more office space or larger manufacturing facilities. The company may even want to acquire another business. All of that shows up in this section as *cash spent.*

A larger business might sell off a division or major equipment, and that would show up as an *inflow of cash*. You'll often see purchases and sales of available-for-sale securities and other cash equivalents, such as U.S. government securities, in this section. If a company has no immediate use for excess cash, it might invest it to get a higher return.

This section of the statement of cash flows will usually be negative, and that's okay. Smart investments can help a company be around for the long haul. In fact, a company that's not spending enough on investments won't be able to sustain its business.

Cash flows from financing activities

This section of the statement of cash flows shows how the company is getting the money it needs, other than the money that it is generating from operations. If the company pays a dividend, buys back stock, or pays off its debt, then it's spending cash for financing purposes. If it takes on more debt or issues new stock, whether through something big like a public offering or something small like employee stock benefits, then it's receiving cash.

The bottom line

Finally, after going through all three sections, the company reports its net change in cash for the year. Over several years, it should be slightly positive. If a company has too much cash, it should be paying dividends, buying back stock, or investing in the business. If it is short of cash, it won't be in business much longer.

No matter how much you love a company's mission and business, if it can't make money, it's a bad investment. It won't improve just because you want it to.

Footnotes

The footnotes to the financial statements are like a treasure map. Following the footnotes can be tedious, but that's how you get to where all the good stuff is hidden.

Like what? Like how much money the company actually paid in taxes. How much money it owes its employee pension plan. Whether it has pending lawsuits that could hurt it. When its debts come due. What kinds of debts — like leases — that it has that aren't reported on the balance sheet.

It's worth the slog through the bog of legalese. Many times, good news or bad news is leaked in the footnotes to those who bother to read them.

Perusing the Precious Proxy

Each year, companies send their shareholders statements of issues for them to vote on. *Proxies* are important sources of information that you can consult before you invest. Chapter 5 tells you everything you need to know about using proxies to create change.

Just like annual reports, proxies are public information that must be filed with the Securities and Exchange Commission. You can often get them from the company, even if you aren't a shareholder, or you can go to the SEC's Web site, www.sec.gov. Proxies contain three key tidbits of interest to prospective investors:

- ✔ Who the members of the board of directors are
- ✔ What potential conflicts of interest exist that might cloud the executives' or the board members' judgments
- ✔ How much money the executives make

Board of directors' information

Legally, companies are owned by shareholders who elect a board of directors that oversees the work of management. The proxy is the medium for electing the board, so the proxy statement includes biographical information about the people in the running. Look it over: Do these seem like people who understand business, finance, and the company's industry? You can even do a little Web searching on the names, if you're so inclined.

Don't be misled by celebrity names on boards. You want to see that the board has members who understand their responsibilities and who have the time to do the work. Some boards nominate glamorous people, maybe because the other board members want to hobnob. Now, a celebrity may well be able to do the job, but do your research to make sure.

After the Who's Who will be a description of the board's committees, with members specializing in compensation, audit, and nominating. Toward the end, you'll see a sentence or two about how often the board members went to meetings. Most governance experts believe that a board member needs to attend at least 75 percent of all meetings to provide good guidance.

Finally, check out the section entitled something like "Committee Interlocks and Related Transactions," which tells you if the board members have any conflicts of interest. A common issue is compensation, because the CEO may well be on a board determining compensation for a board member who is an officer at another company. Then both would have incentives to push for big raises and little oversight. You may also see board members arranging jobs for their children, receiving significant discounts on products that the company sells, or working for customers. Then decide: Are these conflicts great enough that the board member may not be making good decisions for me?

Checking out how much the execs make

The fun part of the proxy is the section on executive compensation. It usually starts with a description of the company's philosophy: Is it to be an industry leader in all aspects, including executive pay? Is the goal to reward top performers? Share gains with all employees? Maintain equity? Promote loyalty? Provide incentives? These different attitudes affect the way that people at all levels are paid. No system is right or wrong, but the choice affects the organization's culture. It may also affect the company's performance, depending on what market conditions it faces.

Following the discussion of how the firm approaches pay, the proxy includes a description of employee stock option programs and other incentive compensation that involves stock. Shareholders care because new stock issued reduces the percentage of the firm that other shareholders have. They want to know if the performance incentives offset that dilution.

The proxy then lists the compensation of the five most highly paid officers in the firm, as well as the compensation for members of the board of directors and the chairman of the board, if the chairman isn't also an executive.

Only the executives' compensation has to be disclosed, even though some companies have a few employees who make more than the CEO. The SEC has proposed the so-called "Katie Couric Rule" that would require companies to also disclose the compensation of employees who earn more than the CEO, named for the most highly paid staffer at CBS Corporation (NYSE: CBS). At press time, the rule hadn't passed.

There's nothing wrong with executives making a lot of money as long as they're generating results for shareholders and as long as all employees are compensated for their work, too. There's a problem if the executives get fat raises while everyone else sees their returns go down.

In my opinion, the best part of the proxy statement's discussion of compensation is usually found near the end under the heading "Certain Relationships and Related Transactions." Here, the executives disclose any conflicts of interest they may have, which can range from owning the office building that the company leases for its headquarters to giving their children summer jobs. Most of these conflicts at most companies are minor, but on occasion, you'll see conflicts that are so large that it's as if management has contempt for the shareholders.

Staying Up-to-Date

The annual report and the proxy tell you the general state of the company at the end of the last fiscal year. But a lot can happen in the intervening 365 — or 360 — days between annual reports. If you're considering investing in a company, you should check out the latest facts. If you own a security, staying on top of the news should be a priority. You can get some of the information from the company in yet more SEC filings, and the rest you can find from reading the news.

Reviewing quarterly reports (10Q)

Every three months, publicly traded companies have to update shareholders on their progress. They usually issue a news release and hold a conference call, but the minimum requirement is to file a quarterly report on form 10Q with the Securities and Exchange Commission. You can get the 10Q from the company or from the SEC's Web site, www.sec.gov.

The 10Q is similar in format to the 10K report but much less detailed. It includes a discussion of what has changed over the quarter, and then includes quarterly financial statements with footnotes. The presentation may have fewer lines than in the annual report, and it isn't audited by any accounting firms, but it should give you enough information to determine how your company is doing relative to the same time period last year.

Most companies have seasonal businesses. Most retailers, for example, post almost all of their sales in December. Hospitals show more admissions in winter months, because of flu and pneumonia, than they do in the summer. That's why you need to compare quarterly results to the same quarter a year ago rather than to the quarter that just passed.

Listening in on conference calls

Many companies hold a conference call for analysts and investors after they report their earnings each quarter. One or two of the senior executives go through the results and explain what happened (with a hefty dose of positive spin, natch), and then take questions. In most cases, only analysts and institutional investors invited by the company can ask questions, but anyone can listen. Companies usually announce these calls on their Web site. If you miss the call, most companies then post a recording or a transcript on their Web sites. (Companies don't have to have conference calls, but if they do, they are required to make the information available to all investors.)

These calls are great sources of information about where the business is headed. The questions — and the answers — give you a good sense of what concerns experienced analysts have about the financial results and the prospects for the future. The managers answering the questions may be cheery, candid, evasive, or even a combination of the three. The information helps you track the progress of the business, or find out where it's been and where it's going if you're a prospective shareholder.

Viewing investor presentations

When you're checking out the investor section of the company's Web site, you may see some presentations that company executives have given to groups of investors, usually at brokerage firm conferences. The brokers hosting these meetings only invite their large clients, so you probably can't get in. However, the SEC requires presenting companies to share their presentations with all investors through transcripts, Webcasts, or slide shows that you can find on their Web sites.

As with the conference calls (see the preceding section), there will be a lot of happy talk about how the company is the best at everything. You'll also get some data and news updates that can give you a sense of how the company is progressing toward its targets. You can use the information to decide if you want to buy, sell, or hold.

Checking up on current report filings (8K)

If a company has significant news to announce between the due dates for its 10K and 10Q filings, the SEC has it issue an *8K report,* also called a *current report of material events or corporate changes.* An 8K may contain information about a management change, a disaster at an operating facility, the announcement of a major new product, or the outcome of a pending lawsuit.

In most cases, the company also issues a press release that you can find online (I cover how to use news databases and other online resources later in the chapter). The 8K filing ensures that the news announcement becomes part of a company's permanent record, available to everyone through the SEC, no matter what happens to the press release or other news archives.

Poring over the prospectuses

Whenever a company issues a significant amount of new securities, it has to issue a *prospectus*. It looks a lot like a 10K report with even more information about the history of the business and the qualifications of the management team. Some companies issue only one prospectus at the time of the initial public offering and never issue another. Other companies may do another public offering of stock, issue public bonds, and make large acquisitions by using enough stock that a prospectus has to be printed.

The company that you're researching may not have any prospectuses. But if it does, be sure to read the most recent one to help you decide if the investment will help you meet your financial and social objectives.

Stock prospectuses

When a company issues stock for the first time in an *initial public offering (IPO)*, it has to issue a prospectus on SEC form S1. This sets out the company's history, gives detailed biographical information on the senior managers and board members, and describes its industry in depth. The idea is to give an investor every bit of information needed to make a smart investment decision. The prospectus stays on file whether or not the company goes through with the offering.

After a company goes public, it may issue small amounts of stock through employee option and purchase plans or through small acquisitions. A prospectus isn't required for those, although other SEC filings might be.

Some companies make other large offerings of stock after the IPO, referred to as a *follow-on offering* if new shares are issued or as a *secondary offering* if current owners are selling large blocks of stock. For these, a new prospectus has to be filed on form S3. This prospectus has a little more information than the most recent 10K report, but it's not as large as an IPO prospectus.

If a company does a major acquisition and has to issue stock to do it, it will issue an S3 prospectus, possibly in combination with a proxy if current shareholders have to vote on the deal. This prospectus describes the combined business, including *pro forma* financial statements that show what the financial results would look like if the companies were already combined. It's usually the best source of information about how a merger will work.

Debt prospectuses

Many companies issue publicly traded bonds. They usually do this through a *shelf registration,* which means they can file a bond offering with the SEC and then sell the bonds as they need to in order to raise the money. A company may file to offer $100 million in debt, and then find that it makes the most sense to issue $50 million now and another $50 million in six months.

If the company's stock is already public, it can usually make the offering under form *FWP,* which stands for *free-writing prospectus* and really isn't a form at all. It's a supplementary statement that explains what the offering is and how the securities will work without going into details about the company and its history, which are available from other filings.

If a company doesn't have public stock but wants to issue public bonds, it has to issue a prospectus with similar information as with a stock offering. Most private companies that want to issue debt usually choose to do a *private placement* instead; the offering prospectus doesn't have to be filed with the SEC, but only high-net-worth investors can buy the bonds.

Mutual fund prospectuses

Open-end mutual funds issue new shares every day to people who want to invest in them. They are sold through prospectuses which are updated at least once a year.

A mutual fund prospectus is a little different from a company prospectus. Instead of giving an extensive history of the fund, it explains what the fund is like right now. It usually starts with an overview of the fund's investment objectives and the strategy it will use to meet them, including what types of securities the fund managers will look at and what criteria they will use to select them. The prospectus usually describes the amount of risk the fund is expected to have so investors can determine if it matches their desires.

The fund will also have information about historic performance, as well as a detailed discussion of the types and amounts of fees that are charged. Chapter 13 has a lot of information on how to assess different mutual funds.

Google and More: Doing a News Search

The SEC filings contain a ridiculous amount of information about a company, but it's all from the company's perspective. That doesn't mean that it's wrong or misleading, but other people outside of the company have different perspectives on the business.

Besides the major newspapers *(The New York Times, The Wall Street Journal, The Financial Times),* many companies are covered in great depth by the media of the town where the headquarters is. Some companies are followed by bloggers who are obsessed with the good, the bad, and everything in between. And sometimes, interesting tidbits about the company come up when you least expect them.

Hence, investors need to be comfortable with online research! Several financial sites let you monitor stock prices during the day, and many of these sites carry press releases announcing corporate news. A simple query through any of the popular search sites can turn up information that you may not have considered.

Google offers a service called Google Alerts (www.google.com/alerts) that lets you place your search terms on file. You'll then receive an e-mail whenever a site with those terms comes up on Google.

But that may not be enough for you. You may also want to consider searching blogs through a service like Technorati (technorati.com); you may even uncover a few related to your investments or to your social activism style that you want to monitor regularly.

Major news databases, such as LexisNexis (www.lexisnexis.com) or ABI/INFORM (www.proquest.com), can help you find articles in smaller newspapers, trade magazines, and other publication that may not offer online access to their archives. Subscriptions to these services are pricey, but most public libraries have subscriptions. Your library may allow you to get access to these databases through its Web site by using your library card. Mine does! Your friendly local librarian may subscribe to other investment databases that you can use to help you find out more about companies before you invest in them.

Narrowing Your Research with Screening

Are you wondering how to turn your newfound knowledge and all the information you've gathered into investment action? One way is through *screening*. With a screen, you set the criteria for your investment, and then you check several companies at once to see which fit and which don't.

Plugging numbers or criteria into a screen

The traditional way to screen is to set up a spreadsheet and enter the data that you've uncovered in your research. Then take your spreadsheet and sort and analyze the data to find investment opportunities that work for you. It's effective, but it's also a lot of work.

The good news is you don't have to do the screening yourself. If you're investing through a brokerage firm, most of them have screening capabilities that their customers can use. Or, if you're a do-it-yourselfer, you can fire up your computer and use one of the online screening services:

✔ Google Finance (`finance.google.com/finance/stockscreener`) has a screen to help you select stocks.

✔ Morningstar (`www.morningstar.com`) has basic stock and mutual fund screeners for free; more powerful ones are available by subscription.

✔ MSN MoneyCentral (`moneycentral.msn.com/investor/finder/customstocksdl.asp`) has a basic stock screener that looks at valuation.

✔ Yahoo! Finance (`finance.yahoo.com`) offers screening for stocks, bonds, and mutual funds.

Most screening systems are set up so you enter the criteria that matters to you, and then wait for the system to generate a list of companies that match. A good screen is primarily financial; it may look for companies that are expected to grow, that are really cheap, or both. Most screeners have few social criteria, although there may be some information on industries, governance, or other criteria.

Table 4-1 shows the result of a screen I ran on general entertainment companies that had at least some inside ownership (to show employee engagement), positive operating cash flow (to demonstrate financial stability), and expected revenue growth next year. It came back with five stocks for me to consider. I can export the information into a spreadsheet, where I can add columns with other statistics that may be important to me.

Table 4-1   Sample Screening on the Entertainment Industry (General)

Held Insiders >= 0

Operating Cash Flow >= 0

Sales Growth Est Next Year >= 2

Ticker	Company Name	Market Capital- ization	Forward P/E Ratio	Sales Growth Est Next Year	Operating Cash Flow	Shares Held by Insiders
CCL	CARNIVAL CORP	30.764B	13.81	7.3	3.845B	30.027
RCL	ROYAL CARIBBEAN C	6.245B	10.5	8.3	1.211B	38.737
FUN	CEDAR FAIR LP	1.249B	16.8	2.9	181.7M	8.681
LYV	LIVE NATION	1.277B	125.08	8.5	49.8M	16.612
WWE	WORLD WRESTLING E	1.158B	18.73	5.8	98.2M	11.958

If your criteria are too high, you may not end up with any results. My first few versions of this screen had higher thresholds for inside ownership and cash flow; they returned no stocks. I had to be less particular in order to have something to show you!

Double-check the data in a screen before you buy or sell any security based on the results. The results can be thrown off by fiscal years that don't match calendar years, acquisitions, one-time transactions, or unusual accounting methods. If the screen generates the name of an intriguing company, the next step is to read the financial statements.

Combining the results with additional research

Screening is both positive and negative. *Negative screening* helps you rule out investments that won't work for you. *Positive screening* helps you find opportunities that meet your criteria that you may not have known about otherwise.

Social investors may have a positive attitude about changing the world, but their investing usually starts with negative screening. That is, they rule out companies, industries, and types of investments that don't fit their values. Whether it's an entertainment company that started a soft-core porn cable channel, the defense industry, or bonds, some investors won't touch certain companies or investment vehicles. Assuming that you haven't narrowed the field to exclude everything, what you have left — family entertainment companies, the entire S&P 500 excluding military contractors, stocks — can be sorted through with positive screening.

Few software packages can handle extensive negative screening. They may not catch that pork-processing division that generates 8 percent of revenues or that employee benefit plan that you're not happy about. That's why you have to do some of your negative screening manually by doing your research.

What the screen doesn't tell you, the 10K report will. (See the earlier section, "Reading and Understanding an Annual Report (10K)," for more details about these reports.)

Instead of trying to rule out companies, many social investors run positive screens. It's also called *inclusion* or the "best in class" approach. The idea is to seek out companies that fit your social goals. Like negative screening, it usually means doing research to find the information you need to make the right decision.

You may be able to simplify your screening by working with the companies in a socially responsible index that matches your style. Identify the index, get the list of securities included in it (usually available from the index publisher's Web site), and use that as a starting point for further screening. Chapter 13, which covers exchange-traded funds, has information on some of the different social indexes that they're based on.

Chapter 5

Lights, Research, Action! Using Your Research to Influence Your Investments

. . . .

In This Chapter

▶ Taking charge for change

▶ Making your case to management

▶ Connecting with other investors

▶ Nominating board members

▶ Requesting change through shareholder resolutions

▶ The lawsuit of last resort

. . . .

*A*ctivist investing is just that: Active. It's not only about finding investments that match your interests, but also about trying to change the world for the better. After all, for many, money is about the best incentive out there! Companies respond to it just like people do. That's the whole point of our fabulous capitalist system. Hence, social investors who can make the case for change may be amply rewarded. Depending on who they are and how much of a security they own, investors can meet with management, propose changes, and make them happen. It doesn't take millions of dollars; smaller investors can work with others to combine their resources and power.

This chapter tells you how to press for changes that can benefit your portfolio, other investors, and the world at large. It's a way of getting closer to that proverbial "doing well while doing good."

Has Anything Changed?

When you make an investment, you consider your needs as well as the prospects and benefits of the different investments that you're considering. Ah, but what happens otherwise? Investing, socially responsible or otherwise, is an active game. You have to stay on top of what's happening and then decide what you want to do about it.

Things change. All the time. Investments that you once wouldn't have considered may now meet your criteria, while investments that were fine fits when you made them may not be performing as you had hoped, either financially or socially.

Part of the fun of social investing is the opportunity to create change in the world, and that requires paying attention, responding, and maybe even taking action to make a difference. In Part II of this book, I cover different styles of social investing, and in Part III, I cover the different types of investments that social investors can consider. But what happens if, for example, you own stock in a company that could be more responsive to shareholders than it is now? What if you want a local bank to pay more attention to customers in the local community? The following sections help you keep an eye on your investments and know what to do if you're not pleased with the changes you see.

Monitoring your investment

The investment business is all about news and information. Several newspapers, such as *The Wall Street Journal* and *Investor's Business Daily*, cover the markets in detail. CNBC brings trading news to your TV. Seemingly hundreds of magazines cover regional, national, and international business, and almost every town has at least one talk radio show where the participants cover investments. Throw in all the Web publications, blogs, and discussion boards, and you can find out just about anything you want to know.

What you're looking for in all this information is what's changed. Is the company still adhering to the values that attracted you to it in the first place? Is the investment performing as well as, better than, or worse than you had expected? Can you live with the changes, or do they affect how the investment works within your portfolio? Everything in life changes, after all.

Are you overwhelmed? Well, I don't blame you. There's a 100-year-flood's worth of information out there, so here are three tips for wading through the water:

✔ Use the free Google Alerts service (www.google.com/alerts) offered by the search engine company. You can enter in the search terms that you care about, such as the company name and a key issue. Whenever a new item using those terms shows up on Google, you'll receive an e-mail so you can check it out.

✔ Most Internet portals let you set up your own custom news section to bring you stories on the companies or issues that you care about. If you use a home or start page offered by your Internet service provider or by one of the major news and search companies (Google, Yahoo!, or MSN, for example), you should be able to do this.

✔ When you start investing, take the time to look through all the different news sources out there. Find the two or three magazines, newsletters, newspapers, Web sites, or blogs that best fit your style, and then make a point of keeping up with them.

Just remember that you'll probably end up with more stories than you know what to do with, so don't get too excited by headlines; take the time to read the article.

Naturally, the annual report and any news announcements from the company should go into your mix of reading materials. (See Chapter 4 for more on these.)

Deciding on your plan of action

If you notice that your investment isn't what it once was, then you have to decide if you can live with that. If you can, great. But if not, you have three choices:

✔ Get more information.

✔ Divest the security.

✔ Try to create change.

You may want to start by getting more information about the situation. Oftentimes, business news is a cycle of rumors in the market countered with spin by the PR managers of the companies involved, and it can take a while to sort out what's really happening. Keep digging, using resources listed in the "Monitoring your investment" section or in Chapter 4 to look for confirmation or context for the news. After all, the company has an incentive to make everything look good, but others can have axes to grind and use them to take unfair slices at a company's reputation and valuation.

In some cases, you may decide to sell, to *divest* of the security completely to get it out of your portfolio and move on. This option is especially attractive if the investment's financial outlook isn't looking so hot. You may end up incurring a tax liability, but you'd have to pay taxes on a gain someday anyway.

But what if you have owned the security for a very long time and would have enormous tax liability if you were to sell? And what if the investment's financial prospects are excellent? Then sticking to your principles isn't so easy. Still, holding your position doesn't mean selling out your values. You may be able to influence the company management. How? Well, keep reading!

Creating the Change You Want

Many investors become activists because they're not happy with how their investments are performing on measures both monetary and moral. Other investors are activists from the get-go; they're willing to buy securities that don't meet their needs with the explicit goal of trying to force change. This is especially true of investors interested in corporate governance (covered in Chapter 7). It's a risky strategy because it may be difficult to get the changes made that you want, and in the meantime, you may be stuck with an investment that is contrary to your ideas.

No matter how much your investment means to you, it's probably small relative to the entire market for the security. The stock doesn't know you own it, as the traders like to say, and it doesn't owe you anything. Sometimes your best option is to sell.

If you want to rev the change engine, first identify a company that has a specific problem that causes it to behave irresponsibly and affects performance. For example, maybe the company is losing market share because it's making products that use a lot of energy when they're used. This is one use of the research techniques covered in Chapter 4.

Next, find out information about the other investors in the fund. The proxy statement will tell you which shareholders own more than 5 percent of the stock, as well as how much stock senior executives and members of the board own. If employees and board members control a lot of the stock, they may be less open to the involvement of outside shareholders than if they own very little.

Many institutional investors, especially mutual funds, have to disclose their holdings in companies. You can find that information on quotation systems, such as Yahoo! Finance (`finance.yahoo.com`), when you look up the company's price quote. You can get a sense of how involved the shareholders are. (For example, if the holders are equity index funds, then the fund managers aren't going to investment conferences and meeting with management. If the holders are affiliated with socially responsible mutual fund companies, then they are almost definitely engaged.)

If you think the people who are investing in the company are pushing for change, then your quest to buy the stock in anticipation of change may be more successful.

Making your votes count at meetings

Shareholders own the company, managers work for shareholders, directors monitor managers, and the purpose of the company is to maximize shareholder value. Those concepts are taught in the very first session of the most basic corporate finance course, and yet, they don't always play out in the real world.

As a small shareholder, the company may not even know your name; your stock may well be held in *street name,* which is the name of your brokerage firm. Nevertheless, you can let yourself be known and get your questions answered. All public companies publish financial reports and hold annual shareholder meetings, and many of them hold periodic conference calls, attend conferences, and accept questions and comments from shareholders.

Attending annual meetings

Each public company is required by law to hold an *annual meeting.* During this meeting, the management gives a report to the board and the shareholders, and shareholder votes are tallied. Shareholders are invited to the meeting and can vote on issues there instead of submitting proxies (see the next section for more on proxies). The agenda, issued on SEC Form DEF 14A (also known as the *proxy statement*), includes time for shareholder questions.

Annual meetings can range from perfunctory two-hour meetings in a company conference room to the days-long extravaganza of shopping, softball, and steak put on by Berkshire Hathaway (NYSE: BRK-A), the investment company controlled by Warren Buffett. Most shareholders skip annual meetings, but folks located in the town where the meeting is held or who have a strong stake in an issue (financial or otherwise) may want to attend.

Information about the date, time, and location of the annual meeting is on the first page of the proxy statement, and you should receive it in plenty of time to book your trip. In many cases, annual meetings are open only to shareholders, and to attend you may be given a ticket, asked to register in advance, or be required to show a brokerage statement.

Any material information discussed at the annual meeting is released to the public, but that doesn't mean that the general public is allowed to attend the meeting.

Although the Internal Revenue Service allows investors to write off many investment expenses, trips to annual meetings aren't included. Why? The IRS was concerned that people were buying one or two shares of stock in companies headquartered in resort areas, and then planning vacations around the annual meeting in order to write off their trip.

Voting proxies

Few shareholders attend annual meetings, but that doesn't mean they give up their say. In fact, that's why the DEF 14A filing is known as a proxy statement: Investors who don't attend the annual meeting use it to make their votes known in advance.

These votes are cast by *proxy,* which means the shareholders authorize someone else, usually a designated member of the management team, to register their votes at the annual meeting. (And don't worry, the votes are cast as you request! Proxy votes are audited and reported.)

The DEF 14A includes information about the members of the board of directors and the company's senior executives, including the amount of stock that each owns. It describes key board policies and committee assignments, gives a report on the management compensation program, and lists any shareholder proposals.

Want to know which board member has a child who received a highly paid summer internship, which executive's spouse provides interior decorating services at above-market rates, and how much everyone used the company's jet for personal use? Then read the proxy statement. It will give you a good sense of the norms within the organization that may or may not benefit shareholders. (Because proxies are such valuable sources of information about a company, I cover them in more detail in Chapter 4.)

The key issues on which shareholders vote are:

- **Members of the board of directors,** who by law are to represent the interests of shareholders and provide oversight to management.

- **The company's audit firm.** Only a handful of firms handle most of the audits of U.S. companies. By necessity, shareholders almost always have to approve the firm recommended by the board.

- **Executive compensation packages,** especially those that involve the issuance of stock directly or through options.

- **Proposals that shareholders — including you — may have brought to the board.** You can find out more about shareholder proposals and resolutions later in the chapter.

Most companies allow for *statutory voting,* which gives you one vote per issue per share held. On each issue, you can vote for or against, or you can abstain. If you don't make a choice, management will vote for you, and you can guess whose interests they'll be representing. Investors who have fiduciary responsibilities, such as pension fund managers, are required to vote proxies. It's a good idea for you to do so as well.

Some companies allow shareholders to engage in *cumulative voting,* sometimes called *preference voting.* That means you can allocate your votes among different board candidates, depending on how strongly you feel about each. If you own 100 shares and four candidates are running, you have 400 votes. You can give them all to one candidate or divide them among the group. This gives activist shareholders more power because they can concentrate their votes to get a new person added to the board.

You may know how you want to vote based on your own research. A few resources that can help you with your decision are ProxyInformation, `www.proxyinformation.com`; As You Sow, `www.asyousow.org`, which specializes in environmental matters; and the California Public Employees Retirement System governance site, `www.calpers-governance.org`.

 If you own a mutual fund, you receive a proxy on issues related to the mutual fund itself. The fund's managers, in turn, are responsible for voting proxies on each of the securities held. Each fund has to disclose how it voted on issues. If you feel strongly about an issue, call or write to the fund to let the management know. It may not affect the vote, but it doesn't hurt to let the fund company know you're paying attention.

Counting on conferences and conference calls

Securities laws require companies to report a great deal of financial information. Most companies have figured out that if they disclose more than the minimum requirements, they'll have happier shareholders and possibly a higher security price.

The cornerstone of most investor relations programs is the quarterly earnings conference call. Companies have to announce their financial results each quarter, and many managers use that as an opportunity to give shareholders an update on what's happening. (Otherwise, the shareholders may reach their own conclusions, and that may not be good for management!) Many hold conference calls.

If a company holds these calls, then anyone must be allowed to listen to them. Most use Webcasting technology, linking to their calls through their Web sites and then making recordings available after the calls are over.

During these calls, the senior executives review financials, discuss their perspectives, and then take questions from listeners. It's one opportunity to get in front of managers.

Individual investors aren't always allowed to ask questions on these calls. But if you have a question, chances are good that someone else does, too. By listening, you can find out more about the company and, quite possibly, receive an answer to your concern.

Many companies appear at investor conferences throughout the year. Some of these are by invitation only (say, only for certain major customers at major brokerage firms), but others are open to anyone. Sometimes the organizer charges a fee; sometimes they're free.

Companies also announce these appearances on the investor relations section of their Web sites, and they make the presentations available afterward. You can find a list of some conferences later in this chapter.

Joining with other investors

Here's the bad news about being an activist investor: You are just one investor among very, very many. Even Bill Gates, the founder of Microsoft, is dwarfed by other holders of the company's stock (including the charitable foundation that he founded). Company management doesn't really care what you think unless a lot of other shareholders feel the same way.

Keep your shareholdings in perspective. Your position may mean a lot to you, but it's probably small relative to the total number of shares outstanding and the stakes held by large mutual fund companies, pension plans, and large endowment funds. Unless you own more than 1 percent of the shares outstanding, it's best to couch your communications in terms of friendly suggestions and requests for information; managers laugh at the 50-share owner who demands satisfaction.

Don't give up hope for change, though. If you join forces with other investors, you may be able to get management to take notice. There are a lot of ways to find these people, too. Some investors use investment message boards, some network at investment conferences, and others belong to coalitions of investors with common goals.

Discussion boards

One way to find like-minded activist investors is online. Every minute of every day, message boards hum with news, rumors, and complaints about different companies. If several people share the same complaints, they can often band together, talk to financial journalists, meet with management, create shareholder resolutions (discussed later in the chapter), and go about convincing management to behave in a more responsible manner.

The conversations themselves can spur changes, or at least make management aware of what shareholders are thinking. That's because sometimes company managers check out discussion boards to see what concerns investors have. And sometimes, company managers participate — often anonymously.

Many discussion boards are for traders, who rarely hold a security long enough to care about making changes. These boards often charge subscription fees that are worth it for the serious trader but not for someone with only an occasional interest in market gossip. Investors, with their longer-term perspective, may find that the boards I list here (all of which are free) can help them find others with a similar view of the world.

- ✔ **AOL Finance** (`money.aol.com`): America Online is an old-timer in the investor message board game, and it still attracts folks who want to gauge what others are saying.

- ✔ **Google Finance** (`finance.google.com`): Google Finance offers quotations, news, information, and discussion boards about different companies.

- ✔ **Investor Village** (`www.investorvillage.com`): This Web site specializes in financial news and information and is aimed at experienced investors. It includes several active message boards.

- ✔ **Morningstar** (`www.morningstar.com`): Morningstar's specialty is mutual funds, although the company offers in-depth research of common stocks, exchange-traded funds, and general investment issues. The site has a discussion board along with its great information.

- ✔ **The Motley Fool** (`boards.fool.com`): The Motley Fool is a great source of information about all aspects of investing. Its columns, blogs, and discussion boards offer plenty of ways for you to bone up on the issues and find others who share your point of view.

- ✔ **MSN Money** (`moneycentral.msn.com/community/message/default.aspx`): MSN Money is the financial section of MSN, Microsoft's go-to collection of news and information. It includes discussion boards covering different stocks and industries. (Disclosure: MSN Money is one of my clients.)

- ✔ **Yahoo! Finance** (`finance.yahoo.com`): Yahoo!'s quotation system includes extensive information about companies, including message boards.

Investment chat rooms and discussion boards can be depressing places, full of people insulting each other and lying in an attempt to get the security price to move in their favor. Some chat rooms and discussion boards are more helpful than others, so tread carefully.

Investor conferences and clubs

Want to get in touch with real, live investors whom you can see and talk, rather than type, to? They're out there! And some of them want to talk to you. Investing doesn't have to be a solitary activity where all interaction occurs through a computer screen. It can involve actual conversations between living people who want to share ideas and, when necessary, join forces so companies will pay attention to them. Activist investors don't hide. They often attend conferences and clubs to gather more information and find others who share their concerns.

Investment conferences are a great way to discover what's new, what's changed, and who's important in the markets. If you attend one of these conferences, you have plenty of opportunities to rub shoulders with the successful and talk to people who may be interested in shareholder activism.

The downside? Most of these conferences are for institutional investors and investment professionals, so they usually take place at expensive hotels and have hefty fees (say of $1,000 or more) for attendance.

Some conference organizers sell tapes of presentations or offer briefing books afterward to those who couldn't attend, often at a lower cost than a ticket to the event. These give you access to the information but not the networking.

Here's a list of some conference organizers that offer programs for social and individual investors:

- **Financial Research Associates** (www.frallc.com) puts on conferences about different aspects of investing. These take place all over the country and have covered such hot topics as faith-based investing, carbon investing, and sustainable investing. Attendees usually pay high fees, so these conferences are good for finding serious investors with serious expense accounts.

- **Institutional Investor Events** (www.iievents.com), like the name indicates, specializes in events for institutions. Individuals willing to pay the institutional-sized fees are welcome to attend. Some of the conference offerings cover socially responsible investing in all of its varied aspects.

- **The Money Show** (www.moneyshow.com) operates a series of investor conferences all over the country. Some are general; others have themes that may interest social investors, such as politics and the stock market. Most events are free; some have a relatively low fee; and others take place on cruises that are most definitely not free. Of course, each Money Show features a lot of vendors looking for customers among the investors who attend. If you can handle a sales pitch or two, this may be a great way to find out more about investing and find other investors who share your activist goals.

✔ **SRI in the Rockies** (www.sriintherockies.com) is a big institutional investing conference held each fall at resorts in the U.S. or the Canadian Rocky Mountains. One of the main sponsors is the Social Investment Forum, a trade organization for socially responsible investors, so it brings together the big names from the big funds. Like the other institutional conferences, it's not cheap to attend.

If you're looking for more regular contact with other investors than you can get at a conference, or if you don't want to spend big bucks to attend the intensive institutional meetings, consider joining groups of individual investors. You can form an activist investing group on your own, possibly as part of a community group or religious organization that you belong to. Or you can link up with investor groups where other birds of the social investing feather flock together.

✔ **The National Association of Investors Corporation** (www.better-investing.org) is the umbrella group for most investing clubs. Members of these clubs are individual investors who meet regularly, contribute a set amount of money each month, research investments, and develop an educational program so everyone becomes a better investor long after the club disbands. For social investors, club members can figure out a strategy for activism as well as for basic investing. The NAIC also offers a newsletter, regional chapter meetings, and a national conference where investors can network and gain insight.

✔ **The American Association of Individual Investors** (www.aaii.com) is for individual investors who want to invest on their own (no clubs required!) but who also want to find out more about how to invest well. The group publishes newsletters, stock reports, and books aimed at helping individuals do as well as the pros. It has several local chapters that put on educational and networking events, and it puts on an annual conference. Those in-person meetings can help activist investors find others with the same interest.

Organized coalitions

Because there is power in numbers, institutional investors often band together to promote their concerns to other investors and press companies for change. You may find inspiration and ideas from their efforts. If you're involved with an eligible group — maybe you serve on your synagogue's endowment board, for example — you may want to join. If you can't be a part of the direct action, you can certainly use the efforts of these groups to help with your own investment choices and activist activities.

- ✔ **CtW Investment Group** (www.ctwinvestmentgroup.com): *CtW* stands for *Change to Win,* and it represents union pension plans with a total asset value of about $1.5 trillion. It has no financial responsibility for any of these investments, but it does have a mission: to increase returns by rooting out companies that have weak management accountability and strong conflicts of interest between the managers and the boards of directors. CtW publishes lists of target companies, which it then notifies of its concerns. It organizes proxy campaigns to encourage shareholders to vote for change, and it publishes a blog about activist investing.

- ✔ **Coalition for Environmentally Responsible Economies** (www.ceres. org): The coalition has an awkward name that creates a cute acronym, CERES, who is the Roman goddess of agriculture. The group represents institutional investors who want to use shareholder activism to improve the environment. It accepts donations from individual investors, and the Web site carries detailed information about its issues and campaigns that you can use to make your own decisions.

- ✔ **Interfaith Center for Corporate Responsibility** (www.iccr.org): This group represents Catholic, Protestant, and Jewish institutional investor groups, including hospital and university endowments, clergy pension funds, and affiliated charitable foundations. Only institutions can be full members, but the center has a group of advocates, many of whom are individual investors, who support its aims. Among their primary issues are access to healthcare, food, and water; environmental justice; human rights; and the militarization of society. Advocate members receive information about the issues and advice on how to participate in different investor action programs.

- ✔ **Social Investment Forum** (www.socialinvest.org): The Social Investment Forum Web site has a wealth of information about almost every possible aspect of social investing. The group operates as a trade organization for people who work in this field, ranging from mutual fund companies to corporate lawyers. Membership isn't cheap; it starts at $475 a year for investment professionals. A broker or financial planner developing a specialty in the field might be interested, though. Everyone can use the Web site.

Nominating members of the board

Most companies allow shareholders to submit names of candidates for the board of directors. Some only accept these nominations at shareholder meetings with advance notice, while others solicit letters from shareholders who may know of good candidates. The procedures for making nominations are listed in the proxy statement.

A good board member has extensive business experience, sound judgment, and the ability to get things done; social investors, of course, would also like to see board members who can do the right thing.

Now the reality is that it's extremely difficult to get a director on the board this way. Most companies hire outside search firms that look for experienced corporate and civic leaders; it helps if the nominee is known personally to someone already on the board or a member of the senior management team. However, because you have the right as a shareholder to make a nomination, you may want to exercise it, if only to let the existing board know how you feel.

Submitting shareholder resolutions

As part owners of the corporation, shareholders can have their say at the annual meeting by filing a *shareholder resolution,* sometimes called a *shareholder proposal.* It costs nothing more than some time and a stamp, although you may want to spring for certified mail.

Shareholders filing resolutions must own at least $2,000 worth of stock for at least one year and have a letter from the broker attesting to that.

Resolutions should cover issues that affect at least 5 percent of the business. You may not be happy that the company generates 1 percent of its sales from revenues from a corrupt government, but that's not enough for a resolution asking the company to pull out of that market. Instead, focus on matters of policy that affect the broader business. In no case should your resolution ask the company to break the law (even if it is for a higher purpose) or to provide redress of a specific grievance.

Yes, the company may have really jerked your best friend around when it laid him off, and as a shareholder you may want to help, but a resolution asking for more severance pay for him will be ignored.

The resolution, which should be no more than 500 words long, should be filed 120 days before the proxy statement is published. You can estimate this by looking at the prior year's proxy statement. Sometimes the company publishes information about filing resolutions in the proxy to make it easier for you.

If your proposal meets Securities and Exchange Commission requirements and is not substantially similar to another proposal that someone else already submitted, it will appear in the proxy statement and be voted upon at the annual meeting. Management doesn't have to listen, but the process may force them to pay attention.

A sample shareholder resolution

Exxon Mobil (NYSE: XOM) had 17 shareholder resolutions included in its 2008 proxy statement. The proposals ranged widely and included one suggesting a change to the company's bylaws to limit the number of shareholder resolutions that could be allowed in any one year! Here's one of the other 16, which may interest you because it raises both environmental and governance issues. It was filed by Neva Rockefeller Goodwin, a descendent of John David Rockefeller, who founded the company that became Exxon Mobil after nearly a century of acquisitions and restructurings. The proposal received only 10.4 percent of the votes, so it wasn't approved. However, given Ms. Goodwin's status as a Rockefeller heir, it attracted a lot of attention to the company's policies. It also serves as a model for what a good shareholder resolution looks like. It's specific, it's factual, and it addresses matters of policy rather than day-to-day operations. More important, the resolution makes a business case in just 492 words.

"Resolved: Shareholders ask Exxon Mobil Corporation's ('ExxonMobil's') Board of Directors to establish a task force, which should include both (a) two or more independent directors and (b) relevant company staff, to investigate and report to shareholders on the likely consequences of global climate change between now and 2030, for emerging countries, and poor communities in these countries and developed countries, and to compare these outcomes with scenarios in which ExxonMobil takes leadership in developing sustainable energy technologies that can be used by and for the benefit of those most threatened by climate change. The report should be prepared at reasonable expense, omitting proprietary information, and should be made available to shareholders by March 31, 2009.

SUPPORTING STATEMENT

The April 2007 Fourth Assessment from the United Nation's Intergovernmental Panel on Climate Change (Working Group II) details the potential climate-change-related devastation that regions like Africa and Asia will suffer. IPCC Chairman Rajendra Pachauri noted that 'It's the poorest of the poor in the world, and this includes poor people even in prosperous societies, who are going to be the worst hit.'

This view is widely shared. As stated by the Prince of Wales Corporate Leaders Group on Climate Change, an organization that includes AIG, Dupont, and GE, in a November 30, 2007, Communiqué: 'The economic and geopolitical costs of unabated climate change could be very severe and globally disruptive. All countries and economies will be affected, but it will be the poorest countries that will suffer earliest and the most'. As witnessed by the destruction brought on by Hurricane Katrina, extreme climate events can devastate poor communities even in the United States.

ExxonMobil often argues that cheap and abundant energy is crucial for the economic advancement of poor economies. These countries are forecast, by ExxonMobil and others, to contribute the largest increase in energy use. However, if, as predicted by ExxonMobil, this energy use is based on continued reliance on hydrocarbons, we will see an unrelenting increase in global CO_2 emissions with devastating consequences especially for those who are poor in resources and influence, whether they live in the rich or the poor countries. To the extent that ExxonMobil's growth continues to rely on the sale of hydrocarbon energy to emerging markets, it faces a painful paradox in the future, and distances itself from its true legacy. Part of John D. Rockefeller's genius was *in recognizing early on the need and opportunity of a transition to a better and cheaper fuel.*

While investment in renewable energy sources and 'clean' technologies has recently accelerated, driven by players as diverse as venture capitalists, chemical companies, Internet companies, and old-fashioned utilities, we believe our company is now lagging in creating solutions for the looming climate and energy crisis. We are concerned that ExxonMobil's current slow course in exploring and promoting low-carbon or carbon-free energy technologies will exacerbate the crisis rather than make ExxonMobil part of the solution.

We urge shareholders to vote for this proposal."

If All Else Fails, Should You Sue?

If you've tried your best to influence a change in the companies you invest in, but nothing has worked, you can file a suit against the company as a last resort. These suits can be expensive, so they only make sense if there is strong evidence that members of the board or management violated their fiduciary responsibilities or engaged in outright fraud.

Attorneys often take these cases on *contingency,* which means that they're paid only if they win, and they need to show significant amounts of damages, so the suits are often organized as class actions.

Typically, if a company announces bad news or poor earnings, a lawyer finds a wronged shareholder (sometimes via Internet or newspaper ads), and then files suit on behalf of that person. If the judge approves the case as a class action, then all potentially affected shareholders are notified. They then submit proof that they owned the stock during the time period in question. If the company is found guilty or reaches a settlement, all the shareholders who joined the suit receive a check for their losses.

Shareholder class action suits are controversial; in one case, the law firm with the leading market share in the business turned out to be paying kickbacks to get shareholders to hire them. Many suits have been filed even though the company did nothing wrong, which leads to costly litigation that benefits lawyers but not shareholders. On the other hand, enough fraud and mismanagement has occurred over the years that these suits are often necessary.

Stanford University's Law School maintains a comprehensive list of securities lawsuits at `securities.stanford.edu`. If you're considering a suit to make yourself heard, you should start there to see what makes for a winning case, what defenses companies use, and which law firms handle these suits.

Part II
Issues to Invest In

The 5th Wave   By Rich Tennant

"Environmental stock? Multinational stock? I say we stick the money in the ground like always, and then feed this guy to the sharks."

In this part . . .

Different social investors have different concerns. Some care about the environment, some are concerned with corporate governance practices, and others want to follow guidelines set by their faith. Furthermore, the hot-button issues that spur socially responsible investing change over time, so having an understanding of what the concerns are can help you change your investment selections as the world changes.

The chapters in this part outline the different guidelines that different sets of investors follow, whether their interest is in sulfur dioxide or sweatshops. This part also helps you understand how investing choices may — or may not — make a difference in how organizations behave.

Chapter 6

Close to Home: Supporting Community Development

Social investing sometimes seems to be about solving enormous issues in faraway places. Investors worry about who's financing what war, or how to ensure a safe habitat for polar bears a hundred years from now, or what God wants them to do. But what's happening right down the street?

World-changing goals may be too lofty for some investors. For many investors, responsibility begins at home. They want to make investments that support their local community. Those investments may help new businesses grow, develop better housing, or support local philanthropies. Community institutions, workers, and businesses have strong ties, no matter what community they call home. If you're one of those folks who wants to straighten things out in your neck of the woods before trying to change the rest of the world, then this is the chapter for you.

Whether you're investing in New York City or a tiny Tanzanian village, you can get some ideas for making more socially responsible decisions from this chapter. It covers the benefits and pitfalls of local investing so you can take a savvy approach to civic support, no matter what assets are in your portfolio.

Beginning Social Responsibility at Home

A community is an interplay of organizations, starting with the federal, state, and local governments and including educational, religious, and nonprofit institutions. Within that framework are people and businesses that work together to make a better place to live.

Community investment covers a lot of different areas, ranging from building airports to helping a neighbor establish a home-based craft business. Although many community development efforts are funded by government agencies, many others are paid for by the private sector. As a socially responsible investor, you have plenty of ways to make money!

To start your investigation of opportunities, think about the community from two perspectives: the institutions in place and the businesses that operate within it.

Supporting community institutions

Although you can't invest in a government agency or nonprofit organization directly, many investment opportunities are related to community institutions. For example:

- A municipal bond investor can help support schools and hospitals.

- A private airport or port operator can give a government a steady stream of income that it can use for other projects.

- A for-profit environmental consulting firm can offer a local government the expertise it needs to provide clean drinking water.

Flip to Chapter 12 to find out more about investing in the stocks and bonds that may accompany these opportunities.

Another way to invest in community institutions is to deposit money in a *community development financial institution* (or *CDFI*), which is a bank that participates in the U.S. government's community development financing program. These banks are committed to offering community loans that support individuals and organizations that may have trouble getting funding from a traditional bank. You can find out more about these banks in Chapter 14, and you can find a list of these institutions at the Coalition of Community Development Financial Institutions, www.cdfi.org.

Investing in local development

Small businesses keep local communities vibrant. Local economic development agencies work to help new companies get established, and investors who are interested in community development often look for ways to help new companies grow. Local companies hire local workers and contribute to the local economy.

In fact, the U.S. Small Business Administration (www.sba.gov) reports that America's 26.8 billion small businesses pay 45 percent of U.S. private sector payroll and create between 60 and 80 percent of new jobs. That's impressive, especially because it's all close to home.

So what development issues are important to a community, and how can you make money supporting them? Well, that will vary from place to place, but one source of ideas about current hot topics in development is the National Association of Development Organizations, www.nado.org. Its members come from development groups in cities and towns across the country to share ideas and research. Whether it's brownfield redevelopment (which you can read more about in the later section "Developing commercial and office space") or public transportation for rural communities, these folks are identifying problems and coming up with solutions.

Growing Local Businesses

One way to invest in your local community is to invest in its businesses. After all, businesses create jobs and bring money into a region. Good business opportunities also keep people from leaving for other places. It's easy to invest in local businesses if your hometown is filled with large public companies; if that's the case, just do your research (see Chapter 4 for some ideas about that) and then buy the stock.

If the companies are small and private, investing is a bit more challenging, but you still have investment opportunities. Chapter 16 covers the high-finance aspects in detail, but in the sections that follow, I explain how local businesses look for capital within their own communities.

If you need leads on opportunities where you live, start by checking with your local economic development organization; you can find a list of organizations across the country at the National Association of Development Organizations' Web site, www.nado.org (I talk more about this group in the preceding section). You can also call your local chamber of commerce to see what activities it has that you may be interested in supporting.

Most local small-business investment opportunities come through venture funds, incubators, and angel networks. Each of these serves investors and entrepreneurs in different ways. Whether you're raising funds for your business or have money to invest, read on to find out the differences.

Entrepreneurs want to raise money from people they know because other financiers, such as banks and major national venture capital firms, want to know that the idea and the people behind it have credibility with those who know them best.

Joining local venture funds

Venture capital is money invested in a very new start-up business to help it get underway. Providing venture capital is risky because many new businesses fail. For this reason you should not invest in venture funds with money you cannot afford to lose. But the returns can be huge for those businesses that make it out of the venture stage and turn into full-fledged companies.

In some communities, venture investors get together and form a fund that has the express purpose of investing in local companies. They research proposals from new companies and then make investments when they see something they like.

These investors may be wealthy individuals (often successful entrepreneurs themselves), or they may be affiliated with local pension funds, foundations, or endowments (see Chapter 3 for more about these). Sometimes large local companies put money into venture funds in hopes of finding a business that will make a nice future acquisition.

Many locally focused venture funds belong to the Community Development Venture Capital Alliance, www.cdvca.org. You can check out that site for more information and for a list of member funds that may be looking for new investors — or new companies.

Not all local venture funds will match your social criteria, of course, so make sure to check out how the fund is designed to benefit the community and aligns with your objectives.

Affiliating with angel investors and angel groups

Angel investors are a special category of venture investor (see the preceding section). These folks are willing to put money directly into very small companies that may not be able to attract funds from traditional sources. Angels are usually high-net-worth individuals who ran businesses themselves, and most of them provide mentoring and advice to the companies they invest in. Interested investors usually find these opportunities through networking with local business and trade groups.

Angel investing is risky, and few investors are in a position to provide significant amounts of capital. And one individual making one investment may well become more of a meddler than a mentor.

To overcome these pitfalls and help even more entrepreneurs, angels in many communities have banded together to form *angel groups*. When angels join forces, they can spread their risk over several companies, and the company gets more contacts in the community. Angel groups also provide forums for entrepreneurs to meet with prospective investors and get ideas about how to run their businesses better.

The Small Business Administration reports that in 2006, the most recent year tracked, 649,000 new companies were formed and 564,900 firms folded. Two-thirds of businesses last at least two years, and 44 percent survive for four years or more. It's far from certain that a company funded with angel money will turn a profit or survive, but those that make it often have a fine return on investment to compensate the angel for the risk.

 Many angel groups are affiliated with the Angel Capital Association, angelcapitalassociation.org. The association's Web site has more information about angel investing and a directory of its members, which may help you find opportunities where you live.

An angel network of investors is not the same as Oprah's Angel Network (www.oprahsangelnetwork.org), a charitable organization founded by Oprah Winfrey. Oprah's Angel Network is committed to community volunteering and support, especially in parts of the world that are struggling economically. It doesn't provide start-up capital to new companies.

Investigating opportunities through incubators

An *incubator* is an organization that helps small businesses get started. It's usually a physical building where companies can set up offices, share such services and facilities as Internet lines and conference rooms, and come into contact with others starting small businesses.

Most incubators are affiliated with universities or community development organizations (or both). They rarely accept outside investors, but they're often a source of opportunities for investors interested in funding small businesses within the community. Some incubators work with local venture funds, while others have opportunities for angel investors to meet incubator residents.

Owning the store through a co-op

A business needs customers to succeed. Some businesses are founded by groups of investors who then go out and find customers. Others are set up by the customers themselves, through a *retail cooperative,* also called a *co-op.* The customers join forces and run the business; if there's sufficient profit at the end of the year, the member customers receive a dividend based on the amount of their purchases. There may be other benefits, like discounts during the year or advance notice of sales. Joining a co-op won't make you rich, but it will save you money while supporting a local business and other local customers.

Retail cooperatives can be huge: REI (www.rei.com), a major seller of outdoor clothing and equipment that generated $1.3 billion in revenue in 2007, is structured as a cooperative. For a $20 lifetime fee, REI members receive a dividend equal to 10 percent of their purchases, and they get to vote on the cooperative's officers and key business issues.

Most co-ops are quite a bit smaller that REI. Many communities have co-op grocery stores that specialize in health food, organic produce, or foodstuffs from local farmers. Cooperative bookstores are often affiliated with universities and help ensure that students and faculty have access to textbooks and offbeat titles that may not be profitable for a traditional bookstore to carry. And some co-ops provide services for businesses, not consumers; many regions that rely on farming have co-ops to keep members stocked with seeds, fertilizers, and agricultural equipment.

If you're interested in a community investment that will pay you back for buying things you would purchase anyway, you may want to investigate co-ops in your area. And if you're really ambitious, starting a co-op can be another way to bring a new business to your community.

You can find out more about business incubators at the National Business Incubation Association, www.nbia.org.

Building Buildings to Build Communities

Communities are set in places (and no, cyberspace doesn't count as far as this chapter is concerned). The people in the community need places to live, places to work, places to learn, places to socialize, and places to shop. That's why many community investment projects are tied to real estate, whether it's residential, commercial, industrial, or institutional.

You can read more about the specifics of real estate investment opportunities in Chapter 15; the following sections give you information on the issues as they affect communities.

Putting down roots in residential housing

Everyone in a community needs a place to live, and ideally, it's not in a car or under a bridge. But what types of housing make a community work? Should people be in single-family homes far away from where they work, or are they better off in apartments or condominiums close to where the action is?

Residential housing as a social investment can fall into several categories:

- ✔ **Low-income housing** is for people who otherwise can't afford to live in the community. This type of housing may be in the form of deeply subsidized rents or assistance with down payments and financing for buyers.

- ✔ **Workforce housing** may be available for people who work for the community's government, such as teachers, firefighters, or police officers, but who might not otherwise be able to afford to live there. This can be an issue in fancy suburbs and expensive cities.

- ✔ **Senior citizen housing** can be home to retirees. Some need financial assistance, some may need medical care, and some just want a smaller place than the one they lived in for years.

- ✔ **Entry-level housing** can attract recent college graduates to the community and encourage them to take jobs, start businesses, and put down roots.

- ✔ **Emergency housing** accommodates residents in the event of a disaster, such as a hurricane or a tornado.

The right kind of housing depends on the residents' current needs as well as the community's future ambitions. But whatever fits, there are opportunities for real estate developers and lenders to participate.

Developing commercial and office space

Although there are a lot of wonderful things about working from home, thriving communities need places where business can take place. Employers need offices, people need places to meet, and everyone needs stores where they can get the things they want and need in town.

Most commercial space is strictly that: commercial and for profit. And many of these developments are socially responsible. The projects that make the cut are in economically underserved communities and are environmentally sensitive. Here are a few examples of what to look for:

✔ **Businesses that serve the underserved community:** Many small towns and inner-city neighborhoods have more people than jobs. People have to leave the area to get to work, and they often have to go elsewhere to shop or have a night out. A commercial project that creates jobs; brings in vital support businesses, such as grocery stores and pharmacies; and gives people a safe and pleasant place to meet, like a coffee shop or café, can be a huge boost to the community's financial health.

✔ **Environmentally sensitive development:** Although environmental issues are covered in depth in Chapter 8, they're a big issue in community development. A lot of commercial projects are ugly, and they waste resources, whether through inefficient lighting or enormous parking lots. A huge regional shopping mall built on a former cornfield miles away from where people live isn't exactly the best thing for the environment. Many commercial projects offer better alternatives:

- They reuse space that may have stayed vacant otherwise.

- They're built near where people already live and work.

- They use energy-efficient and sustainably produced materials.

- They're designed to respect the community and its environment.

Some real estate projects are set up under sustainability guidelines because the developers and managers are committed to improving the environment. Some projects are sustainable because they're cheaper to operate. The result is more important than the reason.

✔ **Brownfield redevelopment:** A *brownfield development project* takes place on an old industrial site. When the former business was in operation, chances are that environmental regulations weren't in place, so the site may be contaminated. Or there may be no contamination at all, but no one knows for sure.

Any buildings on a brownfield site may be in disrepair or have problems, like wiring that's no longer up to code. But if the sites aren't redeveloped, they sit empty, attracting troublemakers and blighting the community. It's a big challenge to redevelop such sites, but challenge creates opportunity. To turn them around, the government often has to clean up the site or take over the liabilities to make the site attractive to someone else. But when it's done well, a brownfield redevelopment creates an attractive space for new businesses that can help rebuild the community.

Boosting communities through industrial development

Industrial jobs tend to be good, high-paying ones that require just a willingness to work hard. That's why many communities want to bring in big industrial projects as part of an economic development program. It's a way to create a lot of middle-class jobs, which creates a ripple effect:

✔ The workers have more money to spend, which helps local stores.

✔ The factory needs services large and small, from vending machines in the break room to paving of the parking lot. These expenditures generate revenue for area service companies.

It seems like a big win. And in some cases it is. But when you're looking to invest in an industrial project, you need to consider two key issues:

✔ Is the management interested in supporting the community, or will it pull out the moment it can find cheaper labor somewhere else?

✔ Is the project designed to minimize the environmental effects on the local community?

Hence, you have to do plenty of research, and Chapter 4 can give you some ideas of how to go about that.

Many communities get so excited about new factories that might hire lots of local workers that they give the companies enormous tax subsidies and breaks on regulations. In some cases, the community gives up more than it will ever get back. If a project requires a community to buy its jobs from a for-profit company, it's not socially responsible for either the town or the business.

Interesting institutional projects

Communities also have institutions that support the people. Whether they are educational, health, or cultural, these institutions become places that the community will unite around. These may be for-profit, philanthropic, or government ventures, but no matter who's providing the funding, you may want to find out more about the project.

You can probably find plenty of opportunities to participate! Some for-profit companies in search of investors are finding ways to provide institutional services better than cash-strapped local governments can. (It's not without controversy; you can break up almost any party very quickly by asking your fellow guests whether for-profit companies can provide a better education than public schools.)

Governments often create public-private partnerships in order to get projects done on budget and on time. Even if the entire job is handled by the government, it may need to issue municipal bonds to raise the money, and lots of investors like those. (You can find out more about municipal bonds in Chapter 12.)

A purely philanthropic project may not have any investment opportunities, but that doesn't mean you shouldn't care about the project. Many companies view philanthropy as an important way to support local communities. Corporations may support local institutions by contributing to the construction of a new hospital, underwriting a building at the local state university, or making a significant donation to the arts center. (The section "Focusing on corporate philanthropy" later in this chapter has more details on this topic.)

One person's blight is another person's job. Is a prison or a nuclear plant or a toxic waste dump a good or bad thing for a community? It all depends.

Contributing to Community Infrastructure

Everyone in a community needs a way to get from place to place. They need basic infrastructure to hold everything together, including transportation, utilities, and communications. This can be as simple as a paved path connecting an office building to a parking lot or as major as an international airport handling thousands of passengers each day.

Infrastructure has long been thought of as a *public good* — those goods and services that many people can use without limiting other people's access and for which it's difficult to exclude people who don't pay. Most public goods don't generate a profit but are necessary to keep a community functioning. (Suppose all roads were toll roads. How expensive would it be to get to work each day?)

Of course, public goods have a cost, and it's borne by taxpayers. And because there are costs, investors have different investing opportunities. These may come from lending money to government organizations, providing services to the agencies in charge, or even buying an existing public infrastructure project and turning it into a private company.

As financial markets become more sophisticated, new methods of financing projects can move more infrastructure from public to private ownership, possibly saving taxpayers money and bringing critical services into communities that need them.

Despite the taxes that people pay, many local governments are short of funds. The governments that have the least amount of money tend to have the greatest needs; if they aren't taking in a lot of tax revenue, it's probably because the communities are economically disadvantaged. That's why many infrastructure projects need creative financing, often in partnership with private companies.

In the following sections, I outline some points to consider when thinking about infrastructure investing opportunities. I cover some of the specifics from an investor's perspective in Chapter 12.

Minding money for municipal projects

Governments face the same problem that everyone in any kind of economic organization does: There are more good ideas for spending the money than money to be spent. But governments have an additional problem: They can't just go out and find new revenue sources. A person can get a second job, a corporation can push a new product line, but a government is pretty much stuck. Sure, the administration can raise fees a bit, but it will take a lot of $1 increases on skate rentals at the local park district rink to pay for a new bridge.

There's another wrinkle. When an individual saves money to spend on something, we view that as a good thing. When a government saves up money, we — the taxpayers — tend to view that as bad. Taxpayers would rather have extra money returned to them because they're concerned that if government officials have extra money floating around, they'll spend it foolishly.

For example, the town council may start saving to build a new bridge, but then a retired hockey player gets elected mayor and decides that it would be better to put a new state-of-the-art ice rink in every neighborhood. Then the money is gone, and even the taxpayers who like to skate end up annoyed.

That's why most government projects start with no money down. They're financed over the course of years through

- Direct borrowing (municipal bonds)
- Revenue bonds (in which the lenders receive a cut of fees generated from the finished project rather than interest payments)
- Lease with purchase arrangements
- Public-private partnerships

You can read more about these types of bond investments in Chapter 12.

Pondering privatization

After a government finishes an infrastructure project, it has something of value, like a big hospital, a toll road, or a port. But the grand new project may not generate any revenue for a community that needs money. Maybe a state built toll roads years ago when it had a lot of tax money coming in, but now it's looking at enormous pension liabilities that are about to come due and voters who aren't happy about paying more in taxes. *Privatization* may be one way to convert the asset into cash.

Privatization comes in two main forms:

- **Operational privatization:** If the operations are being privatized, the government maintains the responsibility for providing the service as well as retains the ownership of any underlying assets, but it contracts with a private company to manage the actual operations. For example, a city may keep ownership of its airport but hire an outside company to operate it. The company makes a bigger profit if it can generate more revenue and keep costs down, so it has an incentive to improve operations, making for a nicer airport at less cost to the city.

- **Outright sale:** With an outright sale, the government may decide that it doesn't make sense to provide a certain service anymore, so it sells the asset. Maybe the town figures that it's nice to have an ice rink, but it's not nearly as important as having modern equipment for the fire department or a safe bridge over the river. It sells the rink to a sports management company that then takes over all responsibility for it, setting whatever fees it thinks the market can bear. The town takes the cash and invests it in other projects.

In many developing countries, the government owns many major businesses in whole or part because, at one time, there wasn't enough capital in the country to support a private airline, bank, or telephone company. As the company modernizes and becomes more attractive to outside investors, it may no longer make sense for the government to own the business. These privatizations may involve distributions of some stock to employees and the sale of the rest to outside investors, with the proceeds going to the government.

Please note, though, that privatization is controversial:

- Maybe the asset being sold is more important than the use of the sales proceeds.

- Outsiders with a profit motive may not always do best by the community; they may tend to cut corners on service or security that a government official, accountable to voters, would not be willing to do.

- In at least a few cases, privatization contracts have gone to political cronies rather than to the highest bidder or best operator.

As with all matters socially responsible, you have to do your research to ensure that an investment lives up to its billing.

A privatization program that takes over a community service so it no longer serves the community isn't socially responsible. If a company privatizes the water utility in a poor community and can lower fees by operating more efficiently than the government agency, that's good. If the company instead raises its rates so that half of the community can no longer afford running water, that's bad. If you're investing in a privatization project, find out what goes into the financial projections and the reputation of the company doing the privatization.

Considering Community Philanthropy

Maybe you're interested in community development from a big-picture perspective. You aren't necessarily interested in investing in any one community, but when you buy stocks and bonds, you want to support companies that support the communities where they do business. In the following sections, I give you information about a few things to look for. (For more about buying stocks and bonds, flip to Chapter 12.)

Checking out worker volunteer programs

Many companies provide additional benefits for employees who volunteer in their community. That may include time off, liability insurance, recognition, and financial contributions. Some companies have organized groups of employees who want to volunteer where they live; others may sponsor a day of volunteering in which all staffers work on a specific project, such as repainting a school or cleaning up a park.

Most companies that offer volunteer programs are proud to promote them on their Web sites and in public relations materials, so a quick Internet search can tell you what a company does or doesn't do.

Many companies know that their community activities give them a positive image with customers and community members. And they know that employees want to live in a strong community and work for a company that values what they do outside of work, creating an important recruitment and retention advantage.

Focusing on corporate philanthropy

Many companies put money back into the community through charitable donations. Some companies do this simply to be good citizens. Others are looking for specific public relations and marketing benefits, supporting those causes that resonate with their customers. And many companies delegate to their employees the decision of what causes to support through *matching gift programs.* By matching donations that employees make, companies help ensure that diverse community needs are met by various organizations. (A matching gift program is also a way to support employee activities, connecting the workers to the company and the company to the community.)

Companies tend to be proud of their charitable activities and report them on their Web sites and in their annual reports. If you care about corporate philanthropy and don't see the information, call the company's investor relations staff and ask for details.

Just because a tax deduction is involved doesn't mean that a contribution to a nonprofit agency is good for shareholders or for the community. Some companies have been known to make big donations to fancy charities to enhance the CEO's social status. Others have supported dubious charities or charities that divide communities rather than unite them. In one notorious case, a brokerage firm made a large donation to a private school in the name of one of its analysts to help get the analyst's children into that school; in exchange, the analyst issued a positive rating on a stock that he didn't really like. That donation wasn't philanthropy; the firm bribed the analyst by bribing the school. You should investigate corporate giving practices to ensure that they represent the wise use of corporate funds.

Examining social enterprises

A *social enterprise* is a small business that's operated by a nonprofit organization. Most have complex sets of goals that may include job training, creating markets for local resources, and raising money for the parent nonprofit.

In most cases, when you invest in a social enterprise, you're really donating to the sponsoring organization, but that doesn't mean that these groups can't generate profitable opportunities. That's why some businesses help fund and launch social enterprises in their communities. Other investors lend money to them, which gives the business the funding it needs to grow and gives the investor the potential for return without making an outright contribution.

Social enterprises work in all kinds of industries, so there are a lot of opportunities for a creative company to support the mission while also contributing to profits. For example, a social enterprise may train specialized workers that a partner company needs. It may make unique goods that give local retailers an edge with customers. It may help local farmers find new ways to market their ingredients.

More information about social enterprises, including examples of some successful ones, is available from the Social Enterprise Alliance, `www.se-alliance.org`.

Chapter 7

Scrutinizing Governance: How Is the Company Run?

*L*ike many shareholders, you may believe that companies that are run well and have good oversight are more likely to behave ethically than those that are run poorly. When you pay attention to how companies are run, you're using different measures of *corporate governance.* Investors interested in governance look at how well companies match current standards and how supportive management is of reforms. This chapter covers the basic concepts of corporate governance to help you understand how good companies should operate.

"What's good for the country is good for General Motors, and vice versa," said Charles Wilson, president of the automaker, during his confirmation hearings before serving as secretary of defense in the Eisenhower administration. And that's exactly right. Companies that have good governance aren't felled by massive scandals. The investors have the information they need to make good decisions, and the management is more concerned with creating a sustainable business than with protecting their fiefdoms.

Of course, General Motors has changed a lot in the last half century, so it's not necessarily the model socially responsible corporation these days. But it's still the industry giant, and its management is working through its problems and developing alternatives to its fuel-hungry SUVs.

Don't confuse performance with governance. In most cases, a well-run company has great performance, but sometimes, a well-run company operates in a terrible industry. Likewise, when a company is doing well, investors and reporters sometimes like to claim the stellar performance is because of superior management ability and a sustainable strategy, when really, it's just luck. Or fraud. It now seems like a sad joke, but Enron was once a darling among investors and the media because of its perceived innovations in the energy market.

Taking Care of Shareholders and Other Constituents

Social investors are investors, first and foremost. No matter how many other concerns you have, you're putting money into the market to get a return that will help you meet your long-term financial goals. That's it. And that means your investment considerations should come first. Companies that operate responsibly may have strategic advantages that help them do better financially over the long haul, but not necessarily.

As part of their drive to maintain a sustainable organization, many businesses have expanded their operating charter to include *constituent analysis* or a *stakeholder value*. This means that management is allowed to consider other groups when making decisions, including employees, customers, and the community at large. Some states require corporations to place non-shareholder constituents first, or at least address their concerns when making major decisions such as whether to proceed with mergers or acquisitions.

Corporations are governed by the laws of the state in which they're incorporated. However, there is very little variation because almost all public companies and many private companies are incorporated in Delaware, which has an easy incorporation process and corporate-friendly laws.

Putting non-shareholder concerns first sounds like a nice idea that would fit with the needs of social investors, doesn't it? Unfortunately, the constituent approach to corporate governance rarely works. In fact, it often gives management an excuse for ongoing underperformance. Managers can argue that it's okay that they're collecting big salaries and not generating profits, because their workers still have jobs. The problem is that if the company goes bankrupt, all of those workers will lose their jobs.

Running a company for shareholders doesn't mean that the managers must be ruthless and cruel. It means managers must accept that, sometimes, short-term pain for certain constituencies is necessary for the business to operate responsibly in the long run.

Good governance starts with transparency and consistency:

- **Transparency** means giving shareholders and employees information they need to make decisions, and part of that means making ethics guidelines clear.
- **Consistency** means that the rules always apply, whether it's the CEO or an entry-level customer service representative.

Making information available

A company never tells shareholders everything. It's a competitive world out there. If shareholders demand specific information about contracts, strategies, and tactics, they could well end up destroying the company. Management needs to give shareholders enough information so they can make informed investment decisions. It's not appropriate for them to give out more than that.

As an investor who cares about corporate governance, you need to check out three things:

- ✔ **How much are the executives being paid relative to their performance?** (Check out the later section "Executives and their compensation and perks" for more details.)

- ✔ **Is the auditing firm doing its job?** (The later section "The auditor's role" has more information.)

- ✔ **Is the board an unbiased overseer of management?** (See the section "The board of directors' responsibilities" later in this chapter.)

You can also turn to a company's own documents, such as annual reports and marketing brochures, to get a feel for how it governs itself. But remember, these are internally produced publications, so a company is going to put its best foot forward.

Many companies have codes of conduct that are lavishly illustrated and printed in gorgeous, four-color brochures showing a veritable rainbow of employee skin tones. But if the code of conduct exists as art and nothing more, then it's worthless. Guidelines are only as good as their enforcement. Are employees who violate rules fired, punished, retrained, or simply given a nudge and a wink? Or does it depend on who the employee is and what department he works in? Without fair and firm follow-up, the pretty pictures and strong words mean nothing.

Some of these matters are governance issues, while others are operational. Chapter 11 has information on how socially responsible corporations go about their daily business.

Annual reports also tend more toward artistry than information. The meaty material is buried in legal and accounting terminology and hidden in clever graphic design. Some companies satisfy the letter of the law, and others give shareholders detailed information that they can use to find out more about the business's prospects. (Chapter 4 has a lot of information on how to read and understand annual reports.)

Following good governance reforms

Some shareholders would be happy if company leaders simply adhered to current governance standards and didn't go to great lengths to protect their jobs. Others would like to see more. They want the companies that they invest in to go beyond the minimum. Even better, they'd like to see the minimum standards for governance raised.

Activists push for three reforms: majority voting, open nomination, and "say on pay." A company can add any of these with shareholder approval, but few companies will make these changes unless they're forced to by regulatory agencies or the stock exchanges. I explain these reforms in the following sections. A company that has instituted these reforms is rare, but if you see them in place, you might have a good investment on your hands.

Majority voting

Shareholders vote for members of boards of directors, but their votes count in different ways. At many companies, a *plurality* voting system is in place. A board member needs only to receive the majority of votes cast, not the votes of the majority of shares outstanding. Shareholders can't vote against a director; rather, they can vote for a director or *withhold* their vote (that is, not cast a vote at all). In a plurality system, only one vote is needed for a director to keep his seat. And because directors are shareholders, they can effectively vote to keep themselves on the board, even if every other shareholder wants to see them go.

Although it's highly unlikely that any director anywhere will be able to stay on a board if he's the only one who wants that, the mere fact that it's possible annoys a lot of shareholders. It doesn't seem right that one shareholder can override the wills of all the others. That's why many shareholders want the vote for directors to move to a *majority* voting system.

Under majority voting, directors can keep their seats only if a majority of shareholders votes for them. If 1 million shares are outstanding, then a director needs 500,001 votes to stay on, not just one.

Because a lot of people throw out their proxy statements rather than submit their votes, some majority voting systems allow directors to stay on if they receive a majority of votes cast, but with a twist: Shareholders are allowed to vote no rather than withhold their vote. Under this system, a director needs more yeses than noes to stay on board.

Open nomination

Companies allow shareholders to submit names for nomination to the board of directors, but these nominations are usually ignored. They aren't publicized. The nominating committee members make a note of the letter and then go about finding directors through their usual networks.

Under *open nomination,* any names submitted by shareholders that meet minimum qualifications (no cartoon characters or dead celebrities allowed!) would have to be included on the proxy statement to be submitted to shareholder vote. Then any directors who receive a majority of the votes would be named to the board. This could create competition among candidates; each candidate would have to explain to shareholders why he would be the best person to provide oversight for the company. It would also bring new people and new ideas to corporate oversight.

"Say on pay"

Shareholders vote on certain types of management compensation packages, especially those that include stock options or grants of shares of stock. Some forms of compensation, especially straight salary, are not voted on. After the shareholders approve a compensation package, they don't get to make changes, even if the manager has proved to be undeserving of the money paid.

Hence, many shareholders are pushing for *say on pay.* Under this reform, the shareholders would get to vote annually on whether they believe the CEO's pay is appropriate. It would be a *nonbinding vote;* the board wouldn't be required to make changes if the shareholders no longer supported the CEO's pay package. However, it would force the board to consider whether there are performance problems — or compensation problems — that should be addressed.

TIP

Ways to invest in governance

Every industry has companies with good governance, and every industry has a few clunkers. Investors who want to invest in companies that have good governance will have to do their research, just as will those who want to invest in companies with poor governance in hopes of profiting by turning things around. Investors interested in either type of governance issues will have no trouble finding suitable candidates, no matter where they look.

That being said, certain types of companies are in general more likely to have good governance than others. These are:

✔ Multinational consumer products companies, which are concerned about their

reputation in the market and are used to reporting information about their operations to governments all over the world

✔ Federal government contractors, which have to meet extensive reporting guidelines about their activities in exchange for receiving taxpayer dollars

Meanwhile, companies that are more likely to have problems tend to be entrepreneurial or have high levels of family ownership. These companies are often run by managers who view shareholders as meddlers, even if they are the legal owners of the companies.

"Shareholder rights" and the rights of shareholders

Corporate executives love their jobs. A CEO is about as much of an alpha dog as a person can be in our capitalist society. The pay is great, the office is the swankiest in the company, and no one reclines their seat in your face on the company's Gulf Stream. Sure, there's constant travel, long hours, and high pressure, but it beats waiting tables any day.

Because CEOs are so happy with their positions, they tend to resist when shareholders want them removed for poor performance. They want to thwart acquirers who may come in and kick them out. Hence, boards and managers often push for corporate bylaw provisions that make it hard for the company to be acquired without management's consent.

The irony? These proposals are often called *shareholder protection* or *shareholder rights* issues. Okay, that may not be quite as cynical as it seems: Investors have often been disappointed to find a company that they really like and that meets their objectives, only to have it merged into another company that doesn't have the same social or financial prospects. It's possible that these shareholders would want to keep their companies from being taken over. But the CEO and other managers usually have far more to lose. That's because a company is most vulnerable to being taken over when the stock is cheap, and a cheap stock is usually associated with performance problems.

Shareholder rights programs are discussed in the company's proxy statement (also known in SEC terms as the DEF14A). Most such programs aren't particularly friendly to shareholders, who would prefer that managers try to keep their jobs by performing well rather than by thwarting shareholders' efforts to improve company performance by kicking them out.

Some shareholder rights programs are more obnoxious to the actual rights of shareholders than others. Most, but not all, have to be approved by shareholders; all have to be approved by the board of directors. The following sections give an overview of some of the more common ones.

Director restrictions

Each year, companies announce candidates for the board of directors, and shareholders get to vote on them. At some companies, all the directors come up for vote every year. At others, they are *staggered* or *classified:* Each director holds a three-year term, but only a third of the directors stands for election in any given year. This helps directors gain experience, which is good, but that's not the only purpose of this arrangement. Instead, it makes it nearly impossible for a hostile bidder to select a new slate of directors for shareholders to support, because only a few directors can be changed in any one year.

A related provision says that after a director is on the board, he can only be removed *for cause* (such as skipping meetings or fraud) or by a *supermajority vote* (that is, by a larger percentage of votes than 50 percent plus one, sometimes set as high as 90 percent). This makes it difficult to bring new faces to the board, some of whom may be more interested in shareholder value than the current team.

Golden parachutes

Under a *golden parachute,* a senior company executive who loses his job after a hostile takeover receives a lush compensation package to help cushion the blow. The idea, of course, is to saddle the acquirer with such a high level of costs that a takeover no longer makes sense. Unfortunately, these have become typical in corporate compensation packages (which shareholders vote on).

A related compensation provision, the *golden handcuff,* is designed to compensate the executive so well over a period of time that he has no incentive to leave. These often include stock options or bonuses that are paid out over several years and that go away if the employee quits.

Greenmail

Some CEOs and boards of directors are so anxious to make a big, bad activist shareholder go away, the one who would cut their perks and make them do better jobs, that they simply buy out the troublemaker. They offer to use company funds to pay the activist for his shares at a price above the current market price. In exchange, the activist agrees to go away for a certain period of time. This is called *greenmail* (think blackmail, only green for the color of money).

A handful of corporate raiders, wise to this tactic, started buying shares in companies for the sole purpose of negotiating greenmail agreements. This has become less common thanks to a U.S. tax code change that places a 50 percent excise tax on greenmail profits. And that's good, because it's unclear how shareholders benefit when a company's board of directors engages in these negotiations.

Many boards have been able to get shareholder rights plans passed by including anti-greenmail provisions. Because greenmail is an egregious use of corporate funds, the shareholders are often happy to go along with any plan that forbids it.

Poison pills

The classic shareholder rights plan is the so-called *poison pill,* which is a deal that the acquirer has to swallow unless, of course, the board approves the transaction. When someone acquires a predetermined percentage of the company's shares, say 10 percent or so, the board of directors votes on whether to support the acquisition attempt. If the board supports the action, then business proceeds as usual. If not, then the pill comes out.

A typical poison pill arrangement gives all shareholders with smaller stakes than the dreaded acquirer *warrants,* which are rights to buy more stock at bargain prices. All of these small purchases drive up the stock's price and make it more expensive for the person attempting the takeover; they also make the person's stake in the company relatively smaller. The smaller stake then makes it more difficult to change directors or force through other changes when shareholders vote at the annual meeting.

Some bonds come with a similar provision, called a *poison put.* These give the bondholders the right to redeem their bonds at face value if a *hostile takeover* takes place. (That is, a takeover that is hostile from the perspective of the management or directors.) This increases the cost of the takeover, because the acquirer has to come up with the money to pay off the loans right now.

Supermajority voting

Shareholders have the right to vote for members of the board of directors and other business matters each year. On almost all issues, the majority rules. In order to win, a board candidate, shareholder proposal, or other issue needs 50 percent plus one of the votes cast.

To deter takeovers, though, some companies have established a higher threshold for certain business matters, such as mergers or acquisitions that the board doesn't support. For these, a *supermajority,* say 80 to 90 percent, of shareholders must vote in favor of the transaction. This makes it hard for such a deal to go through because when do 80 or 90 percent of people agree on anything? (Yes, members of legislative bodies voting themselves a pay raise is the exception!)

Who Is Working for Shareholders?

The skills involved in making investment decisions and running companies are very different. Legally, shareholders own the company and elect a board of directors to represent their interests. The board of directors, in turn, hires the senior managers and oversees their activities. At least, that's the way it's supposed to work. It doesn't always.

Management and shareholders often want different things. They have an inherent conflict known as the *principal-agent problem,* where the shareholders are the *principals* and the managers are the *agents.* If the principals don't pay attention, their agents will work for themselves. And that's not good governance.

In an ideal world, managers are paid for delivering results for shareholders, the auditors verify those results, and the board of directors holds the managers accountable for their actions. This section covers these key governance functions in more depth.

Executives and their compensation and perks

Chief executive officers have big jobs. They have huge responsibilities for setting strategy, promoting the company, and overseeing the work of hundreds or thousands of employees who may be located all over the world. Most CEOs work more or less from sunrise to bedtime; even their social lives may be dominated by client entertainment, dinners with vendors, and golf outings with bankers. Because of the volume and importance of their work, they should be paid a lot of money — and not a penny more.

Shareholders will accept a well-paid CEO as long as the investment returns follow.

Executives also receive *perquisites,* often called *perks.* These are special privileges that go with the job. They range from never having to justify a dinner check to the accounts payable department to plush apartments in world financial capitals, personal use of corporate aircraft, and skybox season tickets for all the local sports teams. Some of these extras may be justifiable; for security and efficiency reasons, it may be a good idea for the CEO to have a car and driver so he can place calls during his daily commute. But most perks are fluffy fringe benefits that come straight out of shareholders' profits.

CEOs may deserve big pay, but only if they're doing the big job that they were hired to do. After all, the CEO's compensation is an operating expense to the firm, so it cuts into the return that shareholders receive. If the CEO's salary is too high, it may cause resentment among the firm's other employees. And sometimes CEOs make decisions that are more about preserving their own power (read: pay and perks) than increasing shareholder value. A content CEO may not take appropriate risks. He may be so busy enjoying his benefits that he lets the business stagnate. At an extreme, he may condone fraud if it gets him the bonus he wants and lets him keep his position.

Every April and May, after annual reports and proxy statements are released, business reporters rank chief executive officers of public companies by investment performance and pay. The highest rankings go to those executives who deliver relatively high rates of return per zero on the paycheck. If you missed the most recent analysis, try doing an Internet search on "CEO pay performance" to find the results.

The auditor's role

People like to think that accountants are boring people who live by the rules and don't ever dare flex them even a teensy bit, let alone break them. The reality is that generally accepted accounting principles (GAAP) and IRS tax regulations give companies a lot of leeway in calculating their earnings and presenting their financial position. They may not allow as much wiggle room as some executives at some companies would like, of course, but accountants have enough legal options that a company's financial performance may look a little better than it actually is.

Public companies are required to have outside accountants come in each year to audit the financial results and certify that they comply with applicable accounting regulations and present a fair picture of the company's performance.

Because shareholders care about the accuracy of the financial results and vote to approve the accounting firm, you may think that the different auditors would compete on how tough they are. "Nine of out ten shareholders surveyed recommend our audits!" they could say, or "We caught more fraud last year than all of our competitors combined!" If only that were the case.

The reality is that there are only a handful of accounting firms, so they aren't exactly ruthless competitors. Almost all public companies use one of four big brand-name auditors: Deloitte Touche Tohmatsu, Ernst & Young, KPMG, or PricewaterhouseCoopers. Few other firms have the resources or the capabilities of examining the books at large companies operating from multiple locations. (Private companies, small public companies, real estate firms, and other investment opportunities that you come across probably use other auditors. Most of the other auditing firms are perfectly fine; they just don't have nearly the market share of the Big Four.)

Accounting firms don't prepare a company's financial reports. The company's employees do. The auditing firm's job is to test and verify that the employees' work is accurate. Because investors need good numbers to make decisions, internal financial controls and external auditor reviews are key corporate governance issues.

Just because a company uses a well-known accounting firm doesn't mean the audit is any good. Auditors can miss a well-constructed fraud built by senior executives. On occasion, the accountant assigned to conduct the audit will be a party to the fraud.

You may not be able to catch fraud on your own, but you don't have to be an accountant to determine if the auditing firm is doing a good job and if the company's books are in good shape. One clue is if the company has *material weaknesses* in its financial reports, which are announced in the auditor's letter. If these weaknesses exist, it's possible that they were a problem a while ago and the auditor missed them or let them slide in the hope that management would fix them fast. Or it's possible that the problem is new, but it's the proverbial tip of the iceberg; fresh eyes on fresh-faced accountants from another accounting firm may be able to find other problems.

The board of directors' responsibilities

Members of boards of directors must be shareholders in a company, although some directors don't become shareholders until they're nominated. Many directors are small shareholders, too, owning just 100 shares, which is the minimum size order that can be traded without paying an extra commission.

Directors fall into two categories:

- ✔ **Affiliated directors** are company employees, recent retirees, or others with close financial ties to the business.

- ✔ **Independent directors** have no material relationship with a company. They are neither employees nor former employees, nor do they work for customers or vendors. They shouldn't be relatives of any of the managers or others with significant relationships with the company, either. They have no financial stake in the business's prospects other than as owners of publicly traded stock.

Interlocking directorships

Even though a director is classified as independent, she may still have important conflicts of interest. The best known is the problem of *interlocking directorships*.

Say there are two people, Susie and Janie. Janie is the CEO of a company where Susie is on the board, and Susie is the CEO of a company that has Janie on the board. How much oversight will Janie place over Susie, knowing that Susie will be overseeing Janie? Probably not much! In fact, they may try hard to keep their dealings friendly, no matter what's in the best interests of either firm's shareholders.

Directors with interlocking relationships to management are generally not considered to be independent, but these relationships are harder to track than more straightforward situations such as a current or former employee.

Responsibility overload and conflict of interest

Some directors become overloaded with too many board responsibilities. Being on a board takes time; it's not a full-time job, but it can take up as much as a day out of every week, depending on the size of the company and the issues that it faces. A director who serves on too many boards can't be expected to keep track of everything at every company.

Also, the more boards a person serves on, the greater the potential for hidden interlocking relationships that may create conflicts of interest. Most investors are all right with a board member who sits on five different boards, using the one-day-a-week guideline and assuming that the director doesn't have other commitments, such as a full-time job.

After someone joins a board, he should go to the meetings. Otherwise, how else will the board member know what's happening with the company in order to give management guidance and provide oversight for the shareholders? Proxy statements show meeting attendance; a board member should be at 75 percent of those unless he has a valid excuse.

A death in the family is a valid excuse; a ski trip that seemed like it would be more fun than sitting in a stuffy meeting talking about banking arrangements is not.

Keeping an Eye on Things: Guidance Standards

Our economy relies on businesses to create jobs, pay taxes, and keep the wheels of commerce humming. Hence, lots of people — not just shareholders — have a stake in ensuring that companies have good governance practices.

Some recommendations have come from general observations about which practices work and which are more likely to lead to trouble. Many others have been codified by stock exchanges and government regulations. When a requirement is set by a leading organization, people pay attention, even if their business isn't directly affected.

For example, when the New York Stock Exchange publishes changes to its corporate governance guidelines for companies that trade there, companies with shares that trade elsewhere have to explain to shareholders why they don't meet the standard. Most change their standards to keep pace.

NYSE and Nasdaq listing standards

The New York Stock Exchange (NYSE) was long the most prestigious trading floor in the world. The NYSE has less luster than it once had because of major changes in the way that stocks are traded, especially the movement toward electronic trading. Along the way, it lost much market share to the Nasdaq, an electronic exchange formerly known as the National Association of Securities Dealers Automated Quotation System.

Both exchanges have high standards for companies listed on them, whether the security trades on the floor at the corner of Broad and Wall streets or over an electronic network. The standards are also good models for private companies and others that aren't traded on the exchanges.

The two exchanges have some minor differences in their standards, but both agree that listed companies should have

- A majority of the members of the board of directors with independent status.

- Regularly scheduled *executive sessions,* which are meetings attended by only those directors who aren't company employees, and no management members are present.

- A nominating committee made up of independent directors to find people who are qualified to become board members.

- A compensation committee made up of independent directors to evaluate the performance of the company's chief executive officer and draw up compensation plans for corporate executives.

- An audit committee made up of three independent directors who have demonstrated financial literacy, including at least one member who has experience in accounting or financial management.

- Corporate governance guidelines that the board has adopted and published for interested shareholders to read.

- A code of business conduct for directors, officers, and employees, with disclosure of any waivers that have been granted. (For example, if employees working in one country are allowed to give and receive gifts because it reflects the local culture, while employees in other countries may not do so, that exception should be disclosed.)

President's Working Group on Capital Markets

After the stock market crashed in 1987, President Ronald Reagan signed an executive order creating the *President's Working Group on Capital Markets.* The group advises the president on domestic and international financial crises and recommends new regulations that can help prevent the situation from happening again. It has often been called in on governance issues, especially in the wake of a series of corporate scandals in the early 2000s.

The group consists of

- the secretary of the Treasury
- the chairman of the board of governors of the Federal Reserve System
- the chairman of the Securities and Exchange Commission
- the chairman of the Commodity Futures Trading Commission

Any of these people can appoint someone to take his place, so many people from outside of government have been a part of this group over the years.

Sarbanes-Oxley Act of 2002

Few laws struck fear into the hearts of corporate executives more than the *Sarbanes-Oxley Act of 2002,* sometimes known as SOX. The U.S. Congress passed the law after some horrendous corporate scandals, including the punch line for all corporate scandals ever, Enron.

Sarbanes-Oxley brings criminal penalties to corporate governance. Before Sarbanes-Oxley, executives could go to prison if they were accused of outright fraud, but they had an excuse if fraud happened elsewhere in the firm, even major fraud. The CEO could always say, "Well, gosh, how was I supposed to know what those bad, bad people over in the retail division were doing?" Well, the CEO is supposed to know because he runs the show. Sarbanes-Oxley returns responsibility to the top dog.

Now surely a sneaky employee can pull one past the chief executive officer. To minimize the risk, the Sarbanes-Oxley Act calls for companies to have detailed financial controls in place that can be tested. That part of the law, Section 404, created a lot of work for a lot of companies. To comply, a business must do such things as have a standard for setting passwords, create a policy for canceling passwords when an employee leaves the firm or changes duties, document how often the passwords were changed according to the policy, and enumerate all cases where exceptions were made and explain why. And that's just for passwords!

Section 404 applies to every process in the firm that affects the reported financial results. If a firm can show that it has effective financial controls, then the CEO can avoid criminal responsibility for fraud committed by other employees. For more information, check out *Sarbanes-Oxley For Dummies,* 2nd Edition, by Jill Gilbert Welytok (Wiley).

Securities and Exchange Commission

The Securities and Exchange Commission (SEC) is the government agency that oversees the stock and bond markets. It approves the corporate governance standards set by Nasdaq and the New York Stock Exchange. It also enforces violations.

Failure to meet legal and exchange-created governance standards can result in fines, civil penalties, and the sort of extreme bad publicity that makes many investors run for the doors (bumping into the activist investors who are rushing in to pressure the company to change).

Corporate raids as investment strategies

The easy thing for a socially responsible investor to do would be to avoid companies with bad governance because so many companies with good governance are out there. Many investors follow what they call the *Wall Street Rule:* If they don't like what a company is doing, they simply sell their shares. They see no need to get involved with any of the hassles of voting proxies or calculating ratios of executive pay to corporate profitability.

But other investors, known as *activist investors,* want to press companies for change. Some of these folks are purer of heart than others. Some find themselves with stock that they have to own, maybe as part of an *index strategy* (one that owns shares in every company in a major stock index, such as the S&P 500) or because of a bequest. These shareholders may push for change to improve the returns on their current investments

Others who lead activist charges often see poor governance as a profit opportunity rather than as a way to change the world. These people, often known as *corporate raiders* or *takeover artists,* find companies that are undervalued because of mismanagement, take a controlling interest in the company, and then make trouble.

Corporate raiders tend to care about good governance only because it helps them make money. They aren't interested in building sustainable businesses or improving returns for long-term investors. And they most definitely don't want to be stuck running the company! Raiders want to get in, get their profit, and get out. In the past, some launched their attacks on companies in hopes of receiving *greenmail,* which are payments designed to get an unwanted investor to go away.

(continued)

(continued)

And yet, corporate raiders aren't all bad. They play an important role in keeping stock markets efficient. To maximize their profits, they identify companies with the worst practices. Experienced lawyers and public relations experts help them press their cases. And, because raiders have been effective in the past, they strike fear in the hearts of CEOs and board members. Sometimes a mere rumor that a well-known corporate raider is interested in a business will force the board and executives to change their ways.

Corporate raiders tend to use the same tactics as any other investors looking for change: submitting shareholder resolutions, nominating members to the board of directors, and recruiting other shareholders to vote with them at annual meetings. You can find out more about these tactics in Chapter 5.

Chapter 8

Evaluating Environmental Investing

Companies produce goods and services every day, and in almost all cases, they use natural resources for free. At least, there's no cost upfront. Many investors — and maybe you're one of them — have real concerns about how a company's operations affect the environment, from the raw materials that go into a product to the way that it's disposed of when it reaches the end of its life. And for good reason. If someone owned the air or the water, that owner would demand compensation for the environmental damage. But because no one owns the environment, everyone suffers from its damage.

No one gets away with harming the air, land, or water forever. If a company isn't using resources wisely, it faces a few very real risks. At some point, government regulators get around to placing restrictions on air, water, and soil pollution. It's not always cheap to comply with the regulations, but it's almost always more expensive to repair past damage. Doing the right thing can save a bundle in the long run. If a company's product relies on a scarce resource for its manufacture or operation, that resource must be used thoughtfully or it may go away, taking the market for the product down with it. Finally, customers care about the effects of the goods and services that they use every day. A company that takes care of the environment may have an advantage in attracting customers.

All of these factors add up to good things for investors who care about the environment, and that's what this chapter is all about. First I give you the basics on sustainability and environmental issues as they relate to business. Then I give you the lowdown on how to put all of that information to use in your investments.

Factoring In Sustainability

I mention sustainability a few times throughout this chapter, so before my editor sends me a note about supplying the definition you need, here it is: *Sustainability* means providing for the needs of the present without compromising the resources available for future generations. And it's a hot buzzword in the investment world right now.

By that definition, any process anywhere that uses nonrenewable resources is not sustainable. Prime example: our oil-based economy. Yes, oil is slowly being created naturally by the chemical transformation of marine organisms under high pressure and temperature, but the amount of oil we're using nowadays far outpaces nature's renewal rate. The same is true for pumping groundwater from aquifers, mining metals, and burning down rain forests for cattle pastures.

However, the sustainability philosophy recognizes that businesses should meet present needs. It's not calling for sacrifice, just change. And change creates opportunities for businesses and investors who can navigate through it.

As a practical matter, sustainability is shorthand for environmental performance, and it includes greenhouse gas (GHG) emissions, energy and resource efficiency, water use and wastewater generation, recycling, pollution prevention, regulatory compliance, and just about any other green concept you can imagine. Is composting part of sustainability? Sure. Compact fluorescent bulbs? You bet. Installing bike racks in front of apartment buildings or office complexes? Why not? I cover most of these topics throughout this chapter, but for now, my goal is to help you fully grasp sustainability so you can better understand environmental business issues.

Operations executives like to talk about the *supply chain,* which is every step involved in getting a product to market. It includes extracting the raw materials from the ground, getting them to the factory, and getting the finished goods to customers. For many companies, the supply chain is a complex series of steps, but efforts to make any part of it more efficient and sustainable pay off when multiplied across all the products the company will make for years to come.

Designing products for sustainability

Sustainability starts with a design that considers what materials will go into the product, how it will be manufactured, how it will be shipped to customers, how it will be used, and then how it will be reused, recycled, or trashed when it's no longer useful. At every step, the product's developer needs to think about how to serve present needs without affecting the future environment. That's a tall order, especially for a product that's been on the market for generations.

Everything can be designed to be sustainable, from the toothpaste you use first thing in the morning to the skyscraper where you work during the day. But it's not easy to design everything to be sustainable, and some industries find it darn near impossible. As with everything in life, working toward the goal certainly gets you further than you are now, even if you don't reach it, so many designers and engineers are working on designing sustainable products because true sustainability starts at the drawing board.

One of the key specifications for sustainability during the design stage is the *identification of the product inputs.* This means finding renewable sources for as many of the materials as possible, with an eye toward how to manage the product at the end of its life. Here are a couple of examples:

- ✔ For a clothing manufacturer, sustainable design may mean finding cotton grown with less water, colored with dyes that don't require rinsing, made with plastic *notions* (buttons, zippers, and the like) designed to biodegrade at the same rate as the cotton, and shipped to retailers on reused and reusable hangers in reused and reusable plastic cartons.

- ✔ For a beverage company, it may mean finding organic sources for sweeteners and flavorings; locating bottling facilities in places with excess local water; and designing bottles and cans that are lightweight to reduce energy used in shipping and are reusable and recyclable to get more use out of a single package.

Rethinking the manufacturing process

The stereotype of factories is that they are dark, grimy, and dusty, spewing heaven only knows what kinds of horrible chemicals into the air and water. Some are exactly like that, too, but the situation is changing. Some companies are driven by regulation, but others just want to do the right thing now so they can keep their business running for the long haul.

Processes that are designed to be sustainable are engineered to be as *closed-loop* as possible. The inputs are matched with the finished product, so there is very little wasted energy, unused raw material, or pollution generated by the time the product hits the shelves (see "Taking a Closer Look at Pollution" later in this chapter). This can involve a complete overhaul of the facility or small changes in the steps along the way.

In most cases, the most difficult step in manufacturing sustainably is managing the pollution. Almost any process creates some waste that has to go somewhere, whether it's solid waste for a landfill, particulates that go into the air, or effluent that ends up in the water. The payoff in managing pollution is huge, though, in terms of reduced worker exposure to harmful chemicals, better relations with the surrounding community, and a business that can grow with minimal balance sheet liabilities (see the later section "Accounting for long-term liabilities" for more on this) and maximum resources at its disposal.

Sustainable manufacturing is easier in some industries than in others. As an investor, you may want to consider companies that have made tremendous progress or that have sustainable practices relative to their industries instead of just going for businesses that find it easy to be sustainable. An accounting firm will have an easier time being sustainable than a chemical company; that's the nature of the different businesses. As long as people need chemicals, though, it's important that these companies make progress on being sustainable. Some investors believe that these initiatives create exciting long-term profit opportunities.

Cogeneration is a great sustainable technique for many manufacturing firms. This process creates big savings by generating electricity as a side effect of the production process. If the manufacturing process generates a lot of heat, some of it can be redirected to keep the building comfortably warm. If the heat is especially intense, as in steel making, it can be used to generate steam for turbines that can provide some of the facility's electricity.

Distribution and consumption

After the goods are made, they have to get into customers' hands somehow, and that, too, uses resources. Sure, a company could have its customers drive to the factory and haul the items away, but that doesn't make the process more sustainable. It simply shifts the responsibility, and that's not good. The whole point of sustainability is to make permanent changes now to protect future resources.

Although no business can force its customers to take public transit to the store, a company can do quite a few things to make product distribution and consumption more sustainable. Take liquid laundry detergent. It used to be sold in big jugs that were heavy to lug around. By reducing the amount of water in the formula, the detergent company can put the same amount of active ingredient in a smaller bottle. The customer uses less product to get the same amount of cleaning. The smaller bottles weigh less, so less energy is used to get them to the store. The smaller bottle is made from less material and leaves less to be recycled. The product isn't perfectly sustainable, but it's an example of how the detergent maker is getting closer to the goal.

Most efforts to make the distribution and consumption processes more sustainable lead to lower costs for the company, which means greater profits for shareholders. And that's the goal!

Waste not, want not: Waste disposal, the sustainable way

After the customer uses the product, what happens? Is it all used up? Or is there a package, a byproduct, or an obsolete item sitting around somewhere? If something has to be done at the end of the product's life, a sustainability issue has to be managed.

For all the progress that's been made in product design and alternative uses, disposal is still the biggest sustainability challenge. Too often, using a product now means having it sit in a landfill for centuries to come. When you're looking at companies to invest in, seek out ones that are finding ways to solve the problem. But sustainable waste disposal is harder to tackle than other steps along the supply chain.

If the product's designers did a good job, they considered the product's disposal in the design specifications. A truly sustainable product is made with materials that can be reused or recycled to avoid the fate of landfilling or deep-sea dumping. For materials that are difficult to recycle, such as plastics, the solution is often to burn the material in power plants (a process known as *waste to energy;* plastic, after all, is mostly petroleum.)

In Europe (and at some companies with some products in the United States), the ruling philosophy is *extended producer responsibility.* That means that the manufacturer, not the consumer, is responsible for ensuring that the product is disposed of safely and without creating environmental damage. This ranges from changes in shampoo bottles to ensure that they're recyclable to operating store-based collection programs for old televisions and computer equipment. As extended producer responsibility becomes the norm in more places for more products, companies will be forced to build in sustainability from the start. The bad news for investors is that doing so increases the cost of doing business.

Industries for the environmental investor

If your interest is in protecting the environment, you may want to start by looking at companies in these industries. Not all companies in these industries will be good ones — and every industry seems to have one or two companies that are standouts in sustainability — but at least this list gives you a starting point.

✔ Alternative energy

✔ Environmental consulting and engineering

✔ Food processing

✔ Ocean shipping

✔ Railroads

✔ Technology

✔ Water utilities

Taking a Closer Look at Pollution

Pollution is produced at every link of the supply chain, creating potential liabilities and a challenge for businesses that want to be sustainable. Whether a product is animal, vegetable, or mineral, its production emits greenhouse gasses into the air, generates chemicals that leech into the ground, or spills byproducts into fresh water. Whenever someone turns one thing into another or extracts something from the ground, waste is created that affects something else.

For most companies, the cheapest option in the absence of regulation is to do nothing and let someone else deal with the pollution problem. Sooner or later, though, the good citizens of the world complain about air that is unhealthy to breathe or water that isn't safe to drink, and they ask their governments to do something. The governments respond with regulations and fines, costing businesses involved a lot of money.

The average person tends to freak out about toxic substances, especially *carcinogens* (cancer-causing substances). The problem is that many items that are perfectly fine or even healthy in small amounts become deadly in huge quantities. (Salt is deadly, for example, and yet we all love it and need it and have a lethal dose of it in our kitchens. It's the difference between consuming a quarter teaspoon and a pound in one sitting.) In many cases, a company may release chemicals in trace amounts so low that regulators and toxicologists have no concern, yet the public overreacts. The risk for investors is that a business with a fine environmental record can get dragged into a public relations quagmire or feel forced to spend excess money to keep constituents happy.

Costs aside, pollution is destructive to the environment that we all share, so a social investor isn't going to want to invest in businesses that willfully pollute. (No less a personage than Pope Benedict XVI has claimed that pollution is a sin.) Most pollution problems can be reduced or prevented, although not for free. An investor who cares about the environment would want proof that a company is working to manage its pollution before buying bonds or shares of stock. And this often means paying attention to news coverage rather than company announcements. For more information on doing research, see Chapter 4.

Controlling carbon and other airborne elements

Air pollution comes in two forms, particulates and gasses:

- ✔ **Particulates** include dust, ash, and other fine bits that are spewed out of smokestacks and exhaust pipes. Many, although not all, of these can be scrubbed or filtered out before they hit the air.

✔ **Gasses** are chemical substances in their gaseous form (as opposed to liquid or solid), and they often can't be screened out. These range from perfectly fine to outright deadly gasses, and they can enter the air through smoke and exhaust or from the evaporation of a liquid.

The hot issue in air pollution these days is carbon, especially in its greenhouse gas form of carbon dioxide. Carbon dioxide is generated whenever liquid or solid carbon is burned — as in coal or gasoline. *Greenhouse gasses* hold in the sun's heat, changing the earth's climate. The possible effects range from positive (Arable land in the Yukon! Tolerable winters in Chicago!) to devastating (extinction of species, drought and famine, skin cancer epidemics). Of course, because you're reading this book, you're probably more interested in preventing climate change than in getting me through another Midwest winter.

Carbon isn't the only substance that ends up in the air and can cause problems for the planet's long-term health. Other gasses implicated in climate change include methane, hydrofluorocarbons, nitrous oxide, and sulfur hexofluoride. When looking at companies that have manufacturing processes that emit chemicals into the air, be sure to ask about all the gasses and particulates involved.

Greenhouse gas reduction

Viewed through the lens of global climate change, reducing greenhouse gasses is a hidden benefit of increasing energy efficiency. Companies can reduce energy use for the simple financial reasons that grow more apparent each time we fill up our gas tank, yet get credit for saving the planet by taking on global warming.

Beyond simple energy efficiency, many companies are addressing the problem through improvements in design, manufacture, and distribution designed to limit the use of electricity, plastics, and gasoline. Some are experimenting with *carbon sequestration,* in which carbon that would have been spewed into the air is collected and injected back into the ground from which it originally came. Others are thinking in more radical ways, working to reduce the reliance on internal combustion altogether. (You can read more about alternative energy later in this chapter.)

The fastest way to reduce greenhouse gasses would be to shut down our economy. Fast, yes, but hardly practical. People all over the world, some of whom lived in dire poverty until very recently, want energy and they want goods.

Examining the Carbon Principles

To meet the demand for energy while reducing greenhouse gas emissions, three of the world's largest investment banks developed *Carbon Principles* to guide their investments in electric power projects. Citi, JPMorgan Chase, and Morgan Stanley announced the principles in February 2008, and they may be useful to investors looking to identify companies that make a difference on this matter. The Carbon Principles are

✔ **Energy efficiency,** which reduces carbon emissions by not emitting them in the first place. Investors should look for projects that include efficiency from the start.

✔ **Renewable and low-carbon energy technologies,** which are often good substitutes for traditional coal-based power generation. Many of these technologies create new businesses and new jobs, so this is a key area for start-up financing.

✔ **Risk assessment** on projects that rely on traditional energy technologies. Future regulations may create liabilities, and investors should consider those at the time of investment.

You can see the full list of policies at www.citigroup.com/citigroup/press/2008/080204a.htm.

Carbon as an asset class

Many nations around the world, but not the United States, have signed the Kyoto Protocol, a treaty under which the signing nations committed to reduce emissions of carbon dioxide and five other greenhouse gasses by 5.2 percent below their 1990 emissions levels by 2012. The Kyoto Protocol calls for a cap-and-trade system for managing greenhouse gas volumes. Under it, companies that emit greenhouse gasses are given a certain amount of credits. They can buy more if they like, instead of spending money to change their facilities, or they can make reductions in their output, and then sell their excess credits to companies that need them. Many state legislatures in the U.S. have passed or proposed similar requirements.

The system was already proved to be successful in the United States. The Clean Air Act, passed in 1990, sought to reduce sulfur dioxide emissions. Sulfur dioxide is a byproduct of burning coal to produce electricity, and it injures plants and fish and damages buildings when it's washed back to earth through precipitation, a phenomenon known as *acid rain*. Under the Clean Air Act, electric utilities were given sulfur dioxide credits that they could buy or sell. The problem was solved in seemingly no time

because utilities had an economic incentive to do the right thing.

Investors can buy and sell carbon credits, and some do. For example, if businesses don't get their emissions under control, which would drive up demand for and the price of credits, a hedge fund looking to speculate on the matter could buy credits now and sell them later when the price might be higher. In effect, the Kyoto Protocol turned carbon into an asset class.

The main carbon exchange is the European Climate Exchange (www.europeanclimateexchange.com), also known as the ECX. It has built-in demand because companies in Europe must operate under the terms of the Kyoto Protocol. In the United States, greenhouse gas reduction is voluntary unless a state law is in place. However, there's an exchange here to create a market, the Chicago Climate Exchange (www.chicagoclimatex.com), also known as the CCX. The founder of the Chicago Climate Exchange, Richard Sandor, developed the sulfur dioxide credit system used in the Clean Air Act and proposed the cap-and-trade system written into the Kyoto Protocol.

Preventing water contamination

Water is necessary for human life. Someday we'll figure out a way to make goods without using petroleum (and, in fact, alternative energy is one of the topics covered later in this chapter), but without water, life will cease. Period. Our planet has barely enough drinkable water, and *desalinization* (removing salt from water) of the oceans uses too much energy to be practical. Perhaps someday the alternative energy people can get together with the desalinization people to come up with a nifty solution, but that day is far off.

Drinking water comes from two places: surface water and ground water. *Surface water* includes lakes, rivers, and other bodies of water that sit on top of the earth's crust. *Ground water* is held in soil deep below the earth, and it comes to the surface through natural springs and man-made wells. Pollutants dumped into ground water and surface water end up in drinking water, and chemists have found that most tap water contains a lot more than dihydrogen oxide (H_2O) with a bit of fluoride mixed in.

The best way to keep water clean is to keep outside contaminants away from it. Companies can do this by developing manufacturing processes that use less water, pretreating water to remove noxious chemicals before it's released from the factory, and properly disposing of all waste so nothing leeches into groundwater.

Bottled water isn't the solution to clean drinking water. Many bottled water brands start with tap water or use the same sources. Then the water is put into bottles (made with petroleum and an array of other chemicals, some of which leech into the water) and carted around the country in trucks that run on gasoline or diesel fuel. Bottled water is rarely better for you than what you can get for a nominal cost out of your tap at home, but it does a lot more environmental damage.

If you're looking for environmentally sensitive investment options, you may want to look at water utilities and engineering consulting firms that specialize in water projects. You should also consider how other companies protect the water used in the course of their businesses. And, of course, you can look for companies that work to reduce their use of and damage to drinking water sources.

Scratching the surface of water

Surface water can be contaminated through a factory's *outfall pipe,* which discharges water from the manufacturing process directly into a lake or river. This water may be polluted; even if it was treated or filtered before being released, some contaminants still may remain. Or water that collects in sewers after a rainstorm can pollute surface water.

The toxins can show up in drinking water, or they can be concentrated in the bodies of fish that may be caught and eaten later. Other chemicals can interfere with the growth of plants in marshy areas (know as *wetlands*) that help control flooding. And fertilizers in fresh water sometimes encourage the growth of bacteria that can make anyone who drinks the contaminated water very sick.

Going down for groundwater

Although people often believe that there are underground lakes and rivers, there aren't. Groundwater, instead, is water stored in little spaces that form between bits of sand, soil, and rocks. It helps keep soil healthy, and it can be collected in wells to be used for drinking water. It's usually contaminated by liquids that are spilled on the ground that then soak through, whether intentionally or accidentally.

If the water stayed in the ground, there wouldn't be a problem, but some of it is brought to the surface for drinking water, and other groundwater shoots through the earth as springs that feed surface water sources. The source of groundwater pollution can be difficult to trace, complicating the problem.

You can't put a point on non-point source pollution

Non-point source pollution is often called *runoff* because it's water that washes away dirt and pollutants after a rainstorm.

Think about a parking lot, which has bits of grease and oil, rubber crumbs from tires, dropped cigarette butts, and spilled fast food on it. Some of it's harmful; some of it's not. After a good rain, all of that crud is rinsed off the parking lot and goes into the surrounding soil, winding up in wells and rivers and other water sources.

Agriculture is another primary source of runoff. Fertilizers, pesticides, and bacteria-laden animal wastes wash away during rain or irrigation and end up in the water supply. Investors who are interested in agricultural companies should ask about runoff issues. Even organic farming operations can have runoff issues if they're raising animals or using manure for fertilizer.

Saving the soil for greater savings

The notion of keeping dirt clean is a bit of an oxymoron. After all, it's supposed to be dirty! But soil holds a lot of not-so-good-for-us substances that can get loose if the land is dug up during construction or disturbed by children playing. Those substances can also show up in fruits or vegetables grown on the land. And some chemicals can destroy the land's ability to produce food or be put to other uses. Every community has vacant lots in locations that would make for good playgrounds if only it were safe for children to play there. If the ground is contaminated by lead, though, the land becomes worthless.

Soil can be contaminated when chemicals are spilled or run onto it, when chemicals in the air fall back to earth in rain, or through improper burial of waste products. Sometimes pollution occurs during the teardown of a previous building or the construction of a new one on the site.

Soil contamination can be expensive to remove. In many cases, the dirt has to be hauled away by the truckload and dumped into a landfill, which is ironic. One way to prevent soil contamination is to recycle more items so fewer things end up in landfills, which sometimes leak and contribute to soil contamination. Hence, sustainable design that considers the end of the product's life is an effective way to reduce soil pollution (see the earlier section "Waste not, want not: Waste disposal, the sustainable way" for more details).

Exploring Alternative and Renewable Energy

Most of our energy comes from coal, natural gas, and petroleum. These are carbon-based fossil fuels found in the earth, and when they're gone, they're gone. They aren't sustainable, and they're the primary contributors to climate change. And they aren't cheap, either! At this writing, huge increases in demand from India, China, and other developing countries, along with a prolonged war in Iraq, are driving oil prices to record high levels. Users of fuel (which is pretty much everyone on this planet) are looking for alternatives, and savvy entrepreneurs are finding ways to make those alternatives viable.

Energy usage falls into two main categories: transportation and in-place. Alternative fuels for transportation are difficult to engineer because they have to be portable and they have to be able to handle rapidly changing rates of use over the time of use. Think of how often your car starts, accelerates, decelerates, and stops over the course of a trip to the grocery store or a road trip to Grandma's. However, transportation is where the big opportunity is for finding alternative sources of energy. *In-place energy,* used for heating, lighting, and machine operation, is more predictable and more amenable to alternatives, so many alternatives are already in use.

REMEMBER

As much as socially responsible investors would like to believe that everyone else wants to make the world better, most consumers care only about prices. Alternative energy will take off when it becomes cheaper than traditional fossil fuels, and that's the metric that will drive the stock prices.

To encourage the market for alternative energy and the development of better technologies to make it work, the federal government and many states offer tax breaks and research subsidies to companies to reduce the costs. Investors should look at the merits of an alternative energy project with and without the subsidies. Few projects make economic sense without them, but some are closer to independent viability than others. The closer a project is to profitability before subsidy, the better it should prove over the long run.

It's back: Nuclear power

In a nuclear plant, radioactive materials generate heat that makes steam. The steam then powers a turbine that creates the power. But nuclear power has two huge drawbacks. The first is that if a plant fails, the radiation emitted can make the area uninhabitable for decades (Chernobyl, anyone?). The second is that after the fuel has been used to generate power, it's still radioactive and can remain dangerous for centuries. No one knows what to do with it, so it sits in holding tanks very near where people live and get their water.

On the other hand (and isn't there always another hand?), nuclear energy is inexpensive as long as nothing goes wrong, and it doesn't contribute to climate change. Newer technologies are reducing the risk of operation and of problems with those spent-fuel holding tanks. Hence, some investors are reconsidering their aversion to nuclear power. Opportunities may come in the form of stock in nuclear utilities and bonds for new construction projects.

The alt-power three: Solar, wind, and water

In an old-fashioned electrical plant, coal heats water in a boiler that creates steam that turns a turbine that generates the power. A nuclear plant works similarly (see the preceding section).

But there are other ways to generate heat and turn turbines. Concentrated sunlight can turn water into steam on a small scale on the roof of a house, or on a huge scale by setting up racks of solar collectors out in a desert. Solar power can also be used to heat water, which is a major use of fuel in residential and institutional settings. (I'm not the only person who gets the best ideas standing under a hot shower!) Right now, solar power is more expensive than coal-generated electricity, although the price may fall as technology improves and more large-scale projects come online. And, by definition, solar power requires the sun to work; it's not practical in regions where the people suffer through days or even weeks of overcast skies.

To harness the wind, giant windmills turn as the wind blows, cranking the turbines that generate electricity. The windmills don't pollute the air, water, or soil, and the power is almost as free as the wind. It's a seemingly perfect, clean system, except of course that it isn't. The problems are mostly aesthetic; some people find that the windmills are noisy, and others think they're ugly. Furthermore, they kill birds that fly into them (although at a much lower rate than coal-fire powered plants do), and they only work when it's windy.

Water power uses rushing water to turn turbines. It can be done on an enormous scale if there's enough water; nature's own Niagara Falls generates 1.6 million kilowatts of electricity each day in Canada and another 2.4 million kilowatts in the United States. Hoover Dam, an enormous man-made structure in Nevada, produces even more power. Excluding the rare and wondrous Niagara Falls, almost all significant hydropower projects involve man-made dams that are expensive to build and usually disrupt the local ecology. Villages have to be relocated, wildlife dies, and acres of land are submerged to create a powerful fall to turn those turbines. But after the dam is built, hydropower is inexpensive to operate and creates no air or water pollution. What's an environmental investor to do?

Social investing involves a lot of trade-offs. Some investors will value clean energy more highly than the landscape effects of solar, wind, or water power. Others will value preservation. You have to make your own decisions, understanding that perfection is an impossible goal.

Alternative energy for transportation

The current crop of alternative energy works great for buildings, but they aren't so great for getting from place to place. There's no good way to put the power of Niagara Falls into your car's tank, but people are trying! Engineers are coming up with a lot of creative ideas for environmentally friendly alternatives to the gasoline-powered internal combustion engine we all know and love, or at least rely on to get from place to place. These alternatives include batteries, biofuels, and hydrogen fuel cells, and the hope is that they'll be more sustainable than petroleum. Read on for a glimpse of how you may be powering your vehicle ten years from now!

Building a better battery

If you lived in southern Ontario or upstate New York, and if there were a way to run your car off of a battery that was powerful enough to get you on the highway, lasted long enough to get you where you needed to go, and recharged fast enough to keep you going, then you could power your car with the electricity generated by Niagara Falls. Better battery technology will make it possible to run a car with clean energy.

Rechargeable batteries can be used now in vehicles that have light-duty cycles and operate at low speeds in a controlled environment, such as forklifts in warehouses or cranes in heavy manufacturing plants. It's likely that someday they'll work in cars, too.

Banking on biofuels

Biofuel seems great on paper: a fuel made from plants that works in cars or electric power plants and grows back! We'd never run out of it. It's been the great goal in alternative fuels for years now, but it's not here yet.

Most of the work has gone into *ethanol,* an alcohol made from corn that can power cars similarly to gasoline. Ethanol works, but right now it's not nearly as efficient as gasoline. When you consider all the energy that goes into growing, harvesting, and processing the corn, along with the fact that ethanol gets fewer miles per gallon in a car than gasoline does, it's a losing proposition. That doesn't mean it always will be a loser, but more work has to go into testing different plants, different processing methods, and different engine designs to make it more efficient.

Relying on biofuel for energy isn't perfect. The primary use of crops is for food and takes priority, especially if the corn yield is poor one season.

Another alternative is *biodiesel,* which is nothing more than vegetable oil used in diesel engines. The oil can be mixed with conventional diesel fuel so it will work in an existing diesel engine, or the diesel engine can be modified to accept any vegetable oil — including leftover French-fry grease from a fast-food restaurant. Biodiesel seems to offer similar efficiency to regular diesel, too, and it can sometimes be had for free. This makes it a viable option for those who drive cars with diesel engines.

One concern with biofuels and other gasoline alternatives is how to get them to the drivers. Gas stations won't carry them until there's demand, but demand is often limited because no gas stations carry the fuel! My bet is that as soon as someone develops a low-cost biofuel that works as well as gasoline in a car, the demand will spike so quickly that every gas station will figure out a way to get the fuel. In the meantime, no less a personage than country singer Willie Nelson is trying to sign up truck stops to offer biodiesel, and many farm communities in the Midwest have gas stations offering an ethanol pump (usually subsidized by the state department of agriculture or other agency, but at least they're out there).

Fine-tuning fuel cells

A *fuel cell* is similar to a battery in that it's a device that stores energy. It's different in that it works by creating a chemical reaction that generates electricity. The chemical that creates the reaction has to be replenished on occasion. Most work to date has been done with hydrogen, and it's still not cost-effective.

Although there's been a lot of excitement about fuel cells for cars, no one has been able to build an efficient fuel-cell vehicle at a reasonable price. In the meantime, engineers are looking at fuel cells for stationary applications, including as backup generators, that may be able to complement other electric car technologies.

Accounting for Animal Welfare

Human beings aren't the only creatures in our environment. We share a planet with lots of animals, but we don't always treat them well. Many investors want to make sure that the businesses they invest in treat animals fairly and humanely — if the businesses have anything at all to do with animals. The two biggest issues are animal testing and the treatment of livestock. In this section, I cover these hot issues so you know what to look for.

Responsible testing

Many products are tested on animals before they're tested on humans. Potential new food additives are tried out in animals first to see whether they're poisonous, and promising pharmaceuticals are tested in animals to see what effects they may have. Scientists have developed mice that are guaranteed to get certain diseases so researchers can learn more about fighting cancer or heart disease. But although there are valid reasons to use animals in testing, not all tests of toxicity and performance have to be done on animals; if animal testing needs to be done, the animals should be treated well and kept free from pain.

The Humane Society of the United States has a lot of information about animal testing and alternatives to it that can help guide your investing decisions. You can find it on the organization's Web site, www.hsus.org/animals_in_research/animal_testing.

How is livestock treated?

Plenty of people are all right with killing animals for food, but they believe that those animals should be treated well before they're slaughtered. Not all animals are, and many investors in restaurant and food-processing companies want to know that animals are raised well before being given a quick death.

One of the leading companies in this area is McDonald's. After years of criticism, the company worked with Temple Grandin, a veterinarian who specializes in the design of livestock-handling facilities. With her help, McDonald's drew up requirements for its suppliers to ensure that the animals used to make its burgers are kept healthy, treated well, and are free from pain at the time of death. It backs up its principles with an inspection program. No matter what you think about Big Macs, McDonald's work has put pressure on other food processors to make improvements.

McDonald's policies, which are considered to be a model for the industry, are published on its Web site, `www.mcdonalds.com/corp/values/purchasing/animalwelfare.html`. You can use them to help evaluate investments in the food business.

Striking a Balance Between the Environment and Investors

The environment is all about warm-and-fuzzy nature loving, while the financial markets are about cold, hard cash, right? Well, sort of. The financial markets are about money and little else, but if money is to be made on taking care of the environment, then the markets love it.

I wish I could say that investing in environmentally responsible companies always generates huge returns for investors, but the statistical evidence is mixed. Investing along environmental lines is no surefire path to riches. But no investment program is. So while finance students write dissertations trying to prove the relationship between the environment and the markets five years ago, you have to do your research and monitor your investments now (I cover those topics in Chapters 4 and 5). In this section, I let you know what to look for and consider so you can make the best environmentally based investment decisions.

Looking at statistics realistically

The research to date on environmental investing is a bit mixed: It shows that environmental investing doesn't necessarily lead to bigger profits, but it doesn't necessarily hurt investment returns, either. That's important to know, because some financial advisors will tell you that social investing always leads to poor performance. Here are the findings of some recent studies:

✔ Andreas Ziegler, Michael Schröder, and Klaus Rennings of the Center for Corporate Responsibility and Sustainability at the University of Zurich found that industries that had better sustainability performance had better stock market performance than industries that were not focused on sustainability efforts. But companies that had better sustainable performance relative to their industry didn't seem to be rewarded by the stock market. ("The Effect of Environmental and Social Performance on the Stock Performance of European Corporations," *Environmental and Resource Economics,* August 2007)

✔ A 2001 study by Shameek Konar and Mark A. Cohen found that a 10 percent reduction in the emission of toxic chemicals led to a $34 million increase in a company's stock market value. ("Does the Market Value Environmental Performance?" *Review of Economics and Statistics,* May 2001)

✔ A paper presented at Oxford University in 2007 by Vanda Roque and Maria Céu Cortez found that the more environmental information that Portuguese companies gave investors, the worse the stocks performed! ("The Relationship between Corporate Environmental and Financial Performance: Evidence for Portuguese listed corporations," working paper)

So does all of this mean the environmentally concerned investor is doomed? No. You just have to do your research to ensure that your environmental investment is also financially sound.

One problem with academic research is that it looks backward. A researcher gets an idea, known as a *hypothesis,* and then goes back to see if the historic data support or refute it. As investors know, past performance does not indicate future results. Just because the research so far doesn't show a great connection between the environment and stock returns doesn't mean that it never will. Nor does it mean that the investment you may be considering is a bad one.

Appealing to consumers for better sales

The first thing a business has to do to make a profit is generate sales. It has to persuade customers that its goods and services are worth paying for. Green (or, as I've called it in this chapter, sustainable) products or services are hot because customers are factoring green credentials into their purchasing decisions.

Beware of greenwashing!

Watch out for *greenwashing,* which is the practice of making it seem like a product is good for the environment even if it isn't. Because so many buyers not only seek out environmentally friendly products, but they'll also pay extra for them, a lot of companies want to be perceived as making environmentally friendly products. And if they don't? Well, the marketing department will create ads showing scenic vistas, redesign packages to use earth tones, and create taglines that talk about caring for the environment — without the company actually making costly or risky changes in product formulation or manufacture.

Some businesses take it further and lie. For example, a gym clothing company claimed to be using a special fiber made from fast-growing, renewable seaweed that had special proteins to destress and detoxify the wearer, but independent testing showed that the material was plain old cotton. The Cone and Boston College study mentioned earlier in this chapter found that 90 percent of consumers surveyed expect companies to prove that their products are good for the environment, not just talk about it.

A 2008 survey conducted by the Boston College Center for Corporate Citizenship and Cone, a marketing communications firm, found that 59 percent of American consumers are concerned about the environment and are either consuming less or are seeking out products that are environmentally friendly. (You can see all the details at www.coneinc.com/content1135.) With more than half of customers thinking about the environment when they shop, a savvy corporation needs to think about the environment, too, or be prepared to watch its revenues go to competitors that show more concern.

By going green, a business can stand out and attract customers who want to shop responsibly. The green movement can help the company grow its top line and, it is hoped, bring some of those gains down as profits.

Controlling costs for bigger profits

Helping the environment doesn't have to cost a lot. In many cases, it can be a real money saver, and that's good for you as an investor. After all, the less money a company spends, the bigger its profits will be, and profits drive returns. Even better, a company can save money lots of ways while helping the environment.

Producing and selling products generates costs. And below the cost-of-goods-sold line come all kinds of operating costs that companies incur but that aren't directly tied to products and services. Some of these costs can be avoided by hugging some trees while running the business. I cover many of these issues in the section "Factoring in Sustainability," earlier in this chapter, but here's a quick-and-dirty breakdown of what you should look for in the ways companies control their costs:

- ✔ **Manufacturing and retailing costs:** For most manufacturing companies, the largest cost item is cost of goods sold, which is everything that goes into making the product. If the company can find ways to save energy and water, use sustainable materials, reduce waste in manufacturing, and then reduce the amount of packaging needed to get the goods out the door, it can generate real cost savings.

  Companies other than manufacturers can employ similar strategies, too. A retailer or a service company can find ways to use more-efficient lighting, insulate space for cheaper and better heating and cooling, and make wiser decisions about office supplies, furniture, and fixtures.

- ✔ **Travel and shipping costs:** Because so many companies have to get people or goods from one point to another, they can find ways to save by using fuel-efficient vehicles, lighter packaging materials that cost less to ship, and possibly by making people stay put from time to time. For example, a round-trip flight between New York and Los Angeles generates 2.46 metric tons of carbon dioxide, not to mention the cost of the ticket and the hotel room. If just one meeting per year can be replaced with a conference call or Webcast, then the environment and the corporation benefits.

  You can calculate estimated carbon usage at www.carboncounter.org, a site put together by the Climate Trust, a nonprofit organization that lets people and businesses purchase offsets for their carbon emissions. Of course, if you don't emit the carbon in the first place, you won't need to pay for the offsets!

- ✔ **Marketing:** It's entirely possible that a company will even save money on marketing expenses after its environmentally conscious consumers find out about its good works through news reports, blog postings, or word of mouth from like-minded friends. (It will save even more if it can avoid the sort of environmental disaster, such as contaminated drinking water or a deadly chemical leak, that requires the use of SWAT teams of damage-control experts.)

- ✔ **Waste management:** Businesses generate trash. Any reduction in trash from less upfront consumption and more reuse and recycling saves money in terms of waste hauling and landfill fees. Some businesses generate hazardous wastes. Handling those so they don't contaminate the environment may cost a little extra money upfront, but it will pay off down the road when the company can avoid the expense of regulatory fines and remediation.

✔ **Insurance:** If a business is run so that it has less risk of creating environmental damage in its business processes, waste management, or products, it may be able to save money on insurance fees. If the company reduces the likelihood that it will have a problem, it will pay less. The shareholders, meanwhile, make more. Hurray!

Accounting for long-term liabilities

The way to hit a corporation where it hurts is to make it record a *balance sheet liability*. First, the company has to take a charge to income to show the expense. Then it has that great big number sitting on its balance sheet for investors to pester it about for years to come. Ouch!

Thanks to Financial Standards Accounting Board Standard 5, known as FASB 5 to its friends (and FASB, by the way, is pronounced *fahz-bee*), companies have to report long-term environmental liabilities on their balance sheets. FASB 5, Accounting for Contingent Liabilities, says a company has to record a liability when it

✔ Has reason to know that it has a liability when the income statement is prepared, and

✔ Has a reasonable estimate of its cost

A related standard, FASB 144, covers the disposal of an asset that is impaired, such as a contaminated parcel of land that the firm wants to sell. It, too, calls for the creation of a liability on the balance sheet.

You can find out about these liabilities by looking at a company's balance sheet and reading the footnotes to its financial statements. (See Chapter 4 for more on financial statements.)

These liabilities may limit the amount of money that a firm can borrow, but they also may not be accurate. If the amount on the balance sheet is too low, the company will have to take another charge at some point to bring it up to size. If it's too large, the company will get to reverse it and show a boost to reported income.

A balance sheet liability for environmental damage isn't created when the damage occurs. Instead, it comes up when some kind of enforcement action or site analysis shows the extent of the problem and a recommendation for remediation gives the company an estimate of the cost. Plenty of companies have environmental problems that aren't on their balance sheets.

You can do all of your homework to ensure that the company you invest in has clean production processes, is an innovator in sustainability, and generally goes out of its way to be a leader on environmental issues, but that doesn't mean you're safe. A company can find itself liable today for pollution that occurred decades ago, before we had a good understanding of the effects of all of these different substances in the air, water, and soil — and before regulation gave companies a reason to do something about them. Sometimes a company will take on a problem through an acquisition.

Because of the long life of environmental contaminants, it's important that companies do the right thing now, even if there's no regulatory incentive to do so. That will lead to better profits over the long haul. On the other hand, investors need to remember that just because a company has environmental liabilities on the balance sheet, it's not necessarily an evil polluter. It may simply be dealing with something that happened years ago under a different management and a different view of the world.

Some line items will rule a company in or out for different social investors. A balance sheet liability is not one of those; it's merely a sign to dig deeper.

Real cost savings from sustainable investments

Being good to the environment can bring money to an organization's bottom line, and that's good for investors. Whether you're buying stocks or bonds, corporate or municipal securities, you may like the looks of these dollar savings:

✔ Hormel Foods (makers of Spam, among other fine products) estimates that it saved more than $1.1 million in 2006 by reducing the amount of waste sent to landfills. Also, Hormel spent about $12.5 million for water in 2006, and has set a goal of reducing water use by 2 percent per year for five years. Anticipated cost savings in 2011: $1.2 million, assuming utilities don't charge Hormel more for the water it uses. Would investors like another $1.2M of profit?

✔ The City of Chicago introduced a recycling program in selected wards in 2007. The city estimates that each ton of recycled waste will generate $110 — partly from the price that vendors will pay for recyclables and partly from the avoided landfill fees. The avoided landfill fees are as important as the revenue from aluminum and recycled paper pulp.

✔ Baxter, maker of medical supplies, estimates that it enjoyed a savings of $8.5 million as a result of its energy conservation initiative in 2005, and $23.6 million in cost avoidance or income from all environmental activities in 2005.

✔ Electronics giant Sony estimates that it recycled or reused 173,000 tons of waste out of a total of 193,000 tons generated in 2007, thus avoiding 173,000 tons of landfill fees. The company has not quantified the savings; because the recycling took place all over the world, it is difficult to apply U.S. rates.

Chapter 9

The World around Us: Following International Affairs

*M*ultinational corporations answer to no one but shareholders (and maybe customers), so shareholders often push companies to do the right thing when deciding whether to do business in nations that don't support human rights or that are engaged in civil conflicts. In fact, social investing gained traction as a protest technique against South Africa's former *apartheid* (discrimination against non-Whites) policies, which have now ended. Morals aside, behaving well, no matter what the laws of the land are, can help a company reduce its risk and enhance its value with customers, warming the hearts of even the most ruthlessly capitalistic investors.

It's not perfect. Some people resent it when a big corporation tells them that the local way of doing business is wrong, even if that local way involves discrimination against minorities and bribes to local officials. Others think that companies shouldn't be doing a government's work. Governments, not mining companies, should provide healthcare; governments, not clothing manufacturers, should provide schools; governments, not engineering-construction firms, should work to prevent corruption. But if the government can't or won't meet its civic duties, it may turn to others with money and power to make a difference, and that's often a multinational corporation.

This chapter starts with an overview of the structure and mission of the typical multinational corporation. I also cover some of the key issues facing global companies, especially when they're doing business in developing nations where human rights may not be respected and where the risk of war may be great. That way, when you do your research (see Chapter 5), you know what to look for. After all, companies won't give you a lot of this information. You have to find much of it yourself from news sources.

The goal is to help investors who care about international relations to determine whether the companies that they're interested in share the goal of a better life for the 6 billion of us who share the planet.

Scrutinizing the Global Mega-Corporation

The biggest corporations in the world are no longer tied to their headquarters location. In 2007, Coca-Cola (NYSE: KO) generated just 26.9 percent of its revenue from North America. McDonald's (NYSE: MCD) took in 34.7 percent of its revenue from the United States, while Unilever (LSE: ULVR.L), based in the UK, collected only 37.8 percent of its revenue from Europe. Even companies that draw most of their revenue in only one nation may have close ties to other countries as sources of raw materials or inventories. The world's biggest companies, and many of its medium and small ones, have such diverse businesses that they no longer belong to any one nation. They are the true global citizens, getting things done all over the world.

In a way, this means that these corporations are beholden to no one nation, either. If the Canadian government starts to be a bother, it's no big deal; there are plenty of sales to be found in Mexico. In a strange way, these multinationals are more accountable to shareholders and customers than to any set of regulators or politicians.

Companies have been known to move headquarters if they don't like what's happening in their hometown. Some set up legal shop in such tax havens as Bermuda; others merge with a company in another country and move the headquarters there. But company management can't force any shareholders to sell unless the entire company is sold, so it can't run from activist investors. Furthermore, any management team worth its salt (or salary) wants to attract customers rather than drive them away.

U.S. companies can be found liable in courts here for violating human rights abroad. That's under the Alien Tort Claims Act of 1789. Yes, it's that old, but it has modern applications. The act gave U.S. courts jurisdiction over the civil actions of U.S. citizens committed in violation of U.S. laws and treaties, no matter where those actions took place. Under U.S. law, a corporation is treated as an individual person for civil actions, so the law applies. If a U.S. company operating overseas has a security guard who falsely imprisons or tortures an employee suspected of theft, the company can be on the hook here.

Maximizing shareholder value (s)

The modern corporation is operated for the benefit of the shareholders, who are legally the owners of the company. It should be run to get as great a profit as possible over the long term, which may involve spending now so the business can thrive for years to come. The shareholders want the business to be run in a responsible way. Otherwise, the company can end up losing customers, spending money on lawyers and fines, and getting taken over by a hostile government.

Some socially responsible shareholders are leery of the biggest and most multi of the major multinational companies because they have so little accountability to any one government. If those companies are accountable to shareholders and if those shareholders have an interest in keeping their investment viable for the long term, then shareholders can drive oversight. (You can read more about corporate governance and the role of shareholders in Chapter 7.)

As the world's markets become more sophisticated and workers in places that were once desperately poor earn their way out of poverty, more national governments will be able to face a multinational corporation from a position of strength. Business can create the economic development that gets people out of poverty. A responsible corporation is an asset to the world, not just to socially responsible shareholders.

The (global) customer is always right

The customer is always right, department-store magnate Marshall Field is supposed to have said. Granted, some customers just want whatever is cheapest, no matter how those savings were attained, but others want some assurance that their money went for fair wages to workers, as well as to profits for the company, and that the goods aren't contaminated with lead paint. Some want an assurance that the goods they purchase were made with sustainable materials (which you can find out more about in Chapter 8).

If the customer is always right, then one reason companies pay workers rock-bottom wages and cut corners on the manufacturing process is to pass on rock-bottom prices to their customers. Are you willing to pay more for a T-shirt or new toy to ensure that the makers receive a fair wage?

The fallout from cutting costs and taking shortcuts can be huge. Two U.S. toymakers, Mattel (NYSE: MAT) and RC2 Corp., recalled millions of toys in 2007 because contractors in China used lead paint on them. In 1996, television personality Kathie Lee Gifford was thrilled to announce her new line of clothing for Wal-Mart (NYSE: WMT); neither she nor the shoppers were thrilled to find out that much of the manufacturing work was done by children in Honduras.

In order to stave off consumer boycotts, other brand-name shoe and clothing companies, including Nike (NYSE: NKE), Gap (NYSE: GPS), and Levi Strauss, have had to change their sourcing practices to assure that products are made by workers who are treated well.

It's not just U.S. consumers who care about how products are made and promoted. Multinational corporations entering new markets have had to hire local workers, use local banks and ad agencies, and participate in local activities to show that they have a commitment to the customers there. McDonald's and Coca-Cola want to be global brands that are loved by people everywhere, not "something better" offered by Americans. That way, they can attract local customers by being local themselves.

How corporations work with governments

Although a global corporation has less government accountability than a corporation that operates in only one nation, that doesn't mean it can ignore governments and regulators. Instead, it has to figure out ways to get things done given the law of the land.

Companies have a way of saying that something is impossible in one market but is doable in another. For example, many multinationals complain that it would be impossible to meet increased environmental regulations in the United States, even though they're already meeting stricter standards in Europe. This is a negotiating tactic. A creative management team finds ways to get things done, so activist shareholders should be skeptical of the "we couldn't possibly" argument.

Big companies often take a different approach to compliance in different countries in order to meet the requirements of a local market. In most cases, this is a fine adjustment to the realities of commerce, but it may not always be. Some companies have been known to resort to bribery (which I cover later in this chapter); others have been known to act against stated corporate values in the interests of expediency.

Internet companies Yahoo! (Nasdaq: YHOO) and Google (Nasdaq: GOOG) have cooperated with the Chinese government by releasing information on users that have helped the government track dissidents and by developing search algorithms that limit the access of Chinese users to certain types of information that the Chinese government views as inappropriate. Both companies argued that it is better to have some presence in China than not, but not all shareholders and customers were convinced. (Note that Google's corporate motto is "Don't be evil.")

Not to pick on Yahoo! and Google, but that's a huge challenge that companies face. Because different nations have different laws, a multinational corporation may find itself in compliance but with angry activist investors.

Many companies go well beyond the letter of law; think of consumer product companies that transfer sustainable practices required in Europe to the U.S., where it's not required, or clothing manufacturers that only hire adults, even if the local law allows them to hire children. Others use their financial power to lobby for changes that make a difference. If shareholders support actions that may be costly in the short term but are the right thing to do in the long run, companies are more likely to do the right thing.

Most companies are scrupulous about at least the appearance of political neutrality. They tend to emphasize good corporate governance instead of any one set of policies or another, because becoming embroiled in a messy political battle can backfire with customers and make operations difficult in years to come. For example, in the United States, where politicians expect businesses to make campaign contributions, most companies simply contribute a more or less equal amount to all candidates in a given race.

Human Rights: What's the Company's Global Approach?

Companies are collections of human beings. The shareholders are human beings; even big institutions, like mutual funds or pensions, manage money for the benefit of individuals. The members of the board of directors are human beings, as are the managers and other employees. The customers are human, too; even business and government buyers are collections of people who actually make the decisions and use the products. The big behemoth corporation will cry when poked!

Ah, but as we all know, human beings don't always treat each other very well. And sometimes, a corporation contributes to the problems. As a social investor looking at international companies, you want to know more about their stances on human rights. This section is a guide to some of the key issues, which include the treatment of minorities, the source of the workers themselves, and the rights of workers in the workplace. (I look at domestic workplace issues in Chapter 11.)

A great resource for investors and managers who are concerned about the human rights issues facing multinational corporations is the Business Leaders Initiative in Human Rights, www.blihr.org. It's a group of 13 multinational corporations chaired by Mary Robinson, the former president of Ireland, and supported by the United Nations. The organization's mission is to help businesses find practical ways to apply the United Nations Universal Declaration of Human Rights. The Web site has some great information on the issues that companies face, as well as some possible solutions.

Speaking for the minorities

For all sorts of reasons, many places in the world have institutionalized discrimination. It may be along racial, ethnic, religious, or social class lines; one group is on top, one is at the bottom, and that's just how it is. Some countries allow it by law and others by custom. But that doesn't make it right.

It's easy for the best-meaning company to make mistakes if it's not paying attention. Offering hiring preferences for friends and relatives of current employees may help a company bring in people who are known to be good workers, but it may also reinforce the demographics of the staff rather than help diversify it (see the later section "Saying no to nepotism — most of the time" for more on this topic). Advertising job openings in just one newspaper, at just one school, or on just one Web site will bring in the readers, students, and users of just one type rather than a greater mix of people.

Employment isn't the only issue. Companies must be sensitive to other cultural norms that are important to their customers. New construction projects may interfere with sacred sites or religious rituals. Advertising campaigns that are funny to one culture may be offensive to another. Food ingredients may contain items that are taboo to some religious groups. Being respectful to others is hard work, but it helps companies maintain strong ties to customers, and they're the people who generate the revenues.

Preventing discrimination with the MacBride Principles

Sean MacBride was an Irish politician who won the Nobel Peace Prize in 1974 for his work in promoting peace in Northern Ireland and elsewhere in the world. In 1984, he and the Irish National Caucus proposed what are known as the *MacBride Principles,* which were designed to help international companies doing business in Northern Ireland avoid discrimination against Roman Catholics, which was rampant in the province and contributed to the violence there. The MacBride Principles are still used as a model to help international companies overcome local prejudices anywhere in the world. They call for

✔ Increasing the representation of individuals from underrepresented groups in the workforce at all levels, including managerial, supervisory, administrative, clerical, and technical jobs.

✔ Providing adequate security for the protection of minority employees at the workplace.

✔ Banning provocative sectarian or political emblems from the workplace.

✔ Providing that all job openings be advertised publicly and providing that special recruitment efforts be made to attract applicants from underrepresented groups.

✔ Providing that layoff, recall, and termination procedures do not favor a particular group.

✔ Abolishing job reservations, apprenticeships restrictions, and differential employment criteria that discriminate. This may mean restricting hiring preferences for relatives of current employees.

✔ Providing for the development of training programs that will prepare substantial numbers of minority employees for skilled jobs, including the expansion of existing

programs and the creation of new programs to train, upgrade, and improve the skills of minority employees.

✔ Establishing procedures to assess, identify, and actively recruit minority employees with the potential for further advancement.

✔ Providing for the appointment of a senior management staff member to be responsible for the employment efforts of the entity and, within a reasonable period of time, the implementation of the principles described above.

Facing the reasons for forced and child labor

Although few businesses engage in outright slavery (often called *forced labor*), some have practices that are mighty close. For example, if a worker has to live in a company dorm and can eat only at the company cafeteria, but if the wages barely cover the cost, it may be construed as slavery. Some companies provide transportation to workers to get them to the job site, and then expect the workers to stay until they pay back the cost — which may roughly equal the wages they would be expected to make over the next five years. In a few countries, prisoners can be hired to do assembly work on a contract basis, and they may be forced to work as a condition of their incarceration.

Related to the issue of forced labor is the use of child labor — workers under the age of 17 and sometimes as young as 4. Some manufacturing plants like to use children because they're obedient; they can be intimidated and don't talk back. Sometimes the parents, not the employer, force the children to work, which creates a forced-labor dynamic even if the company isn't behind it. Although it's true that a child is better off having a job than dying of starvation, it's the responsibility of government, not business, to provide a basic safety net for its people. And it's a corporation's responsibility to pay its adult workers enough that they can provide food for their children.

Note that both of these issues are related to paying workers a fair wage. Pay people enough money, and you won't have to force them to work. Pay them enough money, and they'll be able to earn enough so their children don't have to work. Furthermore, workers should be able to earn that fair wage in a reasonable amount of time. Sure, investment bankers and doctors may work 80 or 100 hours a week, but they're making a lot more than $0.75 per hour, and they're free to quit at any time.

The sticky issue with forced and child labor is the use of *contractors*. Few retailers make what they sell. Many corporations view their strength as being in design and marketing, not in manufacture. These businesses hire other companies (contractors) to do the assembly work. In some cases, those contractors hire subcontractors to do the work. Too often, decisions are made based only on the lowest price, and the lower the price, the less money there is to pay the workers.

Investors in companies that operate manufacturing plants in low-wage countries or that use contractors in those markets should make sure policies are in place against the use of forced and child labor. If a company relies on contractors, it should have a certification process enforced with inspections and the potential loss of the contract to ensure that the work is being performed by adults who can choose the work.

The National Labor Committee, www.nlcnet.org, is a coalition of labor, human rights, and religious organizations that monitors conditions in manufacturing facilities all over the world. The Web site has information on current problems as well as details of past campaigns so investors can find out more about the issues and the companies involved.

Standing up for rights in the workplace

They should be lucky they have a job and not complain, you may say, but workers do complain. And while some of those complaints can be chalked up to human nature, others are valid, and businesses should respect the workers' rights to make them.

A common complaint among workers concerns their security and safety in the workplace. Companies should make sure that their managers aren't taking bribes or asking employees for favors as a condition of employment, that sexual and ethnic harassment isn't tolerated, and that the workplace is safe. Employees should not be locked in, exposed to toxic chemicals, or use dangerous machinery without adequate safety protections. They should have access to bathrooms and be given lunch breaks.

A more challenging right for many companies is the workers' right to organize into labor unions. Some businesses are offended by the idea of unions; the managers want to think that they're doing such a great job that the workers should be happy with what they have. Others see a union as something that will create obstacles to getting work done and lead to significant reductions in profits. To combat unions, companies have done everything from limiting the rights of workers to chat in the lunchroom to hiring private investigators to threaten — or commit — bodily harm against organizers.

A company may very well be able to head off union activity by running a clean workplace and treating employees well. But if there's talk of a union being formed, workers should have the basic right to congregate after hours and to discuss it in the workplace as long as they're getting the job at hand done.

War, Peace, and Profit

In his book *The Lexus and the Olive Tree*, *New York Times* writer Thomas L. Friedman posed the *Golden Arches Theory of Conflict Prevention:* No nation that had a McDonald's had ever declared war on another nation with a McDonald's after both nations had a franchise. The fast-food restaurant's presence was a sign of economic progress that no one wanted to jeopardize with a war. The theory has been disproved: Several different global skirmishes have occurred between French fry–loving nations, including decades of hostilities between Israel and Lebanon and the 1999 U.S. bombing of Kosovo. That doesn't discredit the logic behind Friedman's theory, though. As a nation becomes more economically developed, it has more to lose in a war, so it has a greater incentive to solve its problems through diplomatic means.

Still, the peoples of the world are not all sitting down in harmony to share the toys in their respective Happy Meals. War is an unfortunate reality, and companies doing business across borders need to be careful that their behavior doesn't exacerbate conflicts already in place. And if the company is operating when conflict heats up, it needs to take precautions to protect its employees and its business.

Appropriate appropriation prevention

For a business, the worst thing that can happen is that the business is taken over by the government (this action is called an *appropriation*). It's a real possibility during a war or political revolution. Buildings can be taken over, restaurants burned to the ground, and airlines nationalized in the name of whoever is now in charge. When the soldiers show up, few love their jobs enough to fight.

The usual tactic for businesses facing appropriation is to get employees out, lock up the doors, and then use diplomatic channels to try to get either the business back or get compensation for it. Of course, negotiating for reparations can prolong conflicts; one of the many obstacles to the normalization of relations between the United States and Cuba is determining how to compensate people whose homes and businesses were appropriated by the Communists.

To minimize the cost of appropriation, companies often find ways to spread the investment around. Instead of owning a building in a troubled area, a company may lease it from a local landowner, which passes the risk on to someone else. It may use leases on heavy equipment, so it's easy to walk away from the payments if it also has to give up the use. And a company may try to get as much cash as possible into banks in safer countries by transferring funds; if the government limits funds transfers (a common form of appropriation), a company may be able to get money out of the country by charging the local office fees for such interdepartmental services as information technology, accounting, and human resources management.

Appropriation doesn't have to involve the takeover of a business by force as an act of war. Another form of appropriation is if a government changes its policies to make a business obsolete. If the United States were to offer single-payer national health insurance for all citizens, not just those over the age of 65, the insurance companies may perceive that as appropriation. Hence, appropriation is a risk for all businesses, not just those in conflict areas.

Working in a hot spot

It seems like the logical answer to dealing with war is to pack it up, go home, and let the soldiers fight it out among themselves. Logical, maybe, but not practical. Shutting down the business may be taken as a sign of capitulation to one of the warring parties, and it results in lost livelihood for the workers there. A first step is basic risk assessment: Who is fighting, where, and how? If the fighting is hundreds of miles away, with a desert in between, there's less risk to people or property than if the business is next door. If it's a conflict that plays out in one bombing every six months, then the risk is different than if trench warfare is taking place in the next block. The next step is to ensure that workers are protected.

Every company has to make its own decisions depending on its business and the conflict at hand. The point for you to remember is this: It's not necessarily wrong for a company to operate in a war zone, nor is it necessarily wrong to back out even if it leads to a higher level of destabilization in a region. It depends on the unique circumstances of the war.

Responsibility and the defense contractor

Operating in a war zone takes on a particular urgency for companies in the defense business. Some simply make parts and supplies that soldiers use, but other defense contractors take over military functions, including providing security, managing prisoners of war, and operating certain types of equipment. Many defense contractors get work only when hostilities flair, but they still must be responsible about how they do their jobs.

Promoting peace, one diamond at a time

Diamonds are gorgeous stones, and they're practical, too: They're so hard that they can be worn all the time, unlike such softer gems as opals and emeralds. Unfortunately, diamonds are often found in places suffering from complicated politics and outright war. Because diamonds have great value relative to their size, they can be smuggled between places. In Africa, many military leaders and terrorist groups have used diamonds to finance their military activities, giving the stones the nickname *blood diamonds* or *conflict diamonds*. There's no way to tell where a diamond came from, so concern about trade in conflict diamonds hurts sales of diamonds that come from legitimate dealers.

The *Kimberley Process* was developed by diamond-producing and -importing nations in 2003 to create a certification program for diamonds that weren't used in conflict trade. It requires that diamonds shipped across international borders be carried in tamper-proof containers and accompanied by a government-issued, forgery-resistant certificate that lists each container's contents. The only governments authorized to participate are those that are committed to keeping conflict diamonds out of their inventories, and 74 countries participate now. It's not perfect — conflict diamonds still get traded — but it has made the diamond trade much cleaner. It also shows how businesses and governments can work together to help promote peace.

This is not an issue for some social investors, because many refuse to invest in defense contractors under any circumstances. But other investors will consider military businesses because these companies fit their own definition of social responsibility.

The rules for defense contractors are simple: Nonstate actors, like defense contractors working in a war zone, are bound by international humanitarian laws, including the Geneva Conventions. Defense contractors need to protect people who don't participate in the fighting (such as civilians, medics, and clergy), as well as those who no longer can (injured soldiers, prisoners of war, and ship-wrecked sailors). To behave otherwise is to commit a war crime, no matter what the contract calls for. To read more about the Geneva Conventions, look on the International Committee of the Red Cross's Web site, www.icrc.org/ Web/Eng/siteeng0.nsf/htmlall/genevaconventions.

Transitioning to peace

Businesses have an inherent interest in a peaceful world, because it's a lot easier to get work done when people aren't fighting. However, new peace is fragile and creates challenges for the businesses trying to get back to normal. Not everyone in a country may accept the outcome of the war, and some may see the shaky new start as an opportunity to create more conflict. At the same time, the citizens may be too tired to go back to work, especially if they have lost relatives or houses.

On the other hand, peace creates opportunities, because the nation will probably need to have its infrastructure reconstructed. The World Bank has financed most of the major postwar redevelopment projects in the world over the years, and it has a great collection of information for investors and others at www.worldbank.org/conflict.

Some of the principles that the World Bank promotes for managing in a newly peaceful region include

- ✔ **Hire local labor.** People will want to get back to work, and their involvement will help the project be successful and improve the chance of transitioning to peace.

- ✔ **Accept popular sovereignty.** Even if the new government in charge is not the CEO's first choice, it's still the government, and if the people support it, so should businesses.

- ✔ **Have a strategy for managing corruption.** A postwar region is often awash in aid money, has a weak government with bigger priorities than policing bribes, and is home to a lot of people looking to make a quick buck after a period of deprivation. Businesses working in a postwar region need to expect corruption and head it off.

- ✔ **Manage expectations.** Companies must have a reasonable plan for the project and commit to transparency over the course of the work.

Correcting Corporate Corruption

Human beings are greedy, and that greed can be institutionalized in different ways. For example, it can be institutionalized by socially responsible investors who want to find ways to make money while encouraging good in the world. Good can come from greed, but so can a heck of a lot of bad. Different countries have different attitudes about greed, including differences in the ways that governments handle corruption.

Corruption is defined as the misuse of public power for private benefit. It can include bribery, *nepotism* (hiring of relatives, even if they're not qualified), and insider trading. Corruption undermines confidence in the government and the rule of law, causes money to be diverted away from economically viable projects, distorts the market, and cuts into profits.

To find out more about corruption, its many forms, and the governments and business sectors most likely to participate, go to the Web site of Transparency International, www.transparency.org. Each year, this organization publishes its Corruption Perception Index, which is a list of the countries considered to be the most corrupt. No nation wants to be at the bottom of that list! And that's the organization's point: The more that people pay attention to corruption, the less likely it is to take place.

Battling bribery

Want to get something done? For a fee, it can be taken care of. That's *bribery!* It may be a fee to get something done within the law, like a product passed through customs in a reasonable amount of time, or the fee may be for something outside of the law, like to get around child labor or environmental protection laws.

Bribery can take more subtle forms. Does a senator want a donation to his political action committee in exchange for an earmark in the next federal budget? Would a potential customer be more amenable to signing a contract if his favorite charity received a large donation? Maybe that pesky accountant's child needs a summer internship; can that be arranged?

The problem from an investor's perspective is that bribery costs money that could be put to better use (including paying bigger returns to that investor), and it gives people unfair advantages that aren't based on their ability to run their business or promote their brand.

What's the difference between a bribe and a tip? To many people in the world, the idea that you should have to give extra money to your server after you pay your bill is tacky at best and bribery at worst. To an American server, it's vital compensation that's not covered by the tab or paid by the restaurant's owner.

When developing policies for bribery, companies have to make sure they respect local customs for tips and gifts without crossing the line. It may be accepted etiquette to hold a lavish party with expensive presents for your importing partner; it's probably not acceptable to give the prime minister's brother-in-law a new Mercedes in exchange for helping you land a contract. One way to tell the difference between a bribe and a tip is whether the recipient would mind if everyone knew about the arrangement. Servers brag about the big tips they receive; would politicians?

Saying no to nepotism — most of the time

Nepotism, which is the hiring of relatives, isn't necessarily bad. In many family businesses, the relatives will become the owners someday, so they need to master the ropes now. It can also help ensure a committed work force, because people may do better when they know their relatives are watching what goes on. But nepotism has problems, so investors should pay attention.

The big one is that the relative may not be qualified. If a company keeps hiring ne'er-do-wells whom no one else wants to hire, then its performance will suffer as the relative fails to deliver and as other employees come to resent the special treatment. Nepotism can also institutionalize discrimination by keeping the company from hiring workers of other ethnic or religious groups. Finally, it can be construed as a form of bribery, especially if a jobs-for-contracts or "you hire my kid, I'll hire yours" relationship is established.

You shouldn't panic when you see nepotism, but you should ask tough questions about whether the practice is the best for the business.

Inside insider trading illegalities

Insider trading has a definition that only a lawyer could love. Insider trading involves making investment decisions on material, nonpublic information that would cause a reasonable person to change her investment opinion if she had that information. It often involves a misappropriation of information, ranging from an investment banker selling tips to buddies, a company executive sharing a bit of good news to help a favored politician make money, or managers looking to make a profit from a merger announcement before the news comes out.

Insider trading is illegal in the United States, and the U.S. government investigates suspected insider trading violations and punishes those found guilty. However, it's not illegal everywhere, and the laws aren't enforced everywhere that it's illegal.

A key tenet of academic finance is the *efficient markets hypothesis,* which says that markets respond to all information about an investment. Under the strong form of market efficiency, even insider information is already included in prices. Is it fair that some people have access to information that others do not, or is it fair that that information is kept out of the market?

In general, the cost of capital tends to be lower where insider trading laws are enforced, so companies should want governments to enforce it. Investors should want laws enforced, too, so everyone is trading on the same information. That may not be the case in every international market. Hence, you may not be playing on a level playing field when you invest in certain countries, which increases the risk of your investment.

Debating About Divestment

Divestment occurs when investors decide they can't support the behavior in a country, so they pull out their investments. Divestment became a popular tactic of nonviolent resistance to the apartheid regime in South Africa prior to 1990, in which a minority of the population had rule over the majority, engaging in rampant economic and social discrimination. South Africa had a peaceful transition to majority rule and is now one of the most stable nations on the African continent. Because of divestment's success in South Africa, it's often recommended as a tactic for addressing other troubled places.

Related to divestment is a *boycott,* in which companies refuse to do business with certain countries or consumers refuse to buy products made by different companies or in different places. The goal is the same: to create change by hitting businesses in the pocketbook and to force governments to make changes to maintain economic stability.

Divestment and boycotts are controversial, though. Is it better to stay engaged in an economy or to leave? That's the key issue. Divestment is a signal that there's a problem that needs to be addressed, but it doesn't necessarily lead to change. It may leave the people in a region worse off while creating a challenge to the government. After all, some politicians view divestment as proof that they're right and everyone else in the world is very, very wrong.

By staying in a country that has problems, active investment may lead to change. If a company makes it clear that it won't discriminate, no matter what the law allows, then it may start to change practices in other businesses. But it can't make changes if it doesn't participate.

Finally, divestment and boycotts only work if they are coordinated and well-publicized actions. One person's decision is likely to be offset by someone else's; only by working together can any change happen.

Green bananas

Chiquita Brands International is a prime example of a multinational company that made big changes in its business practices — for the better. Chiquita became notorious for meddling in politics of the Central American countries where it grows its products. Its underhanded tricks in Guatemala in the 1950s and '60s gave birth to the phrase *banana republic.* The brand was known for poor environmental policies, deplorable social policies, and overall lack of corporate responsibility. In the face of pressure from European consumers in the late 1990s, Chiquita was faced with a stark choice: change or wither away.

In a complete corporate turnaround, Chiquita embraced its critics head on and began a transformation that has been both notable and profitable. Chiquita countered the mostly accurate charges of poor environmental management practices by partnering with one of its fiercest critics, the Rainforest Alliance. The Rainforest Alliance now certifies all of Chiquita's banana farms in Latin America for social and environmental performance.

The company initiated a farm management program called the Better Banana Program and found that improved environmental management practices made the farms both more productive and more profitable. In the book *Green to Gold,* Daniel Esty and Andrew Winston report that Chiquita spent $20 million to roll out the Better Banana Program, but realized $100 million in operating cost savings since it began participating, mostly due to decreased spending on pesticides.

In Colombia, 30 of Chiquita's workers were killed between 1995 and 1998. To continue to do business in the country, Chiquita made illegal protection payments to Colombian paramilitary groups, financing their terrorist activities. In

(continued)

(continued)

keeping with its newfound commitment to corporate responsibility, Chiquita owned up to the problem, disclosed the illegal payments to the U.S. Department of Justice in 2003, paid a $25 million fine, and sold its Colombian operations.

Although Chiquita hasn't always been the model multinational, its history shows the types of challenges that companies may face and how different activist and investor groups can hold companies accountable.

Chapter 10

Keeping Your Faith: Investing with Religious Beliefs

In This Chapter
- Following religious principles when investing
- Seeing what different religions advocate

any people want to keep their investments consistent with their faith. Moreover, some religions require that they do so. In this chapter, I outline some general guidelines for major (and some minor) religions, but remember that there are gray areas in every faith as well as plenty of practices that I don't have room to cover. I offer no *fatwa*, no *nil obstat*, just general information to get you started on your quest. A Reform Jew and an Orthodox one may approach their investing differently, and a rank-and-file churchgoer may not care much about where investments are placed, but the board of a missionary society's endowment does.

A *fatwa* is a ruling from an Islamic scholar on whether something fits Muslim law. A *nil obstat* is a ruling from a Catholic theologian that a work is free from doctrinal error.

Investing according to religious principles is a complicated subject, and exact interpretations may vary by denomination and congregation. My information came from sources that I believe to be reliable, but your priest, rabbi, minister, imam, guru, or teacher may have a different take on the subject. If religion is important to your investing, talk to your own clergy to get the guidance that counts.

However, if you're looking for a sense of how people from different religious backgrounds view money and investing, I can help you. That way, you can get started on your own quest, identify like-minded investors when forming activism campaigns, or understand the motivations of your friends and neighbors better.

Religion and Socially Responsible Investing

To many people, the only socially responsible investment is one that is compatible with their religious values. They aren't going to worry about niceties of corporate governance or employee benefits when they have their souls on the line. The traditional interests of socially responsible investors, including human rights, the environment, and corporate responsibility, match those of some religious investors but not of others. Hence, a mutual fund that is labeled "socially responsible" may or may not work for you.

The key: Do your research. (Have I told you that already? If not, take a gander at Chapter 4.) Know what matters to you, and then look for investment opportunities that match.

Bringing Your Faith, or Someone Else's Faith, to the Investment Table

Here's the thing about religious beliefs: What seems normal to someone in the group may seem very strange to someone outside of it. (That's why it's called faith.) What difference does it make if you flip a light switch on Saturday, eat a hamburger on a Friday in March, or take out a loan rather than a lease? It makes a difference to someone, and maybe to you.

If your broker looks at you like you're crazy when you bring up your religion relative to your investments, that's a sign to start looking for a new broker. Likewise, if someone in your office complains about how the 401(k) choices contradict her faith, don't laugh. Show her this book, help her understand the company's issues under ERISA (explained in Chapter 3), and suggest that she recommend some new investment choices.

Examining Investment Practices of Different Faiths

What, exactly, do different religious groups believe about investing? There are many variations among religious investors, depending on the attitudes that a faith has about wealth and community responsibility. And, of course, many local religious communities may have their own interpretation of the larger faith's guidelines. In alphabetical order, here's a list of all the large and many of the smaller faiths, along with a look at their approach to money matters.

Baha'i: Seeking global prosperity

The Baha'i faith is a new one, with approximately 5 million followers. It was started in 1863 when its prophet, a Persian prince named Baha'u'llah, taught that human society had finally matured enough to unite into a just, global society. Baha'is believe that global economic justice and prosperity will occur when everyone recognizes that the spiritual and the practical aspects of life are connected.

To abolish the extremes of poverty and wealth, people who own businesses should share their profits throughout the organization, so Baha'i investors look at how a company treats its workers and suppliers. Baha'is don't drink alcohol or gamble, so investments in those industries are off limits to most followers.

Buddhism: Financial stability leads to happiness

Buddhism is an Asian religion. It was founded in India about 2,500 years ago by Guatama Buddha, a prince who became a great teacher when he discovered the difference between his plush life and his subjects' hard life. He renounced his worldly things and took up meditation in search of enlightenment about why the world was the way it was. He even gave up food until he nearly died. After that, he decided that the ideal path through this world was a middle way, neither too soft nor too hard. He taught that through meditation, people could overcome their greed and hatred to see the world as it was. (To find out more about Buddhism, read *Buddhism For Dummies* by Jonathan Landaw and Stephan Bodian [Wiley].)

The main precepts are *dharma,* which is the importance of right living, and *karma,* which is that all actions have a cause and an effect, even if it's not obvious. Although some Buddhists renounce worldly goods, it's not necessary to do so in most traditions, as long as one isn't too attached to them. In fact, Buddhism recognizes that some material stability is necessary for happiness. Happiness can come from earning a just livelihood, not being in debt, and sharing wealth with others.

There is little in Buddhist texts that affects investment choices, but many who practice the religion are concerned about how their finances influence their dharma and karma. They often think about two other concepts, *karuna,* or nonviolence, and *metta,* or care of the world. Hence, many Buddhists refuse to invest in companies that make military equipment or process meat.

In 2008, the Dow Jones Dharma Indexes were developed to reflect the teachings of Buddhism, Hinduism, Jainism, and Sikhism (I cover the latter three religions later in this chapter). The hope is that mutual funds, exchange-traded funds, and other products will be introduced to reflect the concept of dharma.

Christianity: Applying biblical teachings to investing

Christianity is the largest religion in the world and is one of three religions founded in the Middle East. It shares some texts with the other two, Judaism and Islam. Its main teaching is that God has three forms: God the father, his son Jesus Christ, and the Holy Spirit. Through God, believers will be forgiven and achieve eternal salvation. Jesus Christ, a prophet who lived approximately 2,000 years ago, spoke against many of the laws that the Jews followed, and he promoted new laws emphasizing love, peace, and forgiveness. (If you want more specifics on this religion, check out *Christianity For Dummies* by Richard Wagner and Kurt Warner [Wiley].)

The teachings of Jesus, collected in the Gospels of the New Testament, are deeply ambivalent about money. Jesus says three times that "it is easier for a camel to enter the eye of a needle than for a rich man to enter the kingdom of heaven" (Matthew 19:23–24, Mark 10:24–25, and Luke 18:24–25). But Jesus never says it's impossible for a wealthy person to enter into heaven, and Christians believe that all things are possible with God's help.

That being said, there is no one "Christian" perspective on anything. Denominations have broken up over whether the pope has authority over all churches, and they've broken up over whether it's appropriate to play music during worship services.

Few Christian denominations have explicit rules about investing, but many followers use their church's teachings to help guide their decisions. Here's an overview of some of the concerns that some of the major Christian denominations have about investing, arranged in chronological order of the group's founding.

Roman Catholicism: Promoting equality and the value of human life

The Roman Catholic church is the oldest denomination, founded by Jesus's disciple Peter. It remains the largest, although other Christian churches split off from it for all sorts of doctrinal and political reasons. The church has a centralized, hierarchical organization led by the pope and headquartered in Vatican City, an independent city-state in the middle of Rome, Italy. (To read more about this religion, check out *Catholicism For Dummies* by the Rev. John Trigilio Jr., PhD, and the Rev. Kenneth Brighenti, PhD [Wiley].)

The church's main teachings are based on the Bible, the main Christian text, and found in the *catechism,* a list of major beliefs and sins affecting all parts of life. Only a few financial practices are explicitly listed as wrong; these include committing fraud and encouraging others to do so; speculation and market manipulation that cause one person to make money at the expense of others; tax evasion; and forgery of checks and invoices.

Matters of dictate and matters of conscience

Some religious groups set forth precise rules that adherents must follow to remain in good standing. These are *matters of dictate.* It's not important what the rules are or how they seem to outsiders, only that people who are in the practice must follow them.

Matters of conscience are guidelines that followers of a faith don't necessarily have to meet; they may involve matters that the texts and traditions of a congregation don't address or that can be argued many different ways.

Most religions have matters of dictate and matters of conscience, and investing often falls under conscience. Hence, Catholicism's Jesuit Order of priests may choose not to invest money of affiliated organizations in the stocks of defense contractors, but there is no rule that says Roman Catholics commit sin if they do so.

The Catholic church teaches that social and economic inequality can threaten peace and cause wars, so anything that exacerbates that inequality is a sin. Another teaching is that human life is the most important value in society, so anything that leads to abortion or unnecessary war is a sin. Hence, Catholic investors are often reluctant to be involved with defense contractors or with healthcare companies that make products used in abortion.

Because many institutions affiliated with the Roman Catholic church have significant funds to invest, Catholic church groups are known as aggressive activist investors. They use shareholder resolutions, proxy votes, and meetings with management (see Chapter 5 for more on these) to press for changes in corporate practices that can lead to greater social and economic justice. How significant are those funds? The University of Notre Dame had an endowment of $5.9 billion as of June 2007, making it the 14th largest university endowment in the United States and the largest endowment of any American university with an active religious affiliation. Add to that the money from other Catholic universities, charitable foundations, hospitals, and pension funds for employees, priests, and nuns, and you have a force for social change through investing.

Traditional Protestantism: Succeeding through hard work and thrift

The oldest Protestant churches, including the Congregational, Episcopal, Lutheran, Methodist, and Presbyterian churches, believe in the importance of individual conscience and the guidance of the Bible rather than dictates from a central church leader. They also have a cultural belief in hard work and thrift to show that they're good Christians.

No surprise, hard work and thrift usually lead to financial success. The Puritans, Congregationalist Protestants who were among the first European settlers in the United States, may have set the tone for those who came before and after, no matter what their religion; many historians believe that much of the economic success of the United States is because of the so-called Protestant work ethic.

Hard work aside, Protestant churches themselves tend to be neutral on the issue of social investing. Many liberal Protestants avoid investing in defense companies or those with poor records of worker treatment; many conservative Protestants avoid investing in companies that produce items used in abortion or that sell pornography. Protestant institutions are often activist investors, using the value of their investments to promote social justice and other values of their faith. They often join with investors from other religious institutions to get companies to listen.

Evangelical and Fundamentalist churches: Investing based on beliefs

Evangelicals and Fundamentalist Christians tend to believe in the literal interpretation of the Bible and the importance of demonstrating their beliefs to others. Both movements are associated with American interpretations of Protestantism and tend to have a conservative view of the world. Evangelicals believe that each person must have a personal religious conversion (known as being *born again*); Fundamentalists often believe in *predestination,* or the idea that God has already determined who will achieve salvation.

Although they're often lumped together, Evangelicals and Fundamentalists are very different. Evangelicals believe in going out into the world to convert people. They tend to be conservative about matters of doctrine, although not all Evangelicals are conservative. Fundamentalists are extremely conservative about doctrine, and they sometimes avoid outsiders for fear that they'll be led into sin by the temptations of the wider world.

There are many different church groups associated with Evangelical and Fundamentalist traditions. Although few set out specific investing guidelines, many followers believe that to live their religious commitment and be free of corrupting influences, they should only invest in companies aligned with their beliefs. Hence, many don't invest in businesses associated with abortion, alcohol, gambling, or pornography.

Mormons: Financial security is a priority

The Church of Jesus Christ of Latter-day Saints, whose members are often referred to as *Mormons,* holds that the original teachings of Christianity became corrupted over time. Their main text, the Book of Mormon, is a companion to the Bible, and Mormons believe that it restores the teachings of Jesus Christ to their correct form. (For more details on this religion, pick up a copy of *Mormonism For Dummies* by Jana Riess and Christopher Kimball Bigelow [Wiley].)

The Latter-day Saints church teaches that members have a responsibility to provide financial security for their families; without it, the household can't achieve peace and harmony. Members should strive to be self-reliant financially. After paying off debts, the church recommends that families build a financial reserve. After that is met, members should save money for long-term needs, including retirement and education. Many members also save to cover the costs of missionary service for themselves or relatives. The church isn't concerned with the specifics of the members' investment choices, as long as those investments are prudent and help the investor become more self-reliant. Many church members have the same considerations for specific investments as other conservative Christians: No sin stocks!

Hinduism: Advancing peace and the good of the world

Hinduism is the world's oldest established religion. It's ranked third globally in numbers of adherents, and it is practiced almost exclusively in India or by people of Indian descent who live in other countries.

Some readers may be thinking, hey! Atheism is third! Indeed, most surveys of world religion show that more people have no religion than are Hindu. However, this is a chapter about religion. An atheist won't find much guidance here but will find in Chapters 7, 8, 9, and 11 ideas about other values-based ways to invest.

The Hindu religion is very different from most others because it's not based on a specific text or a specific interpretation of God. Instead, it has a wide collection of texts accumulated over millennia as well as a pantheon of gods. Some Hindus worship only one; others worship several, and a few worship none at all. The common belief, instead, is that the soul, called *atman,* is eternal and will be reborn. One's form in the next life depends on karma, influenced by one's behavior in this life.

Because Hinduism has so many texts and traditions to draw on, a believer looking for guidance on investing will be overwhelmed. Attitudes toward money are shaped by specific congregations and family traditions. For many, two key Hindu concepts influence their investment choices:

- ✔ **Ahimsa,** the Sanskrit word for nonviolence, prohibits anything that harms a living soul, and because souls are reincarnated, an animal soul is the same as a human one. That means that businesses that process or sell meat are prohibited as well as those that make weapons.

- ✔ Under **loka-samgraha,** a Sanskrit term meaning "the good of the world," investments should make the world a better place and be rooted in sustainable economic development rather than greed.

Islam: Money matters are well defined

Islam is the second largest religion in the world; the number of members is growing faster than Christianity, so it may soon be the largest. The religion shares roots with Judaism and Christianity. Islam's prophet, Muhammad, wrote the *Koran,* the religion's main text, about 1,400 years ago. Followers of Islam, known as *Muslims,* believe that Christians and Jews deviated from God; the Koran restores his teachings. (*Islam For Dummies* by Malcolm Clark [Wiley] has more details about this faith.)

Muslims believe that the desperations of poverty can force people to stop believing in God. Therefore, it's all right to have material wealth, but Muslims have an obligation to give money to charity.

Islamic law, known as *Shariah,* has strict guidelines for financial matters. Muslims may not pay or receive interest, known as *riba.* Philosophically, a believer should be a partner in the business and thus take on risk; in a traditional loan, the lender receives regular interest and can claim collateral if the borrower doesn't repay.

To a Muslim, that is an uneven relationship. Instead of borrowing money or buying bonds, Muslims use other forms of financing, including *cost-plus arrangements,* in which someone buys an item for you at one price and resells it to you at a higher price later; lease-to-own arrangements; and joint ownership and shared profits. If the borrower is unable to pay, the arrangement must be forgiven to stop the cycle of borrowing and refinancing that can leave people deeply in debt.

Muslims can and do own stock, but they can't invest in companies involved with alcohol, gambling, pork processing, pornography, or tobacco. And, because they can't charge or receive interest, they can't invest in traditional banks. Several banks in the Middle East operate entirely under Shariah, and more institutions in Europe and the United States are developing business lines to accommodate the needs of their Muslim clients.

Many Muslim scholars will grant exceptions to Shariah out of necessity. If a Muslim wants to buy a house in a place where no Islamic financing arrangement is available, he would probably be allowed to use a traditional mortgage. But if you happen to be a Muslim in this situation, don't take my word for it. Find a scholar or imam, because his definition of necessity might be different from yours.

In situations where Muslims find themselves using prohibited financial arrangements because there are no alternatives, they may be required to purify any profits by giving a share to charity.

Jainism: Building wealth through savings

The Jain religion emerged from Hinduism more than 2,000 years ago. Jains believe that they can stop the otherwise endless cycle of the suffering and rebirth of their soul by living a strict and Spartan life. In that way, their souls will finally have God-consciousness. They emphasize *ahimsa,* or nonviolence in relations with all creatures.

Jains are allowed to accumulate wealth, and many do because their lifestyle encourages hard work and discourages spending. They tend to support educational and religious charities. When Jains invest, they're very careful not to support any businesses that engage in violence against the world, similar to Buddhists, Hindus, and Sikhs (I cover these religions elsewhere in this chapter).

Juche: Investing is unnecessary

Never heard of Juche? Neither had I until I started researching this chapter! Juche is a spiritual belief system practiced in North Korea. It emphasizes self-reliance and obedience to the nation's leader. Because North Korea has a Communist economic system, people who practice Juche don't invest.

Judaism: Accumulating wealth and sharing it with the poor

To be a good Jew, one must be able to read and write. When a child comes of age in a ceremony known as the *bar mitzvah* (for boys) or the *bat mitzvah* (for girls), the honoree must read to the congregation from the *Torah,* which is a key Jewish text. Because of the emphasis on education, Jewish people have often been successful in business and professional life. (Some people have used this success to argue that the Jews must be doing something far more sinister than going to school and working hard.)

A key component of Jewish belief is *tzedakah,* which is similar to charity. Jews are expected to share 10 percent of their wealth with the poor, even if they are impoverished themselves. The money doesn't have to go to a synagogue or Jewish charity; educational and healthcare institutions are also acceptable recipients of tzedakah. The highest degree of tzedakah involves giving money to make someone else self-reliant, which may include investing in his business. (*Microfinance,* which involves lending small amounts of money to small-business people in impoverished countries and is discussed in Chapter 17, is a perfect example.)

Jewish law, known as *halacha,* covers all aspects of life for Orthodox believers. It recognizes that humans have a natural desire to make money and accumulate wealth. Therefore, money is not sinful; instead, it's important that it be earned ethically and that tzedakah be maintained, no matter how much or how little money one has.

There are exceptions to halacha. Certain laws should apply to everyone in all circumstances regardless of religion, such as prohibitions on fraud. Other rules, such as the kosher rules affecting how animals are slaughtered and food is prepared, apply only to Jews. Therefore, it's acceptable for a Jewish person to invest in a company that is open for business on Saturday, the Jewish Sabbath, or that produces non-kosher food, as long as he isn't a majority shareholder.

Like most religions, Judaism is split into different denominations that have different interpretations of halacha. Some, especially Reform Jews, adhere to the ethical components but don't observe the rules about diet, dress, or Sabbath behavior. (For a more comprehensive explanation of the Jewish religion, read *Judaism For Dummies* by Ted Falcon and David Blatner [Wiley].)

Shinto: Focusing on the environment

Shinto is a native Japanese religion heavily influenced by Buddhism (see the earlier section for more on this religion). Believers worship the spirits of places in their country as well as natural features themselves, such as Mount Fuji. Historically, the nation's emperor was also worshipped as a god, a practice that ended after World War II. Adherents believe that nature is sacred, so it should be loved and celebrated.

Rather than participate in specialized rituals once a week, Shinto practitioners believe in formal rituals of respect and appreciation throughout the day. Hence, it's the source of the strict etiquette practiced in Japan. The religion has little to say about investing, but someone who practices strict Shinto invests in companies that protect the environment.

Sikhism: Acquiring wealth is discouraged

The Sikh religion developed out of Hinduism about 500 years ago. The followers believe in one God, the creator of all living beings. Members see themselves as soldiers for God, charged with defending their faith and providing service to all. The military influence means that Sikhs seem to be in uniform. Sikh men and women cover their hair, which they don't cut. Sikh men don't cut their beards, either. Baptized Sikhs wear a small sword called a *kirpan* under their clothes, but the religion teaches nonviolence, using the same Sanskrit word, *ahimsa,* as do Hindus and Jains (see the earlier sections for more on these religions).

Sikhs aren't encouraged to acquire material wealth, and they may not drink or smoke. When investing, Sikhs avoid alcohol and tobacco companies as well as military ventures.

Unitarian Universalism: Practicing social and economic justice

Unitarian Universalism is a religion formed in the United States in the 20th century, although it traces some of its beliefs back to the 18th century. It's based on Jewish and Christian teachings about treating one's neighbors with love and respect, but it doesn't have a formal creed or set of beliefs. Unitarian Universalists believe strongly in social and economic justice throughout the world. As an organization, the church supports sustainable and community investing; many church members do, too.

Wicca: Respect is fundamental

Wicca is the modern-day version of traditional Northern European pagan religions. Followers call themselves pagans, witches, or Wiccans. Wiccans worship a male God and a female Goddess who manifest themselves throughout nature. The basic credo is "Do as ye will, as long as ye harm none." Members accept a variety of different lifestyles and approaches to the world as long as respect for other people and nature is maintained. Wiccans also believe that whatever they do will come back to them threefold, whether good or bad. Many of the religion's rituals are secret, known only to initiates. Initiates also perform spells, which are incantations and rituals designed to bring about change; some are for abundance and wealth.

A Wiccan looks for investments that are friendly toward the environment, promote peace, and protect the rights of other people.

Chapter 11

Social Change and the Responsible Corporation

· ·

· ·

*M*any social investors want the businesses they invest in to behave responsibly. Investors expect the company to sell its product or service fairly and accurately, and they want the company to respect every person who gets that product to market, including vendors, customers, and employees. Few companies get it right. Those that do are often rewarded with happy customers, loyal employees, and rich profits.

Those who want to earn profits are often caricatured as heartless, greedy folks. Think Ebenezer Scrooge, the character in Charles Dickens's classic story *A Christmas Carol.* Scrooge's love of money causes him to lose the people he loves. No matter how much socially successful businesses want to generate big bucks, they know that if they don't provide value or promote societal values, customers and employees will go elsewhere.

Forward-thinking businesses are experimenting with new ways to conduct their basic operations and change the world in the process. In some cases, that means better products. In others, it means revamping the way the corporation operates. This chapter covers the ways that corporations make money and how they improve relationships with customers, suppliers, government regulators, and employees. It includes information on employee ownership, which may be helpful if your investment portfolio includes shares in the company that employs you. However, it doesn't include information on environmental issues (covered in Chapter 8) or international concerns (covered in Chapter 9).

Running a Business to Get its Relationships Right

Every day companies enter into relationships with others. A company must interact with the companies that supply it with inventory and other goods and services needed to make the business run; with its customers, who keep it in business; and with the regulators who ensure that the company follows applicable laws. (Employees are another key group — so key that they get their very own section later in the chapter.)

Companies can choose policies that are good for everyone involved, or they can choose policies that make the company better off while making everyone else worse off. If you care about how companies that you invest in do business, you need to pay attention to these areas.

Building good supplier relationships

A company is in business to make a profit, to be sure, but it's not right to deprive suppliers of a profit, either. For a company to do well over the long haul, it has to have happy suppliers that are willing to work with it. Chiseling on price, sitting on invoices, and demanding unrealistic levels of service from suppliers may help a company generate profits in the short run, but it will hurt in the long run when the suppliers go out of business or move on to better customers. Good supplier relationships tend to be collaborative, with the suppliers helping the customer and the customer paying the supplier for the value added.

Likewise, it's important for companies to keep an eye on suppliers. More than one salesperson has been so desperate to write an order that he offers kickbacks, bribes, or other enticements. Companies work to manage their supplier relations so everyone behaves appropriately.

Some companies go so far as to draw up a *code of conduct* for prospective suppliers, setting out how they expect suppliers to behave when calling on them, and setting forth environmental, labor, quality, and financial standards that they expect their suppliers to meet. These standards may be backed up with a certification program or audits that the supplier must pass if it wants to keep the contract.

Many companies send key functions in their business to outside contractors to save money or get access to people with greater skills than they can afford to hire full time. It's usually good business for both the company and the outsourced service provider; it can be terrible if it's a way for the company to push its responsibilities onto someone else.

Promoting good customer relations

Businesses have to have customers. Some companies sell mostly to other businesses (known as the *business-to-business market,* sometimes shortened as *B2B*), while others sell to individual consumers, and still others sell to both.

These different sets of customers have different sets of expectations. For example, a company selling to another business may have to go through a certification program or agree to honor certain marketing practices (see the preceding section). It's highly unlikely that any company would agree to go through a certification process at the request of an individual, but you as an individual customer can do the research to decide if a company deserves your business, just as you can do the research as an individual investor to decide if a company deserves your investment.

But certification process or not, companies are expected to treat customers well. After all, the customer is the source of revenue. Things are going to go wrong, but a company that can accept responsibility for its problems is a more responsible business overall. A responsible company will stand behind its products and address customer complaints promptly and politely. It will want to keep customers happy so they turn into repeat customers.

Any company in any industry will run into occasional problems. Investors should not view a problem as a sign that a company isn't responsible; instead, they should watch to see how the problem is handled and whether it was an unusual event or an indicator of loose tactics.

In 1982, seven people died when they took Tylenol, a pain reliever, which had been tainted with cyanide. Johnson & Johnson (NYSE: JNJ), the company that makes Tylenol, was not at fault, but the company immediately pulled the drug off the shelves everywhere. The company's managers knew that customers were frightened and that it was pointless to tell them that someone else was responsible. The recall generated tremendous goodwill for Johnson & Johnson, because customers and investors felt that they could trust the company to do right by them.

Beware the fallacy of the anecdote. No company will satisfy 100 percent of its customers, and the cranky ones complain the most. When assessing a company on its responsibility toward customers, look for overall trends rather than a single complaint, even if the complaint is legitimate and even if it was made by your best friend. On the other hand, your buddy may be in love with a business that has managed to disappoint every other customer it has.

Maintaining government relations

Every business faces an army of regulators, whether local, state, or federal. There are taxes to pay, licenses to hold, and rules to follow covering everything from the sizes of entryways to the management of retirement plans. Like them or not (and most businesspeople don't), regulations are a fact of doing business.

The responsible way to approach government regulations is to follow them. The irresponsible way is to ignore regulations as long as possible and then try to bribe one's way out of them. (Hey, I live in Chicago. Don't tell me it doesn't happen.) And then there's an entire range of approaches in between, from aggressive lobbying of elected officials in the hope of receiving more favorable regulations to ignoring the regulation until someone comes around to enforce it.

You can find out which candidates get the most money from different corporations and their employees by searching at www.opensecrets.org. It includes data on *political action committees (PACs),* which are fundraising organizations that allow people to raise money for a cause rather than a candidate; PACs can accept larger donations than candidates can.

Establishing Ideal Employee Conditions

Employees who are treated well are most likely going to do a good job for shareholders. Employees have friends and family; their experiences on the job are part of the company's public face. And work conditions are highly regulated, so an employer that wants to run a legal operation has to comply with regulations that affect wages, hours, and working conditions. Companies that are known for being good places to work have an easier time attracting smart, hardworking staff members.

The law is the law. Just because an employee agrees to wage or hour conditions that are different from what the law requires doesn't mean a company can get away with it.

Obviously, this doesn't mean that employees can do whatever they want. Some people aren't a right fit for the job they are in. However, it's possible to treat people humanely even when disciplining or firing them. (Here's a hint: Firing someone by voice mail or e-mail is a bad idea.)

The following sections cover some key employee issues that may interest social investors, such as discrimination, benefits, wages, and working conditions. Most managers want to believe that they are great bosses, so it can be difficult to get good information about what it's like to work at a company from the company itself. Difficult, but not impossible.

Statistics on employee turnover are usually published in a company's annual report on Form 10K, filed with the Securities and Exchange Commission and made available to investors. A quick Internet news search can often turn up interesting stories, good and bad.

Discouraging discrimination

Most forms of discrimination are illegal. Employers can't favor workers based on race, religion, age, gender, or physical status. And yet, employment discrimination takes place every single day and in far too many workplaces. It goes without saying that it's a bad thing. A company that discriminates isn't going to be able to hire the best person for the job. It's not going to be in touch with a large slice of its potential customers. And it may end up spending too much time defending its practices rather than running its businesses.

Although discrimination goes on, it's difficult for investors to identify which companies are the biggest offenders unless there has been a major public lawsuit or related action. It's easy to find companies that have a good reputation, though, because many business publications prepare annual rankings of the best places overall to work, as well as lists of the best companies for minorities, women, and people with physical disabilities.

Domestic partner benefits

In the United States, people under the age of 65 usually get healthcare coverage for themselves and their families through their employers. (People over age 65 can join a single-payer national healthcare program called Medicare.) Many people, especially gay couples, are in family relationships that aren't legally recognized, effectively limiting their health insurance options. To take care of this inequality, many employers allow their employees to buy health insurance for people with whom they live, even if they aren't married. Some may limit this to same-sex couples where marriage is not an option; in cities and states that allow some form of marriage or civil union for gay couples, employers may limit domestic partner benefits to people who make that commitment.

There's one big problem: Under federal law, employee benefits for heterosexual married couples and their children are deductible from income taxes, but benefits for others are taxable as income to the employee. That makes domestic partner benefits very expensive. Still, in a nation where about 50 million people have no health insurance, it's better than nothing.

Most social investors think that domestic partner benefits are good because they help companies attract and retain good workers, while also doing something important — reducing the number of people without health insurance. A handful of investors have problems with it, especially if their investing style is guided by their religious beliefs and their religion condemns homosexuality.

Offering employee benefits equally

Pity the poor HR manager. She wants to provide benefits that keep most employees happy within a tight budget, knowing that it will make some shareholders unhappy. Allow some employees to buy health benefits for domestic partners? Some shareholders will cheer the firm for being so supportive; others will decry the firm for its lack of morals.

Few employee benefits are mandated by law; the laws usually require only that any benefits that are made available be made available on fair terms. For example, no employer has to offer health insurance, but companies that do face extensive regulation about the ways in which those plans are operated.

One problem that some companies encounter is the trade-off between quality and affordability. Most companies have an enormous range of employee compensation. Entry-level employees may make minimum wage while executive officers have millions. Still, most benefit plans have to apply to all employees. The shop clerk may want health insurance but may not be able to afford the plan with all the bells and whistles that the CEO wants.

At a minimum, companies should provide all employees with sick leave and access to health insurance and retirement plans. It is hoped that most employees would be able to participate in both. Other benefits that can help attract and retain great employees include vacation leave, tuition reimbursement, child-care reimbursement, and extended family leave.

Fair wages and work conditions

A major concern for social investors is how companies treat their employees. Now, you probably have a decent job with an employer that has to compete for workers, so your company treats you and your co-workers in a reasonably humane manner. Thus, it's easy to forget that the annals of labor law are filled with suits filed by employees working for people who would deny them access to a restroom. (In 1998, the U.S. Occupational Safety and Health Administration issued a requirement that employers make restrooms available to all employees to use as needed. Before then, believe it or not, there was no recognized right to use the bathroom during the workday.)

Yes, even in the United States, even today, some employers treat their workers terribly. If you care about how a company that you invest in treats its employees, you'll want to spend some time researching news stories about employee work conditions and wages. Problems with pay are usually related to discrimination, so your findings may uncover other issues that will affect your investment decisions.

Only a small percentage of private sector employees belong to labor unions. Unions came into being when manufacturing employees were treated horribly — in some cases, barely better than slaves. But in the almost two centuries since the first union was established, state and federal regulations have forced companies to improve working conditions, and most employers realized that an employee who was paid fairly and had enough time to eat lunch and use the bathroom would be a better worker than one who didn't have those basics.

Still, many employees have used unions to achieve improved working conditions and better pay, and the threat of unionization has forced many companies to keep workers happy. In general, a labor problem (which is not the same as having a unionized workforce) is really a management problem. If managers aren't taking care of the people who work for them, whether or not they belong to a union, then the company has a lot of other problems.

Many social investors prefer to see companies that have labor unions. Some companies don't have unions because management has thwarted them. However, many companies don't have unions because the employees are treated fairly in the first place.

Sharing the Wealth with Employees

Many companies encourage their employees to work for shareholders by turning employees into owners themselves. Employees who own company stock become shareholders; what is in the shareholder's best interest is in their best interest, too. When employees hold company stock, it reduces the principal-agent problem (discussed in Chapter 2) and distributes wealth throughout the organization. Their ownership status reduces employees' resentment against overpaid CEOs or greedy shareholders, and it may lead to new ideas as employees think more like owners and see how they can profit personally from better sales or lower expenses. For many companies, it's a responsible way to reward everyone who works for the company.

Whether you're an employer thinking of creating ownership benefits for employees, an employee who has shares or options in employer stock, or an investor who wants to know more about these benefits, a great resource is the National Center for Employee Ownership, www.nceo.org.

Employees can be owners of public and private companies.

✔ With **public companies,** the value of the employee's stock and options is set by the investors participating in the stock market.

✔ **Private companies** key the value of stock and options off of other metrics:

- It may use the company's earnings multiplied by the average price/earnings ratios of public companies in the same industry.

- It may be based on the company's book value.

- It could be tied to some other value.

Whatever the company uses, it should be an objective measure that is applied consistently from year to year.

Some of these plans are governed by ERISA, the Employee Retirement Income Security Act of 1974, which I cover in great detail in Chapter 3. So ownership plans must be managed for the benefit of the employees, not the shareholders of the offering company.

Simple and direct ownership

Although the very idea of employee stock options seems to grab people's imaginations, even a decade or so after the initial Internet craze, companies offer employees other ways to own company stock. Many offer actual shares that affect the employee's net worth today. In many cases, companies allow employees to buy stock at a discount, which makes ownership even more attractive.

Employee stock purchase plans

An *employee stock purchase plan,* sometimes called a *423 plan* because of the piece of the tax code that permits it, lets employees buy company stock out of their paychecks. The purchase price is usually a 15 percent discount to the market price, so it's possible for an employee to buy it through the company and sell it immediately for a quick profit. Usually, companies allow employees with at least two years of service to participate.

Restricted stock purchase plans

Under a *restricted stock purchase plan,* only certain employees can buy shares through the program. These are most common in private companies, where people are allowed to buy stock in the firm when they are promoted to a certain level because they're considered to have influence in the company's success. (In fact, they may be required to buy stock in order to accept the promotion, a typical arrangement in many legal and accounting partnerships.)

In some cases, restricted plans are *stock grants* made based on performance or seniority. For example, some companies have a policy of granting shares of stock when employees hit milestone anniversaries, say of 10 or 20 years of service. Employees who receive these grants have to pay tax on the gains as though they were income.

If the company is private, the employee will probably be required to sell the stock back to the company either upon the employer's demand or upon termination. (The employer may demand it if, say, a merger is being negotiated and the buyer wants to deal with one seller rather than all the employee-owners individually.) The employer doesn't always have to pay a lump sum of money for these shares; in some cases, the employer will issue a note and pay the selling employee back over several years. The specific terms will be set out in the agreement that accompanied the share offering. Employees may want to have a lawyer review the terms before committing the cash.

401(k) plans

A *401(k) plan,* named for the section of the law that permits it, is a type of retirement savings plan that allows employees to set aside part of their income before taxes. The employer often matches part of the employee's contribution, sometimes in cash and sometimes in company stock. The employee's contribution usually can be invested in different types of investments, such as a range of mutual funds; sometimes company stock is one of the alternatives. This means that with a 401(k) plan, employees can accumulate company stock at low prices and with pretax dollars.

Companies like it when employees buy company stock in the 401(k) plan because it costs them less money than if the employees elect to put it into mutual funds. The problem is that if the company goes under, employees can lose their jobs and their retirement savings. Ouch! Company stock should never be your only investment. You can show your employer how loyal you are by doing a good job. Don't try to show loyalty by taking huge risks with your financial security.

Employee stock ownership plans

An *employee stock ownership plan (ESOP,* pronounced *eee-sop*) is a type of tax-advantaged retirement plan that invests directly in the employer's company stock. ESOPs are often set up to acquire all or part of the company's shares from the current owner. This could be to prevent a hostile takeover, to spin a division out from a larger company, or to help an entrepreneur sell his company to people who understand it. The key difference between an ESOP and other ways that employees can buy stock is that an ESOP can borrow money to buy the stock that will be distributed to employees. Then the company makes a tax-deductible contribution toward employee retirement benefit to the ESOP each year. The ESOP uses the money to pay down the loan used to acquire the shares.

Now, if you have a sharp eye for tax matters, you may have noticed that ESOPs carry a host of tax advantages. The interest paid on the loan is deductible from income taxes as an operating expense of the business (just as almost all interest is for almost all businesses). The employer's contribution used to pay down the loan is also deductible from taxes (as almost all retirement plan contributions are). And the employee doesn't have to pay taxes on the stock until retirement and possibly not even then, depending on her financial position when that day comes.

Stock options

An *option* is a contract that gives the holder the right, but not the obligation, to buy an asset in the future at a price determined today. The price where the option can be exercised is known as the *strike price.* With a stock option, an employee can pay a premium of $5 today for the right to buy a share of stock at $20 six months from now. If the stock price in six months is more than $20, then the option can be *exercised* and is said to be "in the money." If the price is more than $25, then it makes sense for the option holder to exercise it.

For example, if the stock price were $31, the holder would be able to buy the stock at $20 per share. Because he is already out the $5 option price, the profit would be $31 – $20 – $5 = $6. If the stock stays less than $20 in six months, the option holder loses only the $5 premium.

What makes the stock price go up? Under normal market conditions, good corporate performance leads to a higher stock price, and the collective strong effort of managers and employees can generate that good corporate performance. Employees like options because they represent extra compensation, and the employees don't have to pay tax on them until they sell the stock, which they received when they exercised the option. Companies like them because the options are cheaper than other forms of compensation and they help employees think like the shareholders whom they work for.

Employee option purchase plans

Just as with the employee stock purchase plan described earlier, an *employee option purchase plan* allows employees to buy stock options out of their paychecks. These plans give the employees the right to acquire stock in the future at a price that's determined now, which can be no less than 85 percent of the stock's current market price. Employees don't pay tax until they sell the stock that they acquired when they exercised the option. Employee option purchase plans are *broad-based,* meaning that they are open to just about everyone at the company, instead of distributed as a bonus.

Incentive stock options

Incentive stock options are designed to encourage employees to do a good job and help the company grow, and they're regulated by section 424(c) of the tax code. Hence, they are a very specific type of option with very specific regulations.

These plans must be approved by shareholders, and they don't have to apply to all employees; in practice, most incentive stock option plans are limited to senior executives. Employees given incentive stock options have to exercise the stock while they work at the company or within three months of leaving. Some companies will even lend employees the money they need to exercise the options. (Although strangely enough, based on many proxies that I have read, it seems like the employees who are in most of need of the extra cash are the most highly paid executives. Go figure.)

In some cases, exercising incentive stock options will trigger a liability under the alternative minimum tax, which is higher than ordinary tax rates. Many an employee at a formerly high-flying company has been stuck with a huge tax bill on now-worthless stock. If you have significant incentive stock options, you probably need an experienced tax accountant to help you.

Nonqualified options

Unlike incentive stock options, *nonqualified options* aren't qualified to receive special tax treatment — hence, the name. They are popular as a way to give incentive options to a broad group of employees.

In most cases, employees don't pay any tax when they receive the option. Instead, the difference between the value of the stock when the option is exercised and the price of the option (often zero) is taxed as ordinary income earned at the time of exercise, with the tax due that year. If the stock is held after it is exercised, the difference between the sale price and the value of the stock at the time of exercise is taxed as a capital gain.

Stock appreciation rights and phantom stock

Some private companies don't have stock to give. Other companies want to create rewards based on the performance of its divisions relative to their competitors, rather than on the performance of the company as a whole. They can do this by creating *stock appreciation rights,* which reward employees for an increase in company value without giving them a stake in the company itself, or with *phantom stock,* which is an artificial security based on the value of a company or division. Employees pay tax on ordinary income calculated on the cash they receive when the rights are exercised or the phantom stock is sold.

Ways to invest for social change

Investors who care about the relationship that a company has with all of its stakeholders will find attractive investments in just about any industry. However, a few sectors are more likely to have responsible relationships with customers, vendors, and employees.

✔ **High technology:** Microsoft's founders gave options in the company's stock to all employees, creating an estimated 10,000 millionaires in the process. Boy, did that set a precedent! Most technology companies treat employees well, and their workers have come to expect to be pampered in exchange for working long hours on groundbreaking ideas.

✔ **Small businesses:** Many small businesses are trying to do business in new ways, and that often means taking a responsible approach to products, customers, and employees. They do this to get a competitive advantage over their older, more staid competitors. Some of these companies will be publicly traded; others will still be in the venture capital or angel investing stage (see Chapter 6 for more about these start-up pursuits).

✔ **Service companies:** A firm with a business that requires a great deal of one-on-one customer contact, such as a hotel, is somewhat more likely to behave responsibly because it needs to keep so many people happy. It has to treat employees well or they'll be surly, and it has to keep customers happy because they'll be able to find employees to complain to when there are problems. No hiding here!

Part III
Putting Your Socially Responsible Choices into Action

The 5th Wave   By Rich Tennant

"Sell."

In this part . . .

Think that as a social investor you're limited to under-performing mutual funds and safe but dull bank accounts? Think again.

Depending on your style, social investors can find a full range of investment products to suit their personal needs. You can choose stocks and bonds, real estate, or hedge funds, not to mention top mutual funds and feder-ally insured profit-sharing accounts at Shariah-compliant banks. Some social investors may even want to take the route of microfinance, making small loans to small-business owners around the world. This part explores the range of options out there for meeting your financial and personal goals.

Chapter 12

Buying and Selling Responsible Stocks and Bonds

. . . .

In This Chapter

▶ A bird's-eye view of the stock and bond markets

▶ Setting the stage for owning stocks

▶ Brushing up on buying bonds

▶ Touching on related securities that you may see

. . . .

Stocks and bonds are the most basic and traditional of investments. Other types of investments that you may consider, whether they're as common as mutual fund or exchange-traded funds (covered in Chapter 13) or as fancy as hedge funds and venture capital (discussed in Chapter 16), use stocks and bonds.

Whether a stock or bond is responsible depends on your style and the performance of the company that issues it. This chapter tells you how these securities are structured and how they trade so you can make better decisions about how to work them into your portfolio. It also helps you understand how the information that you uncover in your research (see Chapter 4) affects the value of the stocks and bonds that you're interested in buying.

What You Need to Know about Securities Markets

Companies and governments need to raise money all the time. They have factories to build, new products to bring to market, and payrolls to meet. To do this, they can sell part ownership of the company to someone else by issuing stock, or they can borrow money by issuing bonds.

Because investors often have extra money, they can buy these shares of stock or these bonds to get back more money in the future. (You may not think you have extra money, but if you're putting even a little bit away today to pay for retirement or something else special down the road, then you have something extra! Doesn't that make you feel a little bit better about your financial condition?)

The *securities markets* are where companies that need money and investors who have money to spare meet and fulfill each other's needs. Historically, it was a physical location, such as the New York Stock Exchange, where brokers would match the trades between the buyers and the sellers. Now these transactions mostly take place electronically, although the New York Stock Exchange still has some floor operations.

For most investors, stocks and bonds themselves are socially neutral. (The primary exception would be for investors following Islam's prohibition on paying or receiving interest; they wouldn't want to invest in bonds.) Instead, it's the responsibility of the issuing company that determines which stock or bond you want to include in your portfolio.

One way to find these companies is through research. A second way is to get a list through an index or service of those companies that meet your social criteria, and then do the research on their investment suitability. (Chapter 4 covers investment research in great detail.)

Things change very quickly; a company that may have made your social cut a year ago might not now, and vice versa.

Getting your return

Investors buy stocks and bonds because they want to make money. It's nice if you can support the underlying business or help a fine company grow, but the name of the game is still profit.

Profits come in two main forms:

- ✔ **Income:** Income is a regular payment, such as interest or a dividend.
- ✔ **Capital appreciation:** Capital appreciation happens when you can sell something for more than you paid for it.

The two have different effects on portfolios and taxes. I cover them in more detail in the following sections.

Incoming income

Investment income is the regular stream of payments generated by the stocks, bonds, and other securities that you own. For tax purposes, it's handled differently from *earned income,* which is the money you make from your job or your business.

Interest income, which comes from bonds, certificates of deposit, and bank accounts, is money paid to compensate you for lending money to someone else. When it's paid by a bond, it is called a *coupon* (a term left over from the days when securities were printed on paper rather than traded electronically). Coupon payments usually arrive twice a year in your brokerage account.

Dividends are payments that corporations make to their shareholders out of their profits. Companies don't have to pay dividends, and many don't. Most dividend-paying companies declare their payments quarterly; the funds show up in your brokerage account.

Interest is a tax-deductible business expense to a corporation. Dividends are not deductible; they are paid out of after-tax income. Then the holder of the bond and the owner of the stock pay taxes on the interest and dividends received. Because the corporation doesn't pay tax on interest but the bondholders do, interest is taxed just once. Because the corporation pays tax on the income that goes toward dividends, and then the shareholders pay tax again, dividends are taxed twice.

As of this writing, bond income is taxed at the regular earned income rate, which is currently a maximum of 35 percent. Dividend income is taxed at a lower rate, 15 percent. Even if you reinvest interest or dividends, the tax is paid in the same year that they are paid to you. Because tax laws change, be sure to check for the most recent information if you're generating income in a taxable account.

Counting on capital gains

When you make an investment, you hope to buy low and sell high. The difference between the low and the high is a *capital gain.* The gain is realized only when you sell the security that you hold; until you do that, your gain exists only on paper — hence, capital gains are called *paper gains* until the stock is sold.

Capital gains are the primary way that stock investors make money. Although there's some risk to having a big gain on paper that may or may not be realized, there's also a huge advantage: Investors don't have to pay tax on their capital gains until they are realized.

When dealing with the IRS, you'll need to segregate your short-term capital gains from your long-term ones. *Short-term gains* are gains on assets held for less than one year (under the current tax law); *long-term gains* are held for more than a year. The big difference is that under current law, short-term gains are taxed at your regular income rate, which could be as high at 35 percent, while long-term gains are taxed at just 15 percent.

If you end up selling your investment for less money than you paid for it, then you have a *capital loss.* Capital losses aren't all bad, though; they can be used to offset your capital gains, reducing the amount of taxes you owe. You can get all the details on how to do this in "IRS Publication 550, Investment Income and Expenses," which is available at www.irs.gov.

If you buy a bond when it's issued and hold on to it until maturity, you'll have no capital gains or losses. However, if you buy a bond at any time after issue or sell it at any time before maturity, there may well be a price difference. If it's in your favor, then you have a taxable capital gain.

Working with a broker

When you're ready to start investing, you have to purchase most stocks and bonds through a brokerage firm that can take your order, find someone to take the other side (to sell if you're buying or buy if you're selling), make the trade, and then transfer the securities to you.

It's technically possible to make trades without involving a brokerage firm, and many large investment companies have set up electronic communications networks to let you do just that. Those same firms use brokers, too, and so will you if you want to play with these securities.

Although you have to set up an account with some sort of broker, you can choose from several different types:

- ✔ Full service
- ✔ Discount
- ✔ Financial planner

Any of these professionals can support your financial social goals. Want to find out more about each? Keep reading!

Not all brokers and financial planners are convinced that social investing has any advantages, and they may well try to talk you out of it. Be sure to ask your adviser's opinion, and keep looking if you don't like the answer. And you can always send that narrow-minded broker a copy of this book. . . .

You may see firms described as *broker* or *dealer* or both. The terms are often used interchangeably, but there is a difference. A *broker* matches buyers and sellers of securities, while a *dealer* buys and sells securities out of its own account. Almost all brokerage firms are both brokers and dealers.

Full-service brokers

A *full-service broker,* also called a *registered representative* or an *account executive,* gives customers advice on their investment portfolios. He makes recommendations about what to buy and what to sell, often providing research to support that advice. These people often work for full-service brokerage firms with household names, such as Merrill Lynch or Morgan Stanley, but they may also work for banks or small, regional brokerage firms.

As compensation for their services, full-service brokers charge a range of fees. Some firms charge an annual account fee, some charge a percentage of assets under management, and others charge a commission for each transaction made. Make sure that you understand how you're being charged and that the advice you're receiving is worth it. The fee schedule may be buried deep in a lot of boring legalese in your account paperwork, so it's easier to ask. Full-service brokers aren't the cheapest way to invest, but their services pay off for many customers.

Brokers have to pass examinations and submit to background checks administered by FINRA, the Financial Industry Regulatory Authority. (And yes, the fingerprints really are checked against arrest records, as more than one prospective broker has found to his chagrin.) You can go online to look up the registration and disciplinary status of a broker you're considering working with. Go to www.finra.org, and click the link for "FINRA BrokerCheck."

In general, the broker is more important than the firm he works for. Every firm has a few outstanding employees and a few bad apples. You want to make sure that the broker you use will help you manage your money according to your investment style and will ensure that the products in your account are right for you, not just those that pay the highest commissions to the broker. After you check out a broker through FINRA, sit down with him and ask a few questions:

- ✔ How do you feel about my socially responsible investment style?
- ✔ How many of your clients invest socially?
- ✔ How do you choose socially responsible stocks and mutual funds?
- ✔ What types of clients do you prefer to work with? What's your trading and investment philosophy?
- ✔ How much experience do you have? What did you do before you became a broker? What training and qualifications do you have?

✔ How much education do you provide your clients about their financial strategy and investment choices?

✔ How quickly do you usually return calls? Will you meet with me in person? How do you prefer to communicate with clients?

✔ What is your minimum account size and minimum order size?

✔ What products pay you the highest commissions? What mutual fund companies do you recommend and why?

✔ Do you charge an annual fee, or do you charge commissions? If I have a choice, what type of account do you recommend for me and why?

✔ Do you have any references whom I can contact?

If you don't like the answers, keep looking; there are plenty of good brokers out there, so you don't have to deal with someone who isn't a good fit for you. You can ask friends for referrals, or you can call the brokerage firm office and ask for advice. You may get sent to the first available broker rather than one who is your dream registered representative, but that's okay as long as you're willing to ask questions and walk away if necessary.

Discount brokers

Many investors make their own decisions about what stocks and bonds they want to buy and sell. They may have small accounts and thus not be able to get the value of a full-service broker (see the preceding section for more about these folks). Or they may be primarily interested in mutual funds. If any of these descriptions apply to you, you may want to check out a *discount brokerage firm*. These firms charge much lower fees and commissions than full-service brokers do. They don't provide as much service, either. No one will take you to lunch, but then, no one will use that lunch to sell you a mutual fund with a high commission that isn't a great fit for your investment goals.

Discount brokers provide some services, just not as many as full-service brokers do. Many have online calculators and investment guides that can help you figure out how to set and reach your financial goals. Some provide a range of research services, such as access to newsletters or ratings services. A few even have registered representatives on staff who can provide you with information about different investments, if not specific recommendations. Still, your primary relationship will be with the firm, not any one employee, so you need to check out how the roster of services that you'll use compares to the fees charged. Some of the questions to ask are:

✔ What is your commission schedule? Do you also charge account maintenance or other fees?

✔ What is the minimum account size? What is the minimum order size? Do I have to make a minimum number of trades each year?

✔ What research services do you offer? Do you have analytical tools or calculators?

✔ Do you offer educational services or seminars?

✔ What markets and securities can I trade through your firm?

✔ Can I buy mutual funds through you? Which mutual fund companies do you deal with?

✔ What types of investors do you cater to? Are you a better option for day traders, small investors, or wealthy investors who make their own decisions?

✔ Can I talk to a human being? Does your staff offer investment advice or technical support? Where are they located?

The cheapest discount broker may not be the best for you. Some online brokers charge no commission. They make money on trading, and they don't offer a full range of services.

Financial planners

Many people want and need a lot of advice. They want to deal with someone who can help them manage their budgets, their savings, their insurance, and their taxes. The solution is a *financial planner,* who can look at all of your assets and liabilities and make detailed recommendations about how you should manage your money. Many financial planners specialize in different socially responsible investment strategies, so they can come up with recommendations that suit your needs and values.

Some financial planners work independently. Some are on staff at larger financial planning firms, and still others may be full-service brokers, insurance agents, or accountants. An ideal financial planner will take an objective look at your current financial position, assess your goals, and make an objective recommendation for how you should invest your money. The reality is that many financial planners push certain products or financial strategies no matter what your needs are. And, no surprise, these recommendations tend to involve high commissions.

Yet because their services are so comprehensive, most financial planners tend to charge high fees or recommend products that carry high commissions. That's fine if the recommendations improve your financial position enough to offset the fee. Good financial planners are worth the money. Bad ones are not. You need to make sure that the person you're hiring is going to be able to do a good job for you. Some questions to ask are:

✔ How do you feel about my socially responsible investment style?

✔ How many of your clients invest with social guidelines?

✔ What types of clients do you prefer to work with? What is your financial planning philosophy? What is your minimum account size?

✔ How much experience do you have? When did you become a financial planner? What training and qualifications do you have?

✔ Are there certain types of products that you think everyone should have? Why?

✔ Do you charge a fee, earn commissions, or both? If you charge a fee, is it based on assets, is it a flat fee, or is it an hourly rate? What fee would you charge me for your services?

✔ How often would you want to meet with me? How do you prefer that clients contact you?

✔ Will other people work on my financial plan? Who are these people, what do they do, and how do they get paid?

✔ Can I see a sample financial plan?

✔ What products pay you the highest commissions? What mutual fund and insurance companies do you recommend, and why?

✔ Do you have any references whom I can contact?

Using margin for leverage

Many stock and bond investors goose up their returns with *leverage* — using borrowed money to get a higher return. This arrangement is called *margin*, and almost every brokerage firm offers it. Of course, margin means taking on more risk, so it's not suitable for all investors.

Here's how it works: You decide to buy 100 shares of stock worth $20 each, for a total investment of $2,000. You put up $1,000 of your own money and borrow $1,000 from the broker at 10 percent interest. If the stock goes up to $31 per share, then you have a profit of $1,000 after paying off the loan and interest, doubling the amount of your initial investment. If the stock goes down to $11, though, you still have to pay back the loan and the interest, so you're left with nothing.

Of course, the brokerage firm probably won't let you lose everything; as your losses mount, you'll receive a *margin call* ordering you to put more money in your account. If you don't, the broker will sell your stock for you. The broker does this to ensure that the loan is paid off.

Minimum margin requirements are set by the Federal Reserve Board and are designed to keep the financial system stable, so begging and pleading won't work. Many an investor has been forced to sell a security to meet a margin call, only to watch it go up in price a week later.

If you're an experienced investor who wants to take some risk and who has no objection to paying interest, than margin may be right for you. If you aren't sure that it's appropriate, then it probably isn't.

Buying Socially Responsible Stocks

A share of *common stock,* also called *equity,* is a security that represents a fractional interest in the ownership of a company. It allows a company to raise the money to grow while sharing ownership among thousands of people. Buy one share of Hershey (NYSE: HSY), and you're a partial owner of the company. Of course, your stake will be small relative to that of the Milton Hershey School, a boarding school for orphaned and disadvantaged children that owns 79.9 percent of the voting stock of the company. The Milton Hershey School may have voting control, but you still have a stake in the company. Instead of making direct decisions about how the company should be run, stockholders elect a board of directors to represent their interests.

A key feature of stock is that it has *limited liability.* If the company goes bankrupt, shareholders can lose all of their investment — and not a penny more. The lenders can't come after the shareholders' personal assets for the money they're owed.

Your company may pay you a *dividend,* which is a small cash payment made out of its profits. Most of your return (you hope) will come from *capital gains,* which is an increase in the price of the stock between when you buy it and when you sell it. (See the earlier section, "Getting your return," for more about dividends and capital gains.)

The social responsibility of any stock, of course, is determined by the company's policies relative to your goals.

How stocks trade

Stocks are priced based on a single share, but they almost always trade in groups of 100 shares, known as a *round lot.* If you buy less than a round lot, you'll probably have to pay a higher commission.

A stock's price is determined by the supply and demand for the shares, and that's usually a function of expected performance. If people expect a company to do well, they'll want to buy the stock, and that will drive the price up. If they aren't excited about its prospects, then they'll sell shares, and that will take the price down.

There are lots of reasons to sell a stock. There is only one reason to buy: because you think the stock is going to increase in price.

Every stock has two prices: a bid and an ask. The *bid* is the price at which the broker buys stock from you if you're selling; the *ask* is the price at which the broker sells to you if you're the one buying. The difference, known as the *spread,* is the broker's profit.

Here's an example of a price quote:

> WFMI $22.03 $22.17

This is a quote for Whole Foods Market (Nasdaq: WFMI). The bid price is $22.03, and the ask is $22.17. Spreads may be as small as a penny, but they can be higher, especially if the company's stock doesn't trade often or if there's news that's bringing a lot of buyers or sellers to the market.

The brokerage firm makes money from the commission and from the spread. When interviewing brokers and financial planners, make sure to ask about the commission that you'll be charged to trade. However, the commission is only one part of the cost. Some brokerage firms do a better job than others of keeping a small spread. If you expect to trade often, you need to consider the firm's ability to execute the trade with a narrow spread as well as the cost of the commission. Firms that work with active traders make their execution data available for the asking.

Where U.S. stocks trade

U.S. stocks trade mostly on organized exchanges like the New York Stock Exchange and Nasdaq. Many brokerage firms belong to the exchanges themselves. Smaller brokerage firms and financial planning companies often use a correspondent firm for trading, receiving a cut of the commission but giving the work to someone else.

No matter how you contact your brokerage firm to place an order, the firm's trading staff will execute it wherever it can get the best deal. But is that the best deal for you or for the brokerage firm? It's tough to know the right answer. In general, firms that do the most trading and participate in several exchanges and electronic communications networks can get you the best execution.

The New York Stock Exchange (NYSE)

The *New York Stock Exchange* has been synonymous with big money for more than 200 years. Most of the largest U.S. corporations trade on it, paying handsomely to do so. Besides paying the listing fee, a New York Stock Exchange company usually needs to have at least 2,200 shareholders, trade at least 100,000 shares a month, carry a *market capitalization* (number of shares outstanding multiplied by price per share) of at least $100 million, and generate annual revenues of at least $75 million.

Much NYSE trading takes place the old-fashioned way: on the trading floor at the exchange's building at the corner of Broad and Wall streets in New York City. That style of trading is becoming obsolete, so the NYSE has developed its own electronic communications networks to accommodate traders who value the faster, easier trading possible over an Internet connection.

Nasdaq

Nasdaq used to stand for the National Association of Securities Dealers Automated Quotation System, but now it's just a name, not an acronym (pronounced *naz-dak*). It was founded as an electronic communications network, almost like an Internet for traders before the Internet was available. At first, it handled companies that were too small or too speculative to meet New York Stock Exchange listing requirements. Over time, brokers liked using the Nasdaq network, and technology companies that were once small became international behemoths that saw no reason to move their stock listing to the NYSE.

When a customer order to buy or sell comes in, the brokerage firm's traders use the Nasdaq system to search for a matching order. If one exists, then the trader can execute the order. If not, he can send a message to traders at other firms to see if they have interest in picking up the order. To ensure a regular flow of order activity, Nasdaq has several *market makers.* They are employees of member brokerage firms who agree to buy and sell some shares of a designated stock every day to ensure that there's some supply and demand in the market.

Over-the-Counter Bulletin Board (OTC BB)

The *Over-the-Counter Bulletin Board* is the market for public companies that don't qualify for Nasdaq listing. Some of these are foreign stocks that trade in the U.S. but that aren't listed on the New York Stock Exchange or on Nasdaq. American Bulletin Board companies will have four-letter ticker symbols followed by ".OB". For example, ICP Solar Technologies' ticker symbol is ICPR. OB. Foreign issuers trade with five-letter symbols — four letters followed by an F. ACS Motion Control, based in Israel, trades as ACSEF.

Your broker will get quotes for Over-the-Counter Bulletin Board stocks through Nasdaq. Although these stocks don't trade on Nasdaq, the communication system allows traders to find the current prices and locate buyers and sellers.

Many Over-the-Counter Bulletin Board companies are fine, but others used to be on Nasdaq and were delisted because they lost a lot of money. Tread carefully.

Pink Sheets

Before trading went electronic, there wasn't an easy place to trade many companies' shares. Shares in some smaller companies would go for days without seeing a buy or sell order. To value these stocks, brokerage firms subscribed to a weekly newsletter that listed the prices for those companies. It was printed on pink paper, hence the common name was the *Pink Sheets*.

Over the years, Nasdaq expanded so it could list more companies, while the Over-the-Counter Bulletin Board was created for companies that couldn't be listed on Nasdaq. Hence, the number of public companies that weren't listed anywhere and that didn't trade very often became very small.

The Pink Sheets are now available online (www.pinksheets.com). Pink Sheet companies don't have listing requirements. The companies are public, but they don't qualify for listing on Nasdaq or Over-the-Counter Bulletin Board, usually because they are behind on their filings with the Securities and Exchange Commission. These companies have four- or five-letter ticker symbols and are sometimes shown with the suffix ".PK" after the ticker. Most brokerage firms can handle orders for Pink Sheet stocks.

Some Pink Sheet companies are frauds. Because the listing requirements are so few, the Pink Sheets are filled with penny stocks (those trading at less than $1 per share), shell companies, and securities with prices that can be easily manipulated by a crooked broker. Many investors have been burned when they start trading in this market. There are some good businesses in the pinks, but it's a market for sophisticated traders only.

Buying, otherwise known as going long

When you buy a stock, you are said to be *long* it. When you sell it, you are *short*, and I'll talk about that later in the chapter.

Buying a stock is pretty simple: You open a brokerage account, you place the order, you put the money in your account (you have three business days to pay), and then you're a happy shareholder. You won't receive a certificate; the stock itself will be held in electronic form. It will also be held in the name of the brokerage firm, known as *street name*. The brokerage firm is responsible for sending you annual reports, proxy statements, and any correspondence about your holding. It maintains the transaction record and credits any dividends to your account.

If you need to have the stock certificate or want the holding to be registered in your own name, you can do both, but your brokerage firm will almost definitely charge you extra. Electronic order entry and street name have been the norm for decades and work well, so opt for the extras only if you have a specific reason.

Buying and holding

Many investors buy stock with the hope of holding it for a long time. They do lots of ongoing research (see Chapter 4) to make sure that the company is still a good one and still matches their social goals, but they keep owning it. And that's a fine approach to owning stocks. Holding is cheap — brokerages charge commissions to buy and sell, not to hold — and the capital gains accumulate free of taxes until you sell.

Although you can make huge profits by buying and holding good growth companies (wouldn't you like to have been in on the initial public offering of something like Johnson & Johnson?), not all companies stay good and growing forever. Don't fall in love with a stock, because it will not love you back. If the situation changes, it may be time to sell.

When you hold a stock for a while, you may notice one day that you own more shares, but the price is lower. You have received a *stock split*. The company simply increases the number of shares that each shareholder has, and the price falls by the same amount. If you held 100 shares worth $30 each, and the company announced a 2-for-1 stock split, you'd end up with 200 shares worth $15 each. Your total value hasn't changed. Because there's no change in total value, a stock split isn't a taxable event; in fact, it's more of a nonevent.

A company with a low stock price might do a *reverse split* in an attempt to make the stock look better in the market. Hence, you may start with 100 shares worth $1 each; then the company announces a 1-for-5 reverse split, and you have 20 shares worth $5 each with no change in total value. Reverse splits tend to be viewed badly. True, there's been no change in value, but the thought is that the company has run out of ideas for building the business and is now reduced to playing games to make the stock price look good.

Trading

Many of the people in the stock market aren't investors; they are *traders*. The difference is that investors tend to hold good stocks for a long time, while traders have a short-term mentality. Some traders, known as *day traders,* only plan on holding a company for a few minutes! Others may be interested in holding a position for a few weeks or months, but rarely more than a year.

Trading isn't terribly compatible with most socially responsible investment styles. The incompatibility has nothing to do with trading itself, which is important for keeping markets liquid. Rather, socially responsible restrictions make trading difficult, and the short holding period for trading limits the ability to be an activist investor.

A trader needs to have a large universe of securities to look at; on any given day, only a handful of stocks may present good short-term opportunities. That pool of stocks may be further limited by excluding companies because of their revenue sources or their governance practices. After all of those restrictions are applied, the selection of socially responsible stocks can be too limiting.

The second reason why trading and social investing don't fit well together is that social investors often use the powers of capitalism to encourage companies to do the right thing. If you hold a stock for a very short time period, the company won't notice any effect on long-term value from appealing to your better nature, nor will you have any ability to influence the company's choices.

Profiting when stocks go down: Short selling

Normally, investors buy stocks in the hopes that they'll make money when the stock goes up in price. Unfortunately, stocks also go down, as many investors have found to their chagrin. Wouldn't it be great if you could make money on a declining company?

Well, you can, through the magic of *short selling*. Short selling allows you to bet on a future decline in the price of a security, just as going long lets you bet on a future gain (see the previous section). It's risky, though.

When you want to sell short, you first need to do some research. This helps you know exactly why a security is overvalued and what it will take for the rest of the market to realize that. For example, does a company use unusual accounting methods? Is it making money while other companies in the same industry are struggling? Has management been hyping the potential of its product beyond any reasonable rate of sales? If so, you may be able to profit from an overvalued situation.

Sell something short only if you have done thorough research that indicates that the stock is overvalued in the market. Do not sell short simply because you don't like the company. Short selling is risky even for people who do the work; it's a quick way for others to lose a lot of money.

All brokerage firms can handle short sales. You have to have an account that is approved for margin, because you'll be borrowing stock to make the trade. You place a sell order and indicate that it's a short sale. The broker arranges for you to borrow stock from another holder in the firm. (This is easy to do when all the shares are held in the broker's name, and no, the lender rarely knows that his shares have been lent out.) After the stock is borrowed, it's sold. The short seller waits for the price to fall and then buys back the stock at the lower price to repay the loan. The profit is the difference between the price sold and the price of the repurchase, less the interest charged on the loan.

Of course, if the stock goes up, the short seller has to pay a higher price when buying back the stock, and he still has to pay the interest. Ouch! And the interest accumulates while waiting for the price to go down, so if it takes a long time, that can offset the profit.

Traders can't be both long and short at the same time on the same stock. If you short a stock you already own, you are in effect selling it, and your return is the difference between where you bought the stock and where you shorted it. Stock investors can protect themselves from declining share prices. It's beyond the scope of this book, but some of the guides to stock investing listed in the appendix can give you the information you need.

Buying Socially Responsible Bonds

A *bond* is nothing more than a loan that is standardized for easy trading. When an investor buys a bond, the money goes to the issuer. In exchange for the use of the money, the issuer agrees to pay interest on a regular basis, usually twice a year. Each payment is known as a *coupon,* a convention that goes back more than 30 years to a time when bonds had little coupons attached to them. When each was due, the bond holder would cut off the coupon and take it to the bank.

Because of these steady coupon payments, bonds are often referred to as *fixed-income investments.* The money that's borrowed in the first place, called the *principal,* isn't repaid until the date that the bond comes due, known as the *maturity.* Most bonds have a maturity of more than ten years; if they come due in a shorter amount of time, they are often called *notes* instead. A bond that matures in one year or less is usually called a *bill.*

Sometimes, the principal is split from the interest payments so investors who want regular payments can get those while an investor who wants a single sum at a future date can get that.

The coupon part of the bond is known as a *strip,* while the remaining principal is called a *zero-coupon bond.* Related to the zero-coupon bond is the *discount bond,* which is sold at the principal value less the amount of interest that will accrue while the bond is held. When the bond matures, the holder receives the full face value. Treasury bills are sold as discount bonds.

If a bond issuer goes bankrupt, the bondholders get their money before any shareholders do. Often, the shareholders are left with nothing. That's one reason that bonds have less risk than stocks.

Bonds are popular with conservative investors who want low risk and steady cash flow. Many retirees keep part of their savings in bonds to give them the money they need to enjoy their work-free years. During inflationary times, bonds may offer higher returns than other types of investments.

As with stocks, the social responsibility of the bond is related to the behavior of the bond's issuer rather than the bond itself.

Types of bonds

Bonds are classified according to the issuer: a domestic company, the federal government, a local government, or someone in another country. Each of these groups has some different nuances to consider as you think of how the investment suits your financial goals as well as your social ones.

Corporate bonds

Corporate bonds are issued by companies that need to borrow money. These businesses tend to be large enough and established enough that bond buyers will be interested in their deal. (Many companies work with banks rather than issue bonds, often because they don't need to raise enough money to make a bond offering worthwhile.)

Bonds are often issued to finance major construction projects, such as a new manufacturing plant, or to help a company make an acquisition. You can choose from a few different types of corporate bonds to complement your socially responsible style.

High-grade bonds

When a company wants to issue a bond, it's given a rating, or grade, by a rating agency, such as Moody's or Standard & Poor's. Analysts at these firms research the company's financial situation and then assign a rating. The rating is similar to the score that credit bureaus assign to individuals that affects how easy it will be for them to get a mortgage at a good rate.

The best rating, usually shown as AAA or Aaa, depending on the agency, is awarded to companies that have the best credit. These companies are the least likely to need money and the most likely to pay back whatever they do borrow. Hence, these borrowers have little risk, so they pay the lowest rates of interest.

Borrowers that are still considered to be good risks but don't meet the highest rating are assigned slightly lower rates, usually arranged as AA, A, and BBB in descending order.

Junk bonds

Companies with low credit ratings, usually two Bs or less, are considered to be less likely to pay back their debt. This doesn't mean that they won't pay the debt back, just that they are less of a sure thing. In exchange for the risk, buyers of these bonds demand higher rates of interest. These low-rated bonds are usually referred to as _junk bonds,_ even though people who actually work with the bonds prefer the nicer-sounding term _high-yield bonds._ Nevertheless, the not-so-nice term has stuck.

Junk bonds are often issued by companies as parts of acquisitions, when the buyer needs to borrow a lot of money to complete the purchase. In many cases, these are hostile transactions in which the seller doesn't want to be bought and thus won't cooperate in financing the deal. Other junk bonds are those of companies that used to have a higher rating but are now facing fading financial fortunes.

Government bonds

Government bonds are issued by the U.S. government. Are these bonds responsible? Some social investors avoid U.S. government bonds because they disagree with many of the government's uses of funds, especially military spending. Others like these bonds because they avoid the problems that may arise with private companies, such as sources of revenue or corporate governance.

Because of the gap between what the government takes in from taxes and what it has committed to spend, the U.S. government is constantly issuing bonds. It's easy to buy them, too. Treasury bond buyers can go straight to the government's Web site, `www.treasurydirect.gov`, to open an account and place orders.

International bonds

International bonds are issued by governments and corporations outside of the United States. The dynamics are similar to those of corporate and government bonds issued in the U.S., with one major exception: They usually have exposure to foreign currency. Is this good or bad? Well, it depends on where the U.S. dollar is on any given day. If the dollar is weak, then an international bond can have a higher dollar return than a similar U.S. security; but if the dollar is strong, the opposite will happen. Managers of international bond mutual funds often use different risk-management techniques to reduce the negative effects of exchange-rate changes. It may be difficult, but not impossible, for individuals to do the same. That makes mutual funds a great option for international bond investors, and those are discussed in Chapter 13.

Municipal bonds

Municipal bonds are issued by state and local governments, often to support infrastructure spending or economic development projects. The beauty of these issues is that the interest is exempt from federal income taxes and may be exempt from state taxes, too. That's a nifty little bonus! To find out more about how municipal bonds are used, turn to Chapter 6.

How bonds trade

A single bond usually has a face value of $1,000. Many brokers will trade only one at a time, but some require a minimum trade of ten of the same bonds at a time. Most bondholders want steady income and hold their bonds until they mature, so bonds don't trade as often as stocks do. The market value of a bond is mostly determined by the level of interest rates in the economy. When interest rates go up, bond prices go down; when rates go down, bond prices go up. Bond prices are also affected by how likely the loan is to be repaid. If traders think that the bond issuer is near bankruptcy, then the bond price will fall.

Generally speaking, only corporate and municipal bonds have repayment risk; the U.S. government can always print money to meet its obligations. Most international government bonds have similarly low default risk because their governments also have printing presses, but that hasn't stopped some nations from defaulting. Russia did just that in 1998, setting off much turmoil in financial markets, including the collapse of a major hedge fund, Long-Term Capital Management.

A bond price quote looks like this:

3.375 2009 Oct 15 n 101:08 101:09

This is a U.S. Treasury note maturing on October 15, 2009, and carrying an interest rate of 3.375 percent. The number right after the "n" (for "note") is the *bid*. As with a stock, the bid is the price at which the dealer will buy the bond from you if you're selling. The second number is the *ask,* and it's the price the dealer will charge you if you're buying. The difference is the dealer's profit, known as the *spread.*

Corporate bonds trade in 8ths of a percentage point, and Treasury bonds trade in 32nds. The bid of 101:08 means that the bond's bid price is 101 $\frac{8}{32}$ percent of the face value of $1,000, or $1,012.50.

The use of eighths and fractions of eighths, by the way, is nearly ancient; it dates back to before the American Revolution, when the main currency in the Americas was the Spanish doubloon, a large gold coin that could be cut into pieces for easy trade. Hence, they were known as "pieces of eight." U.S. stocks traded in eighths until 2001; they now trade in orderly decimals.

Where U.S. bonds trade

Investment banks and the federal government sell new bonds directly to investors. If you want to buy a bond that has already been issued, or you want to sell a bond that you already own, you have to turn to the secondary market — the different ways of trading a bond by using a broker. Some bonds trade on organized exchanges, while others trade over-the-counter.

Listed bonds

Bonds issued by very large corporations often trade on the New York Stock Exchange. To buy or sell a listed bond, you place an order through your brokerage firm, which sends an order to its broker working on the floor of the exchange. The process is almost identical to the trading of listed stocks (see the earlier section "How stocks trade" for more details).

Over-the-counter trading

Most corporate and municipal bonds trade over-the-counter. Instead of working with an organized exchange, brokerage firms use electronic communications networks, like Nasdaq services, to find buyers and sellers for different bonds. Because bonds don't trade often, brokers often refer to a bond order as a *search;* the customer specifies the type of bond, the interest rate, and the maturity, and then the broker searches through the list of bonds to find one that comes close.

Treasury dealers

Unlike the corporate and municipal bond market, the Treasury market is one of the most liquid in the world. The best way for most individual investors to buy a new Treasury bond is directly from the government, because no commission is involved.

After Treasury bonds are issued, they trade on a secondary market made up of Treasury dealers. These are large brokerage firms registered with the government who agree to buy and sell bonds and maintain a stable market for them. If your brokerage firm isn't a Treasury dealer, it will have a relationship with one that it can send your order to.

Neither Fish nor Fowl: Other Securities

Whenever there's a stream of cash and a rate of risk, an investment banker can create a new type of security to meet the needs of borrowers and investors alike. These alternatives aren't as common as stocks and bonds, but you may well come across them. Sometimes they'll be more suitable ways for you to invest, depending on market conditions, your financial goals, and your investment style.

I describe some of these securities in the following sections, but don't worry: There will be others, as long as people keep dreaming up new ways for companies to finance growth and for investors to make money.

Collateralized debt obligations

A *collateralized debt obligation (CDO),* likes its cousins, the *collateralized bond obligation (CBO)* and the *collateralized mortgage obligation (CMO),* is a pool of different loans sold in shares to investors. For example, a bank may take all of its car loans, put them into a single pool, and then sell investors certificates entitling them to a share of the pool. The investors then receive the principal and interest payments; if the borrowers skip out on their obligations, the certificate holders lose out. These investments offer investors a higher rate of return than with a traditional bond because they carry more risk.

Collateralized debt obligations picked up a bad name when the subprime mortgage crisis hit, and some big banks that should have understood the risks better were burned. These aren't inherently irresponsible securities; they traded with few problems for decades. If the people selling the loans deal responsibly with borrowers and disclose accurate information to borrowers, they can be an appropriate investment in the right situation. Still, it's a tricky market, and it's not for investors who can't take risk.

Convertible stocks and bonds

Convertible securities are combinations of stocks and bonds. They're issued as bonds or preferred stock (which I describe in the next section), but investors have the right to convert them into common stock at a predetermined price.

For example, you may be able to exchange a convertible security with a face value of $1,000 for 40 shares of stock at $20 each. If the stock is trading at less than $20, the holder would rather have the convertible because it pays interest (for a convertible bond) or a regular dividend (for convertible preferred bonds). If the stock is trading at more than $25, then it may make sense to convert because the shares would be worth more than the bond. Convertibles aren't very common, but if you come across some, you now know what they are.

Preferred stock

Preferred stock is a security that pays its holders a regular, preset dividend. It's a type of fixed-income security because the payment is predictable, but it's not exactly the same.

First, a company has to pay its bond interest; it if misses a payment, the bondholders can force it into bankruptcy. If a company misses a preferred dividend, the preferred holders can't order payment. The missed dividends are accrued and have to be paid before any common dividends are paid, but that may never happen. If the company does go bankrupt, bondholders are repaid before the preferred stockholders. The preferred stockholders, in turn, are repaid before common stock holders.

Some classes of preferred stock carry voting rights; they may be lesser or greater than the voting rights of common stock. As with convertibles, you may not see preferred stock very much, but when you do, you'll understand it.

Sukuk

Under Islamic law, a Muslim may neither pay nor charge interest. Instead, returns are to be based on shared investment risk. Yet all over the world, Muslims want to buy houses, build factories, or improve roads, and they need financing to do it. To give people, companies, and governments the money they need to expand and to offer investors the low-risk, predictable returns that many of them want, the *Sukuk* was developed.

Sukuk financing is often based on revenue that accrues from the construction of a physical asset. Instead of a mortgage, for example, a lease-to-own arrangement may be structured, with the Sukuk holders being the legal owners of the property until all lease payments are received. Few such contracts trade in the United States, but they're common in Europe, the Middle East, and Asia, and are likely to become more popular here.

You don't have to be Muslim to use Sukuk financing, by the way; these securities may be purchased or issued by any investor who sees the value.

Chapter 13

Mutual Funds and Exchange-Traded Funds (ETFs)

*A*lthough you should have exposure to the stock markets, it's tough for an individual investor to make money trading single stocks. It's hard enough to find good companies to invest in, but adding a social screen throws in an extra level of work that may be intimidating. And, to reduce the risk in your portfolio, you should hold about 30 stocks. It takes a lot of money and time to accumulate those. Buying bonds poses similar problems. Minimum prices start at $1,000, making it costly to diversify across a range of maturities, rates, and issuers. (More on stocks and bonds in Chapter 12.)

Is the cliché right: Does it take money to make money? Well, you need to have a little bit of money to get started investing, but you don't need to have a lot. Instead, consider mutual funds and exchange-traded funds (ETFs), which allow investors to reap the benefits of the stock and bond markets for a relatively low amount of money. And these funds aren't just for people with small portfolios; they offer many benefits for people with lots of money socked away.

Successful investing in mutual funds and exchange-traded funds involves a little upfront work, though. This chapter covers the information you need to know as you look for more ways to invest responsibly.

No Matter What Type of Fund You Choose . . .

Mutual funds and ETFs (exchange-traded funds, described later in this chapter) are great ways for individual investors to leave the hard work of choosing securities to someone else. But you still have to do some work. Later in this chapter, I explain the specific issues involved with the different types of funds, but here are a few concerns that may crop up no matter if you choose mutual funds, ETFs, or a mix of both.

Figuring out your investment needs

Funds are a great way to get started in investing, and they may be all that most individual investors will ever need. But simply owning a mutual fund is not a financial plan. This book is not so much about investing in general as it is about social investing. If you aren't quite sure what your needs are or how to meet them, you may want to pick up a copy of *Personal Finance For Dummies* (Wiley) or meet with a financial planner. You certainly don't want to invest willy-nilly, or you may give up fees and miss out on good opportunities.

The longer it is until you need the money, the more risk you can afford to take. (Risk is the likelihood of losing money or otherwise getting a return that you don't expect.) A 28-year-old can take a lot of risk with retirement savings, but should not take risk with money being saved for the down payment on a house. That basic relationship between time and risk underlies most personal financial decisions.

Monitoring performance

Not all mutual funds and ETFs are the same, even if they have the same investment objective. Two different *large-cap value* mutual funds (mutual funds that invest in larger companies that are inexpensive relative to the market) can have different performance, as can two different *emerging markets* ETFs (exchange-traded funds that invest in lesser-developed countries) based on different indexes. The initial investment decision isn't your only investment decision; you want to check the performance of your funds relative to similar investments to make sure you're invested where you want to be. One good source for tracking mutual fund and ETF performance is Morningstar, www.morningstar.com.

There's a fine line between adjusting your holdings based on performance and constantly selling low and buying high. If your stock mutual fund is down when the entire stock market is, that doesn't make it a bad investment. In fact, that may be a good time to buy so you have money invested when the market inevitably turns around.

Working with a retirement plan

Many people use mutual funds as part of their retirement plan. If you're managing your own retirement funds, say through an IRA account, you can make your own decisions about where you put your money. Most mutual fund companies and brokerage firms can set up these accounts for you, usually charging a small annual fee for the service; once established, you can buy and sell funds as needed until you're ready to chuck your job and move to the beach.

If you're saving through an employer retirement plan, such as a 401(k) plan, then you're limited to the fund choices that the company offers. The funds may not fit your social goals. You can request that your employer add a suitable social fund to its array; but keep in mind that the employer has to meet federal regulations concerning retirement plan performance (see Chapter 3 for more information), so you'll have more luck if you can recommend a fund with good performance and low fees.

Getting acquainted with the different funds

Mutual funds and exchange-traded funds have some significant differences, but they have a few things in common. Both types of funds collect money from large numbers of investors, and then hire professional managers to manage it. The money is invested in broader portfolios (a concept known as *diversification*) than would be possible for almost any of the individual investors to create on their own. Funds are available in a wide range of investment objectives and investment styles, so they can help investors diversify or help them pick up exposure to a narrow market sector.

Mutual funds and exchange-traded funds are easy to buy. Write the check, place the order, and you're a shareholder! Of course, that assumes you've done the research to know what your investment needs are and how any particular fund meets them. Each type of fund has almost countless variations (with new ones coming to market every day, it seems). The result can be a precise fit with your investment needs, but it can also be a bit overwhelming. Hey, that's why I'm here. In the rest of this chapter, I help you navigate your way through the mutual fund and ETF jungle.

Grasping the Basics of Mutual Funds

In the United States, *mutual funds* are investment pools that are required to register with the Securities and Exchange Commission under the Investment Company Act of 1940. The operators of these funds collect investments from large numbers of investors, and then hire investment managers who buy and sell securities for everyone's benefit.

Legally, a mutual fund is a separate corporation that doesn't pay taxes. Instead, the tax liability is passed on to the investors, who may or may not owe anything.

Mutual funds are a good fit for many individual investors, but they have some quirks that you'll want to understand before taking the plunge. You can find the information in the *prospectus,* a legal document that mutual fund companies must file with the Securities and Exchange Commission and give to prospective investors, but the facts are buried in a lot of legalese. In the following sections, I give you a handy guide to some of the structural issues that can help you ask good questions and find the facts you need. If you're going to pay a sales charge, transfer money, or pay taxes on your gains, you'll want to know why and how! First, though, you need to get acquainted with the two main types of mutual funds.

Mutual funds fall into two types, open-end and closed-end. Open-end funds are far more common; most socially responsible options fall into this category.

Open-end mutual funds

Most mutual funds sold in the United States are *open-end mutual funds.* The funds buy and sell shares directly to shareholders, using prices at the end of every business day, issuing and redeeming shares as necessary. Invest $1,000 in the fund, and the fund size grows by $1,000. Cash in $1,000 of your shares, and the fund shrinks by $1,000.

The good news? There's always a market for your fund shares, no matter what's happening in the financial markets. Of course, the fund manager may need to sell securities if the amount of the day's redemptions exceeds the amount of cash on hand.

An open-end fund's shares trade at its *net asset value (NAV),* which is the total market value of all the securities held in the fund divided by the total number of shares that the fund has issued. The fund will never sell for more or for less than the NAV. There may be an additional sales charge, called a *load,* which I explain in the "Loaded from the start" section later in this chapter.

Closed-end mutual funds

Closed-end funds are relatively rare, making up less than 10 percent of all the mutual funds tracked by the Investment Company Institute (www.ici.org), the trade organization for mutual fund and ETF companies. A closed-end fund issues a set number of shares when it goes public, and then doesn't buy or sell any more. The fund managers invest the money but never have to deal with influxes or outflows of cash. Those interested in buying shares of a closed-end fund place orders through their brokers, who turn to the stock exchange to find existing shareholders who are selling.

Closed-end fund managers report the *net asset value* (or *NAV;* the value of all the securities divided by the total number of shares outstanding) to the different securities pricing services, so you'd think that a closed-end fund's share price would match the net asset value. And yet, it rarely does. Instead, most closed-end funds trade at prices below their net asset values. It's not what you would expect, but it's a big draw to investors who are looking to buy stocks at a bargain.

Some closed-end fund shareholders have forced the fund managers to disband the fund or convert it to an open-end fund in order to profit when the discount is eliminated. You shouldn't count on that if you choose to invest in closed-end funds, unless of course your activist charge is corporate governance (discussed in Chapter 7).

If you want to find out more about closed-end and open-end mutual funds, there's always *Mutual Funds for Dummies* (Wiley)!

Within open- and closed-end funds are different categories of funds you can choose from for your portfolio. I cover these categories in detail in "Choosing Your Mutual Funds," later in the chapter.

Complexes, social and otherwise

Each mutual fund is its own corporation, but very few funds stand alone. Almost all are sponsored by *mutual fund complexes,* which can be the household-name investment companies, like Fidelity and Vanguard, or small firms offering just two or three funds, like some of the socially responsible mutual fund companies listed later in this chapter. Those companies, also called *fund families,* organize different mutual funds based on where they see the market going. They hire the investment staff, market the funds, and manage customer relations. In exchange, each of the mutual funds pays a fee to the fund complex for its services. The fund complex often allows certain privileges to shareholders of its different funds, including unified statements and easy exchanges between its funds as a customer's investment needs change.

As a legally distinct corporation, each fund has its own board of directors. In almost all cases, the board of directors rubber-stamps the fund management complex's decisions. Note that I said "almost all." That's because every now and again, the fund company management gets greedy, and the board of directors votes to give the fund's management contract to a different firm. A handful of mutual fund companies avoid this problem by hiring outside investment managers as a matter of policy, giving the fund's board more leverage.

Some fund families offer nothing but socially responsible funds, and several of those are covered in this chapter. However, a lot of general mutual fund companies have a few socially responsible funds on offer. One decision you have to make is just how pure you want to be. Will it bother you to do business with a fund company that has funds that invest in ways you don't like as well as funds that invest in ways that you do? Or will you find that the convenience — and the opportunity for the social fund to inspire others on staff managing other funds — outweighs your quest for purity?

Fee structure: Pay now, or pay later

Mutual funds aren't free. Some funds charge a fee when you buy shares, some charge a fee when you sell shares, and all charge at least some fees while you own the fund to cover the costs of operation. Fees come out of performance and can add up over time, so you should pay attention to them.

Some sponsors of socially responsible mutual funds believe that investors will be so happy to find a fund that fits their values that they won't pay attention to all the fees being levied. Promise me that you'll pay attention. Almost all social investors have more than one fund or investment option to choose from.

Loaded from the start

The first fee you may, or may not, pay is called a *load.* That's a sales charge incurred when you buy or sell shares. Many mutual funds have *no load,* and you can buy those directly through the mutual fund company offering the fund. Other funds come with *front loads,* which are sales charges that can be as high as 8.5 percent of the amount invested. More typically, front-end loads for stock funds will be in the 4 to 5 percent range. Some mutual funds have no front load but come with a *contingent deferred sales charge,* also called a *back-end load,* which is charged when the fund is sold. The percentage charged often goes down each year you own the fund.

Load funds are almost always sold by brokers or financial planners, and they keep most of it as their commission. If you're working with someone who is giving you good financial advice, then he should be compensated for the time and effort involved. That's fair. But if you aren't getting advice, you shouldn't pay.

The hard-to-avoid 12b-1 fee

A *12b-1 fee,* named for the paragraph of the law that allows it to be charged, is a fee charged to mutual fund shareholders to compensate the mutual fund companies for their marketing activities. Now, I don't know about you, but I consider advertising and marketing to be part of a company's cost of doing business. I'd be really ticked off if, say, my grocery store tacked a surcharge on my total to cover the costs of its weekly ads. Nevertheless, mutual funds are allowed to charge the fee, and most do. Legally, they can charge up to 0.75 percent of assets each year under this rule, although most funds found that a really high fee leads to really low performance. A more typical 12b-1 fee is 0.25 percent of assets; back-end load funds often charge much more.

Management fees and operating expenses

Managing a mutual fund can be an expensive proposition. The managers need access to data to evaluate a company's investment prospects. They want to travel to meet a company's managers and check out its facilities. And, of course, the fund staff expects to be paid for what it does! In addition, an accounting firm has to audit investment results, and a lawyer will ensure that the fund's paperwork is right. These fees are charged to the fund in the form of management fees and other expenses.

Management fees can be quite low — around 0.20 percent of assets — for some types of funds, such as index funds (I explain these later in the chapter). For a fund with a complex strategy that requires intensive research, such as one that specializes in stock issued in developing countries, it wouldn't be unusual to see management fees of 2 percent or so. The other expenses for legal, accounting, and related work can be low enough to be nearly negligible for a very large mutual fund, but they may be material for a small one.

All the fees charged to a fund each year, including the 12b-1 fee and other expenses, are summed up in the *expense ratio.* That's the total percentage of assets paid to cover the costs associated with the fund. Obviously, the lower the better, but sometimes, it takes money to make money. (Loads aren't included in the expense ratio.)

You can't avoid paying fees, but you shouldn't pay fees that are so high that they drag down the fund's performance. Check out the fund's performance after fees to make sure that you're getting your money's worth.

How to purchase a mutual fund

Buying a mutual fund is quite easy. For a no-load fund, which has no sales charge, you buy shares from the fund directly. You often fill out a paper form and mail in a check; some larger fund companies will let you transfer money from your checking account through their Web sites.

For load funds, you work through your broker or financial planner, who will transfer money from your account to the fund company.

If you have an account with an online brokerage firm, you can buy many load and no-load funds through it. Charles Schwab (www.schwab.com), for example, has a mutual fund marketplace that allows its customers to buy a wide range of mutual funds through their existing Schwab accounts.

Tax considerations

Although a mutual fund is its own corporation, it's exempt from income taxes. Instead, it passes its tax liabilities on to its investors. Each year, the mutual fund company sends you a statement telling you how much you earned. If the money is in a taxable account, then you'll list those amounts on your tax return and pay the applicable taxes. If the account is sheltered, as with an IRA, you won't owe anything now, although you may when you retire.

Your returns from a mutual fund are the same as the returns from the underlying assets, whether they be stocks or bonds. You can find out more about them in Chapter 12.

When you sell the mutual fund, you may trigger another taxable event, a *gain* on the sale. If the net asset value of the fund when you sold it is greater than it was when you bought it, you'll pay a *capital gains tax* on that difference. In the United States, the capital gains tax is pretty low as of this writing (15 percent) — low, but not zero for most people.

Choosing Your Mutual Funds

When you invest your money in a mutual fund, you probably have some specific social and investment goals in mind. And that's fair. The fund companies spend countless hours developing strategies and promoting funds to show how each works for specific investors. Furthermore, under that ancient Investment Company Act of 1940, mutual fund companies must file a document with the Securities and Exchange Commission called a prospectus that explains all the policies followed by the fund. They have to follow them, too. In 2008, the SEC fined a socially responsible mutual fund company $500,000 for failing to follow its own policies.

Prospectuses are written by lawyers, and very few lawyers write like Scott Turow and John Grisham. Nevertheless, prospectuses are important, so you should read them when you make mutual fund decisions.

Mutual funds invest in stocks and bonds, discussed in Chapter 12. They fall into broad categories based on the types of securities that go into them. Social policies are secondary. Hence, a responsible aggressive growth fund will invest in stocks that are expected to appreciate in value, with those stocks also fitting predetermined social criteria. It wouldn't be appropriate for such a fund to invest in a model company that was growing slowly and paying a high dividend, because that company would not fit the definition of "aggressive growth." (And that would be a company that is expected to grow much faster than the economy in general.)

Later in the chapter, I supply you with a list of some of the many funds for socially responsible investing. For now, though, the following sections give you a rundown of the different fund categories.

Which type of category is right for you? That depends on your ability to tolerate risk, how much money you have to invest, and how long before you need the money. In general, people who are investing their money for a long time are best off in stocks, and those who can't tolerate much risk should invest in bonds. Most people are best off in a mix of the two; one way to get that is through a total return fund.

Stock funds

Stock funds, also called *equity funds,* invest in shares of stock of different companies. (Stock is covered in great detail in Chapter 12.) They are relatively inexpensive, relatively low-stress vehicles for getting exposure to a full range of companies, which usually leads to better long-term performance than most investors can achieve on their own. The objective is usually capital gains (from increases in the stock price), which mean that the fund managers try to generate profits by buying the stock low and selling it high. And yes, that's a little easier said than done!

Within the world of stocks, different funds concentrate on different sectors of the securities markets and follow different types of investment styles, ranging from conservative to risky. Because just about any investment strategy can be socially responsible, look through the following sections to see which strategies may fit your investment needs.

Growth funds

Growth funds invest in the stocks (also called equities) of companies that have faster-than-average profit growth, usually because they're focused on new products, new markets, and good expense control. These funds can be a bit risky; some years, the stock market will lose money or show a lower return than the market as a whole. When held for years, though, the down years tend to be more than offset by the up years. Hence, growth funds are often a good choice for retirement savings and other needs where the money can be put away for a long time.

Return is your reward for taking risk. The higher the risk, the higher the expected return. Of course, no return is guaranteed.

Index funds

When people talk about the market being up or down, they are talking about the performance of the *market indexes.* These are representative collections of stocks designed to measure the performance of the market in general. Among the better-known indexes are the *Standard & Poor's 500 Index (S&P 500),* which aggregates the prices of 500 large American companies; the *Dow Jones Industrial Average,* which tracks 30 very large companies; and the *Russell 3000,* which shows the average price performance of the 3,000 largest American public companies.

An *index fund* is designed to match the performance of one of the indexes, as good or as bad as that may be in any given year. To do this, the fund manager buys all the securities in the index, matching the proportion of each stock in the fund to its proportion in the index.

Many general investors love index funds because they're a low-cost way to pick up market performance. They can be problematic for social investors, though, because the fund managers buy good and bad companies because they need to buy everything that's included in the index. Nevertheless, there are index funds (and exchange-traded funds, which are special types of index funds discussed in more detail later in this chapter) that invest in specially designed socially responsible indexes or that invest in what's left of an index after offending companies are screened out.

International funds

International funds invest in companies that are based outside of the United States. Some funds specialize in certain regions, like Europe, or in certain types of markets, such as developing economies.

One class of international funds, known as *global funds,* invests in the United States as well as in other countries. All of these funds may offer exposure to higher returns from faster market growth and currency appreciation than may be available at home, although they may also have higher risk. This gives social investors a broader array of companies to choose from.

Specialty funds

Although the prototypical mutual fund invests in a diversified portfolio of stocks, some concentrate on certain market sectors, such as electric utilities, technology, or natural resources. These are known as *specialty funds,* and the fund managers tend to understand their chosen industry better than just about anyone else. These funds aren't diversified, though, so they can be riskier.

Some people consider socially responsible funds to be specialty funds because they target a narrow investing audience. That's not strictly accurate, though, because most social funds are willing to look at a broad range of stocks as long as they fit within the predetermined social criteria. Morningstar (www.morningstar.com), a company that analyzes mutual fund performance, sorts social funds into categories based on investments, not based on responsibility.

Value funds

The name of the game is buying low and selling high, so many mutual fund managers look for stocks that are cheap. The price of a stock may be low because the company runs into problems with a product, management screws up, or the business is out of favor for some reason. (Because these fund managers are often looking at troubled companies, value investing is often popular with investors who care about corporate governance, discussed in Chapter 7.)

Value investing requires a lot of patience while the shareholders wait for the company to turn around or for other investors to see how great the business really is.

Bond funds

Bonds, which are discussed in Chapter 12, are loans. The issuing company or government borrows money from the bond investor when the bond investor buys the bond. The bond itself is a contract in which the borrower agrees to pay regular interest and then repay the loan, known as the *principal,* at some point in the future. Bond funds combine money from many investors to buy bonds. Some bond fund managers buy a wide range of issues, while others concentrate in bonds from specific types of issuers or with a target maturity date. As with all mutual funds, the advantages of owning a fund instead of a bond itself are diversification and professional management.

Bond funds aren't appropriate for Muslim investors who can't receive interest, but most other social investors can find a bond fund that suits their needs.

Corporate bond funds

Companies need money to grow. They may need to build new warehouses, acquire related businesses, or make sure that they meet payroll while waiting for customers to pay. Many companies get the funds they need by issuing bonds. The key risk is repayment; if the company goes bankrupt, the bondholders may not get back the money that they loaned out.

Just as individual borrowers have their credit scored by a credit bureau, so too do corporations receive a score from a rating agency. Higher rated bonds have less risk but pay lower interest rates. The least creditworthy are known as *junk bonds* or *high-yield bonds,* and generally pay the highest interest as an incentive to the purchaser to take on the additional risk. Some bond funds specialize in bonds with specific ratings.

International bond funds

International bond funds invest in bonds issued by corporations and governments outside of the United States. (*World bond funds* invest both inside and outside of U.S. borders.) Some international bond funds concentrate on one currency or one region, while others focus on either government bonds or corporate bonds.

Municipal bond funds

State and local governments often issue bonds to raise money. These are known as *municipal bonds* (often shortened to *munis*), even if the issuer is a state rather than a municipality. To give these issuers a break on the interest cost, the federal government exempts the interest income paid to the bondholders from federal taxes. Many states offer a similar deal. Municipal bond funds usually appeal to individual investors in a high tax bracket. They're not appropriate for tax-advantaged savings plans used for retirement or college.

Some municipal bond funds look for good securities anywhere in the country, and others invest in certain states, such as New York or California. State-specific funds rarely make sense for investors in other states because the tax advantage will probably be smaller.

U.S. government bond funds

The U.S. government is the biggest borrower in the world. Although it spends more money than it takes in, it's also considered to be the least risky borrower in the world. After all, it controls printing presses that can be used to make money to meet its bills. Hence, many investors looking for safety turn to U.S. government bonds, and hundreds of mutual funds can help them with their investment. To distinguish themselves from that vast pack, many of the funds specialize. For example, some U.S. government bond funds only invest in bonds that mature more than ten years into the future, while others specialize in treasury bills, which mature in just one year.

Along with government debt, the U.S. government backs bonds issued by government agencies that guarantee mortgages, such as Fannie Mae, Freddie Mac, and Ginnie Mae. Some mutual funds, often known as *U.S. government securities funds,* specialize in these.

Total return funds

The goal of most stock funds is capital gains, while bond funds are usually managed for interest income. But what if you want both? The mutual fund industry wants to help you! The combo category is *total return funds,* also called *balanced funds.* These invest in both stocks and bonds, aiming for a greater return than is possible with bonds but at less risk than is found in most stock funds.

Some total return funds are structured as *target funds,* also called *lifecycle funds.* These are managed to deliver money at a set future date, usually when the fund investor plans to retire. The investment strategy changes over time to shift from riskier investments in the earlier years to more conservative ones as the target date approaches.

Money market funds

Money market mutual funds are similar to bank accounts in that they are managed for a safe return and can often be redeemed simply by writing a check. They usually pay a higher rate of interest than a bank account does, but they're not federally insured. These funds invest in uninsured bank CDs and short-term corporate and U.S. government securities. You can find out a lot more about them in Chapter 14.

Recommended mutual funds for social investors

Several mutual fund companies specialize in funds for the socially responsible investor, using different definitions for what makes an investment responsible. Here's a list of some that you can use to start your research. It's hardly definitive, and you may well uncover more funds, and new funds, as you do your research. This section has a list of a few of the many mutual fund families specializing in different social investing styles.

- **Amana** (www.amanafunds.com): Amana funds are managed to meet the standards of Shariah, the requirements followed by Muslims. The no-load funds don't invest in any bonds or stocks of companies involved in gambling, pornography, alcohol, or banking; these restrictions make them popular with some non-Muslim social investors, too. Amana offers two funds, a growth fund and a non-bond income fund. One of the company's more unusual savings programs is one to help people save money to make the *hajj,* the pilgrimage to Mecca that Muslims are expected to make at least once in their lives. Muslims are also expected to give a percentage of their gains to charity, and Amana will calculate that amount along with income, capital gains, and other investment performance numbers.

- **Ariel** (www.arielinvestments.com): Ariel funds have a strong value bias, which means the fund managers look for stocks that are cheap. They also look for companies that match the firm's values, as set by its founder, John Rogers. Ariel doesn't invest in companies that produce tobacco products, handguns, or nuclear power. Instead, it looks for undervalued companies that have a strong environmental record, are active in their communities, and have hiring practices encouraging diversity. Ariel has three no-load mutual funds, and it manages money for pensions, endowments, and high-net-worth individuals.

- **Ave Maria** (www.avemariafund.com): These no-load mutual funds target devout Roman Catholics who don't want to invest in companies that offer goods or services used in abortions or pornography or that provide domestic partner benefits. The company offers four equity funds, a bond fund, and a money market fund. The fund's advisory board members include former Notre Dame football coach Lou Holtz and Equal Rights Amendment opponent Phyllis Schlafly.

- **Calvert** (www.calvert.com): Calvert, founded in 1976, is one of the biggest and oldest names in socially responsible investment management. The company has a range of mutual funds, manages money for pensions and endowments (see Chapter 3 for more on these), and even handles microfinance investments (covered in Chapter 17). Its 28 mutual funds are sold through brokers and cover just about the full range of risk and return possibilities. Calvert analysts look at how companies rate on environmental standards, workplace conditions, human rights, indigenous peoples' rights, community relations, product safety and impact, and governance/business ethics. The firm also engages in shareholder advocacy, supports community banks and related development programs, and invests in early-stage companies developing new products or technologies that might solve various social ills.

✔ **Domini** (www.domini.com): Amy Domini started her career as a stockbroker who worked with clients who cared about the companies that they invested in. In 1984, she wrote a book on the subject (see the appendix for more information), and in 1989, she created an index that would track the performance of companies that had good records for their treatment of employees, customers, communities, the environment, and shareholders. The Domini 400 Social Index is often used to evaluate the performance of social investing relative to the stock market as a whole. Those interested in Domini's style can choose from the company's six no-load funds investing in domestic and international equity, bonds, and money market securities.

✔ **GuideStone** (www.guidestonefunds.org): These funds are designed to follow the precepts of Southern Baptists. GuideStone hires outside money managers to invest for the funds; they agree not to invest in any company operating in the liquor, tobacco, gambling, pornography, or abortion industries or that otherwise behaves in ways that would be antithetical to members of the Southern Baptist Convention. GuideStone offers 24 no-load stock and bond funds with a mix of investment objectives. One interesting offering is an S&P 500 index fund with only 486 stocks in it, designed to match the performance of the index without buying companies in the index that don't meet GuideStone's social restrictions. There's no Anheuser-Busch (NYSE: BUD) for you!

✔ **New Covenant** (www.newcovenantfunds.com): New Covenant funds are affiliated with the Presbyterian Church (USA) and don't invest money in shares of defense contractors, distillers of alcoholic beverages, tobacco companies, gambling companies, manufacturers of gambling equipment, and manufacturers of firearms. The funds instead prefer companies that treat employees well, support customers and their communities, and have a good environmental record. Among other features, New Covenant offers a program that lets investors use their mutual fund to fund their philanthropy, directing their profits to their church or other charities. The company has five mutual funds, all of which are sold at no load.

✔ **Parnassus** (www.parnassus.com): The investment staff at Parnassus starts by ruling out businesses that manufacture tobacco or alcohol, are engaged in gambling, manufacture weapons, or produce nuclear energy. With what's left over, they look for companies that protect the environment, respect employees, promote diversity, contribute to their communities, and do business ethically. The company has six no-load funds. One, the Parnassus Workplace Fund, specializes in companies that are recognized as great places to work.

✔ **Pax World** (www.paxworld.com): Pax World looks for companies that are all-around good. The company's two no-load funds aren't directly affiliated with the United Methodist Church, but the company's founders came out of that tradition. The fund's managers use a long list of social criteria to choose investments, including environmental performance, workplace conditions, corporate governance, product integrity, and community relations. Pax World's managers use proxies and other forms of shareholder activism to press companies for change, and they're committed to community economic development.

✔ **Timothy Plan** (www.timothyplan.com): Timothy Plan operates a series of ten mutual funds, sold with a load through financial advisors, aimed at conservative Christians of any denomination. The funds don't invest in companies that produce alcohol, tobacco, or pornography; that are involved in gambling, abortion, or impure entertainment; or that support gay rights. Timothy Plan offers variable and charitable gift annuities (discussed in Chapter 14) that follow the same investment principles. The company's Web site includes a referral form if you're looking for a financial planner who supports these investing principles.

Working with Exchange-Traded Funds

An *exchange-traded fund,* or *ETF,* is a fund that is traded on a stock exchange. Like mutual funds, they are regulated under the Investment Company Act of 1940, but they operate very differently. They are relatively new, with the first ETF coming to market in 1993.

Shares of these funds can be bought or sold at any time during the trading day by using a broker. The company that organizes the ETF joins forces with different institutional investor and trading firms. Those firms buy all the securities in the index, and then either sell shares in the ETF to others or hold them for their own accounts.

The price of each share of the ETF should track the performance of the index that it's based on, but it can also vary with supply and demand for the ETF itself. If the price of a share in the ETF falls below where it should be, the institutions that bought the securities to create the ETF can go to the sponsoring organization and exchange ETF shares for the underlying securities, then sell the securities themselves, locking in a neat low-risk profit. This is a key difference between an ETF and its closest sibling, the closed-end mutual fund (see the section earlier in the chapter for more on these). It gives the institutions an incentive to participate and helps keep the ETF shares trading at prices in line with the value of the underlying index.

Because ETFs invest in stocks and bonds, you can find more in Chapter 12 about how they get their returns.

Although the first ETFs were based on such long-standing and commonly used indexes as the S&P 500 and the Dow Jones Industrial Average, newer indexes are designed all the time to track very narrow market sectors or investor concerns. This way, new ETFs can be developed to meet new investor interests, nearly matching the array of specialized and sector mutual funds.

The big advantage of an ETF is that investors can buy or sell during the day to take advantage of short-term market changes. This makes them attractive to day traders. Another advantage is that ETFs can be sold *short* (borrowing shares from a broker and then selling them) for those who want to bet that an index will go down in value, or they can be bought on *margin* (money borrowed from the broker). Finally, ETFs are available on currencies and commodities that may be difficult for an individual investor to buy otherwise.

For lots more information about exchange-traded funds, consider *Exchange-Traded Funds For Dummies* (Wiley).

Exchange-traded funds are popular with many fund investors because they offer a lot of trading flexibility. They can also be cheap to operate, leaving more money for investors when all is said and done.

Unlike with mutual funds, there is no family of exchange-traded funds that specializes in socially responsible funds to the exclusion of all others. However, many ETFs appeal to different social investing styles. If you can accept that the sponsor wants to reach a range of investor issues, then read on for more information about buying, selling, and owning these funds.

Fees and expenses

ETFs tend to be cheap because index funds are cheap to manage. The company that develops the index does all the work of figuring out what should go into it and in what proportion, so the ETF firm simply has to match that. It's not unusual for an ETF to charge 0.10 percent or less of assets for management services, compared to 1.00 percent or more at many mutual funds.

However, to meet the demand for ETFs, new indexes are being developed that aren't exactly simple. The first ETFs were on well-known indexes like the S&P 500. Now, there are ETFs that specialize only in solar or wind power, or in intellectual property, or in value stocks. The more work that goes into developing and managing the underlying index, the higher the fees that will be charged. The narrower the ETF's niche, the more likely it is to have high fees.

Although ETFs charge management fees, they don't charge 12b-1 fees, the bane of many a mutual fund investor, nor do they charge sales loads. However, they can only be purchased and sold through a brokerage firm. Many brokers charge low commissions, sometimes as low at $10, to buy or sell an ETF.

Buying ETFs

ETFs can only be purchased through brokerage firms, although these firms vary widely in services and costs offered. Chapter 12 contains some information about this. These firms charge a commission or transaction fee each time an ETF is bought or sold, and some charge account service fees, too. To buy or sell an ETF, you simply call your broker or go to the firm's Web site and place an order.

When you buy shares of an ETF, or of any stock, you are said to be *long*. When you sell, you are *short*. It's possible to sell shares you don't own if you believe that the price is going to go down, and this is a crucial difference between an ETF and a mutual fund. To short an ETF, you borrow shares from the broker (for which the broker will charge a fee), and then sell those borrowed shares. Eventually, you'll have to buy shares in the ETF to repay the loan; if the repurchase price is below where you sold those borrowed shares, you can keep the difference as a profit.

Shorting is risky, because you have to repay the loan no matter what the ETF price does. In theory, a security can go up infinitely, leaving the short seller with infinite losses. Don't short anything unless you can afford to lose the money.

Don't short an industry just because you don't like it. For example, if you believe that entertainment companies encourage excessive consumption and immoral lifestyles and are run by people who care about their own power and perks rather than shareholder value, you may be thinking about shorting something like the Power Shares Dynamic Leisure and Entertainment ETF (Amex: PEJ). The problem is that even though you don't like an industry doesn't mean everyone else will shun it, too. You'll be short, they'll keep buying, and you'll lose a ton of money. Yikes! You're better off being affirmative, buying what you like rather than betting against what you don't.

ETF shares can be purchased on *margin,* which is a loan made by the brokerage firm (for a fee). Margin allows you to buy more shares in the ETF than you would be able to otherwise. This is great if the ETF goes up in value, and not so good if it goes down. After all, the brokerage firm will expect you to repay the loan no matter what happens.

ETFs trade throughout the day, so your purchase or sale will take place when the broker executes the order. This may be more or less than the price at the end of the day. For a long-term investor, this shouldn't be an issue one way or the other. For a short-term investor or a day trader, this can create opportunities for better profits.

Tax considerations

ETFs don't pay taxes themselves. Instead, any tax liabilities that the fund generates are passed along to investors, who then settle up with the IRS. In general, the ETF itself will have few tax liabilities, but a fund can post losses or gains when the securities in the underlying index change, often due to a company being acquired. This means that the fund has to sell the old security and buy the new one, triggering a capital gain for taxable investors.

The object of your ETF affection

ETFs don't come in nearly as many shapes and sizes as open-ended mutual funds, but the situation is changing rapidly. ETFs have become so popular with investors that new indexes are being developed specifically so investors will be able to find ETFs to meet their every need. The following sections offer handy descriptions of the major ETF categories to give you a sense of how you can use them in your investment portfolio.

Broad domestic equity

Once upon a time, all ETFs were in this category, which consists of funds that invest in a wide range of larger U.S. companies. After all, the ETFs were tied to the major stock market indexes, and they remain popular. (These early ETFs include SPDRs, for S&P Depository Receipts, on the S&P 500, and Diamonds, for Dow Jones Industrial Trust, on the Dow Jones Industrial Average.)

The traditional equity index ETF invests in too many different companies to be thought of as socially responsible. However, a handful of broad domestic equity ETFs invest in socially responsible indexes, which consist of a large, diverse array of companies that meet some predetermined criteria.

Sector domestic equity

A *sector equity ETF* invests in a group of stocks from a single industry or with a single investment strategy. For example, an investor may be interested in solar power, but that industry is so new that it may be difficult to select any one stock. An ETF on the solar industry invests in several different companies, reducing the risk of investing in any one.

Likewise, ETF investors who care about value stocks or growth stocks or technology companies can find ETFs that fit those objectives. This gives them the advantages of focused mutual funds with the flexibility of the ETF structure. Some may fit nicely into a set of social restrictions, too.

Global and international equity

U.S. investors took to U.S. ETFs almost immediately, and then they started looking for ways to use the ETF structure to invest overseas. Voilá! New ETFs were introduced to invest in stocks of companies around the world. Some of these ETFs invest in specific markets, such as Europe or China. Others invest in industries such as pharmaceuticals that are multinational in scope, so the leading companies are located all over the world. These ETFs make it easy to pick up exposure to international markets with good diversification to reduce risk.

Bonds

ETFs trade as shares of stock, but it's possible to buy ETFs on bonds. These funds invest in a portfolio of bonds designed to match the performance of a bond index. Although they're not as well known as the big stock market indexes, several indexes measure the performance of different sectors of the bond market.

Buyers of these ETFs end up with a diversified array of bonds to help them better weather interest rate and credit risks; they pay regular interest, too. Depending on one's social style, these can fit in many activist portfolios.

Specialty

Specialty ETFs invest in assets that can be difficult for smaller investors to get exposure to otherwise, such as commodities and currencies. These funds invest in *futures contracts,* which trade based on the underlying value of the asset, so the fund holder can invest in agriculture, precious metals, or the Australian dollar simply by purchasing shares of the ETF.

These funds have made it far easier for individual investors to diversify their assets. Because these sectors tend to be socially neutral, they may be appropriate in a socially responsible portfolio. As with any investment, do your research first to make sure the fund matches your social concerns.

Selecting socially responsible ETFs

If you are interested in socially responsible investing through exchange-traded funds, here's a list of several to check out. Consider it a starting point; new ETFs come on the market all the time, while others are pulled if the sponsor doesn't find enough interest from investors.

- ✔ **Claymore/MAC Global Solar ETF (NYSE: TAN):** Solar power combines clean energy and support for new businesses and technologies, both themes of interest to many social investors. This ETF tracks the MAC Global Solar Index, which tracks 25 companies from around the world that are developing products and technologies to make solar power viable.

✔ **Claymore/Ocean Tomo Patent (NYSE: OTP):** Many investors are inspired by the opportunity to be part of emerging technologies that can change the world for the better. Ocean Tomo, an investment bank that specializes in deals involving patents and intellectual property, created the Ocean Tomo 300 Index to track the 300 companies that have the most valuable patents relative to the book value of their assets. Claymore's ETF lets investors get exposure to all 300 companies in one transaction.

✔ **Claymore/S&P Global Water Index (NYSE: CGW):** Water is a huge concern for both the sustainability of the planet and the economic health of certain regions. The S&P Global Water Index measures the performance of 50 companies that supply water quality equipment and materials or that operate water utilities and related infrastructure. No one can make more water, and it's necessary for life, so this ETF may appeal to people who want to profit from improvements in water quality.

✔ **iShares MSCI USA Islamic (London: ISUS):** A handful of Shariah-compliant ETFs are on the market, but none trade in the United States as of this writing. However, most brokerage firms make it easy to trade overseas, and it doesn't hurt that the New York Stock Exchange owns the Euronext Exchange. Hence, this fund is an option for an investor interested in Islamic principles and exchange-traded funds. It is based on the Morgan Stanley Capital International USA Islamic index of major U.S. companies whose business practices meet Islamic law.

✔ **First Trust Nasdaq Clean Edge U.S. Liquid Series ETF (NASDAQ: QCLN):** The Clean Edge index invests in companies that develop advanced materials, energy management technologies, energy storage systems, or renewable energy. The liquid in this index's name has nothing to do with fuel; instead, it consists of stocks that are listed on the U.S. exchanges and have enough shares outstanding that they trade easily. This ETF may make sense for investors who care about energy and the environment.

✔ **iShares KLD 400 Social Index Fund (NYSE: DSI):** The Domini 400 index is possibly the oldest and best-known index of socially responsible companies; those who want to invest in it can use this ETF. It consists of 250 large, 100 medium, and 50 small companies that aren't involved in alcohol, tobacco, firearms, gambling, nuclear power, and military weapons but that do have strong, positive records on community relations, diversity, employee relations, human rights, product quality and safety, environment, and corporate governance.

✔ **iShares KLD Select Social Index Fund (NYSE: KLD):** The KLD Select Social Index measures the performance of companies that have similar characteristics to those in the Russell 1000 (the 1,000 largest American stocks) or the S&P 500 (an index of 500 large companies). If you're looking to invest in companies with strong environmental and social performance while avoiding those involved with tobacco, check out this ETF.

✔ **PowerShares Cleantech Portfolio (AMEX: PZD):** The Cleantech Index is used to evaluate the performance of 75 companies that are using technology to find alternative sources of energy, use energy more efficiently, purify air and water, grow crops in environmentally friendly fashions, and otherwise contribute to a cleaner planet. This ETF lets investors profit — or not — along with these companies.

✔ **Power-Shares WilderHill Clean Energy Portfolio (AMEX: PBW):** Concerned about carbon? Want to make money from the transition to cleaner energy? Then this ETF may be the right one for you. The WilderHill Clean Energy Index invests in companies that produce or will profit from clean energy and energy conservation. It holds a mix of battery producers, solar companies, biofuel producers, and related businesses.

✔ **Van Eck Market Vectors Environmental Services (AMEX: EVX):** Some environmental businesses are dedicated to preventing future problems by developing new technologies and commercializing alternative fuels. Others are dedicated to evaluating and cleaning up messes, which may be of interest to investors who care about the environment and community redevelopment. This ETF is based on the Amex Environmental Services Index, which is made up of publicly traded companies that handle consumer waste disposal, removal and storage of industrial byproducts, and the management of soil and water.

Chapter 14

Banking on Social Responsibility (and Insuring It, Too)

Social investing isn't limited to stocks, bonds, and mutual funds. After all, even your little federally insured bank savings account paying low interest is invested in something, but what? Is it an investment that supports your goals and values?

You can make socially responsible investment choices with more conservative parts of your portfolio, including cash and insurance, and that's what this chapter is about. You can also find socially responsible options for loans, because most of us need to borrow money at some point. Even if you're opposed to interest and think of insurance as a form of gambling, the ever-creative financial services industry has figured out a way to help you meet your financial goals.

In this chapter, I cover banks, banking alternatives, and insurance. After you know more about the role of banks, you may decide to move your CDs and money market investments to accounts at a community development financial institution. You may find new sources of funds that your church can use to finance its much-needed new roof. Or you may decide that you just want to buy stock in the bank itself. Any option is fine; many social investors find that there are a lot of different ways to invest after they clarify their goals.

Stashing Your Cash Socially

Nowadays it seems like all banks are merging into one or two humongous international institutions that have no interest in small customers, except to collect their ATM fees. Wouldn't it be nice if there were banks that still cared about the community?

Well, there are a lot of community banks out there, but they don't have Midtown Manhattan skyscrapers, they don't bail out hedge funds, and they probably don't even advertise on TV. Instead, they collect deposits from people in their area who are looking for checking and savings accounts, and then they lend the money to neighborhood homeowners, small businesses, and community institutions. These community banks really are like the building and loan in Frank Capra's 1946 movie *It's a Wonderful Life,* but without the suicide attempt and the incompetent Uncle Billy.

Work at a community bank isn't nearly as glamorous as it is at the go-go, high finance, global household-name bank. But what it lacks in gloss it makes up for in social responsibility. Many community banks provide financial services to underserved populations, work closely with small businesses and non-profit institutions to help them expand responsibly, and develop better housing to reduce blight and keep people committed to their neighborhood. They collect deposits from people in the community and elsewhere who want to earn a safe, federally insured return and make a difference at the same time.

That's not to say that the mega-banks can't be socially responsible. Many of the country's largest banks are improving their environmental, governance, and sustainability standards (see Chapters 7 and 8 for more on these standards). Not only do they trumpet their accomplishments on their Web sites and in advertisements, but they also have to meet federal requirements for community performance. Under the Fair Housing Act, banks may not discriminate on the basis of race, color, national origin, religion, sex, familial status, or handicap when customers apply for a mortgage; under the Community Reinvestment Act, banks must show how they're lending in their communities, and that information is rated by the relevant reporting agencies. You can look up a bank's status at www.ffiec.gov/cra/ratings.htm.

With most banks, you have no idea how your deposit is invested. Banks use deposit money to back home loans and commercial loans, or to invest in certain types of bonds (generally U.S. government securities and agency mortgage-backed securities; they are highly regulated institutions backed with federal deposit insurance, and only a few specific types of outside investments are allowed). Some banks offer linked deposits, in which the money in your savings account or CD will be used for predefined types of loans, ranging from agriculture to community redevelopment, but most banks won't tell you where your money is going.

That being said, three types of banks may be of particular interest to investors with a social style:

- ✔ Community development financial institutions (CDFIs), which commit to investing in up-and-coming neighborhoods

- ✔ Credit unions, which collect deposits from and make loans to a specific group of people

- ✔ Small Business Administration (SBA) lenders, which specialize in loans to emerging businesses

I explain each of these types of banks in the following sections.

Before getting excited about the different types of banks where you can hold responsible cash investments, remember your long-term financial goals. Bank accounts rarely offer a return that beats inflation. If you're like most people, a bank account should contain only a small amount of your total assets — enough for an emergency fund or money toward a big expenditure that you plan to make in a year or two. Of course, your situation may be very different.

CDFIs: A little help from the Feds

The U.S. Treasury Department regulates U.S. banks, and it has a special category of financial institution known as a *community development financial institution,* or *CDFI.* These banks are committed to the economic development of the communities they serve.

Most were founded as parts of urban renewal programs in the late 1960s and early 1970s to provide mortgages to homeowners who wanted to stay in their neighborhoods even as the big commercial banks were pulling out for the suburbs, leaving no local lenders. By 1994, Congress created the CDFI Fund to support the activities of these banks and their community development partners.

A CDFI accepts checking, CD, and savings account deposits from interested investors, and then it uses the money to make loans to homeowners, real estate developers, small businesses, churches, and nonprofit organizations in the community.

Many CDFIs even take deposits from major banks that want to participate in economic development (and earn credit toward meeting their Community Reinvestment Act requirements — it counts!). Depositors don't have to be located in the neighborhood; many of these banks will happily open a savings or CD account for an investor on the other side of the country who's looking for an investment that supports community development. CDFIs participate in the Federal Deposit Insurance Corporation (FDIC), so deposits are insured against loss.

You can find a list of banks that participate in the CDFI program at the Coalition of Community Development Financial Institutions Web site, www. cdfi.org. Some may even be where you live!

Earning credit at a credit union

A *credit union* is a nonprofit cooperative organization that works more or less like a bank. The members pool their savings for deposits and then lend the money to those who need it. In general, credit unions pay higher interest on deposits and charge lower interest on loans than traditional banks. Deposits are insured up to $100,000 by the National Credit Union Administration (NCUA), a federal agency.

Most credit unions are affiliated with large employers, but some are designed to draw customers from within community boundaries. The goal of community development credit unions is to provide easy access to financial services that help a community grow.

Often founded by churches or community activist groups, credit unions usually offer financial education in addition to low-cost services. Their services range from traditional checking, savings, and mortgage products to such specialized loans as *payday advances,* which are loans with a term of just a few days to a week used by people who run out of money before they get paid.

Needless to say, a community development credit union charges much lower rates and fees on these advances than for-profit storefront payday lenders, which often charge annual percentage rates approaching 300 percent! These alternative services aren't of interest to traditional banks, but they can really help people who are skating on the edge of solvency. (I hope that's not you.)

You can find information about community development credit unions at the National Federation of Community Credit Unions Web site, www.natfed.org. It not only includes a directory that you can use to find a credit union near you, but it also has information on investment opportunities for people looking to take more risk by helping community development credit unions expand.

Taking care of (small) business

Small businesses drive economic growth in many communities. In this very book you hold in your hands, I have one chapter on community development in general that discusses them (see Chapter 6), and another on *microfinance,* which is the process of providing very small loans to people in impoverished countries (see Chapter 17).

But what do you do if you want to support small-business investment or if you want to take out a small-business loan yourself? You go to a bank that is a certified small-business lender with the Small Business Administration (SBA, www.sba.gov). The standard loan program is called 7A; applicants work with participating local banks to borrow money.

Most commercial banks participate, but you can find the names of some near you by checking with your local SBA office. A directory is on the SBA Web site. You can make deposits with these banks to help support their financing activities. The more money on account, the more a bank can lend.

Shariah Banking

Islam is guided by a set of laws known as *Shariah*. It forbids its followers from charging or paying interest (Chapter 10 has more details on Shariah). That's okay for most ventures because Muslims usually can find acceptable alternatives: leasing a car, using a debit card or writing checks, working through college, taking on a business partner.

Buying real estate is tough though. It's hard to save up enough money for a house while also paying rent, but there may not be many suitable places to rent in the town where you want to live. Financing arrangements are available, though, and they include:

✔ **Murabaha financing:** This is cost-plus financing. The bank buys the house from the seller and then resells it to the prospective homeowner at a price that reflects the bank's costs of carrying it for several years. The homeowner repays the bank with a fixed payment each month.

✔ **Ijara financing:** Ijara is a lease-to-own arrangement. The bank buys the property and then rents it back to the occupants for a set number of years. At the end of the period, the occupants take the title to the property, in some cases after paying an additional but very low purchase price. Because the lease terms can be reset over the life of the loan, this can be similar to an adjustable-rate mortgage.

✔ **Musharaka financing:** In this arrangement, the homeowner and the bank buy the property together, and the homeowner then pays rent to the bank for the use of the bank's stake. With each payment, the homeowner also buys a small portion of the bank's share and eventually owns the whole property.

These arrangements are usually a little more expensive than a traditional American mortgage, so a non-Muslim would probably not be interested.

One of the largest providers of Shariah mortgages in the United States is Devon Bank (www.devonbank.com; pronounced *de-vonn* and not like the county in England), which developed the products in response to changing neighborhood demographics. The bank is in Chicago's West Rogers Park neighborhood, which was once solidly Jewish. The area is now home to Indians and Pakistanis, many of whom were first attracted to the neighborhood by the presence of kosher butchers.

Devon Bank provides real estate financing to Muslims in 31 states; it has competition in some markets as other banks see just how popular these products can be.

It's difficult to find Shariah-compliant bank accounts in the United States because of the prohibition on receiving interest, but it's not impossible. University Bank (www.universityislamicfinancial.com) in Ann Arbor, Michigan, has developed federally insured profit-sharing accounts that are similar to traditional bank accounts, but they invest directly in properties financed though ijara or murabaha arrangements, rather than in the loans themselves.

Mixing in Some Money Market Funds

The key advantage of bank savings accounts is that they carry federal deposit insurance of up to $100,000. If the bank fails, you get your money back. But in exchange, banks tend to offer the lowest interest rates in the market.

One alternative to a bank savings account is a money market mutual fund. These accounts are offered by mutual fund companies that invest your money in such very short-term, low-risk securities as U.S. treasury bills, jumbo bank CDs (which are too large to qualify for federal deposit insurance), and bonds that are about to mature. Most of the securities have a time horizon of one month or less, so there are few unknowns that trip up investors. Any major American company may be bankrupt in 50 years, but how many will go under without warning in the next 25 days?

Given the nature of the investments, there are few opportunities not to be socially responsible. Unless you don't believe in receiving interest, don't want to fund the federal government any more than you already do with taxes, or have deep concerns about the banks that issue the CDs, you're probably okay with almost any of the thousands of money market funds out there. And, in fact, most of the money market funds that bill themselves as socially responsible simply invest in U.S. government securities, making the investment decision nice and easy.

But many investors want social benefits from their investments, and that's what this book is about. A handful of money market mutual funds have a dedicated, socially responsible investment style. They are mostly affiliated with mutual fund companies that organize all of their investing around a social or activist theme.

For example, the Timothy Plan (www.timothyplan.com) offers mutual funds for conservative Christians who don't want their money invested in companies that produce pornography, support gambling, or otherwise operate in markets that are counter to their values. The money market fund carries that position through to its choice of corporate bonds that supplement the government securities and bank CD holdings.

Money market mutual funds aren't federally insured, but they rarely fail, either. Because most are affiliated with larger mutual fund companies, the companies have been self-insured against losses in those very few cases where a problem emerges. To do otherwise means a horrible loss in reputation and business, because investors assume that only the worst investment managers could lose money in the money market. The fund company's managers would rather pay out of the firm's profits than see that happen.

Some of the many mutual fund companies offering dedicated socially responsible money market mutual funds are

- ✔ Ave Maria (www.avemariafund.com)
- ✔ Calvert (www.calvertgroup.com)
- ✔ Domini (www.domini.com)
- ✔ Sentinel (www.sentinelinvestments.com)
- ✔ Timothy Plan (www.timothyplan.com)

You can find out more about the big, socially responsible mutual fund companies in Chapter 13.

Shifting Your Savings into Annuities

An *annuity* is a long-term contract that guarantees a payment over a set future time period. For example, you might buy an annuity today to pay you $10,000 per year for the next 20 years. When the time is up, you don't get any more money. Some annuities are based on your remaining years of expected life, which is a nice deal if you live as long as — or longer than — the insurance company expects.

If you want to supplement your retirement income or bridge your finances between an early retirement and the day you become eligible for Social Security, then an annuity may be right for you. Also, if you work for a non-profit organization or government agency, your employee retirement plan may be in the form of an annuity.

Annuities are usually offered by life insurance companies and sometimes include a death benefit that pays out if you die before you collect a given percentage of the money paid in. To some extent, an annuity is a cross between a mutual fund and a life insurance policy, and many of them have socially responsible investment alternatives. For more detailed information, you can check out *Annuities For Dummies* by Kerry Pechter (Wiley). Here, though, I give you the basics.

Examining fixed and variable annuities

Annuities come in two flavors, fixed and variable. A *fixed annuity* pays a set amount of money each time period, while a *variable annuity* pays a fixed number of units (kind of like shares), but each unit can vary in price. So if your annuity pays you 1,000 units per year, and the units fluctuate in value between $8.50 and $12.00, then your receipts can vary between $8,500 and $12,000. Because of the potential for appreciation, variable annuities may be a good choice for long-term retirement savings.

In a retirement plan, employees may be able to choose between a fixed annuity and a group of variable annuities with different investment options, including some with a socially responsible investment style.

Most of the annuities on the market are *deferred*. That is, you purchase them now, but they don't start paying off until several years into the future. If you pay into an annuity over time, say every month between now and the day you retire, you may be able to accumulate a nice chunk of savings. An annuity that starts paying from the get-go is called an *immediate annuity*. Investors often buy them when they receive a lump sum of money, such as a payout from a 401(k) plan or other type of pension.

Some of the many annuity companies with socially responsible options include:

- ✔ AIG Retirement (www.aigretirement.com)
- ✔ Thrivent (www.thrivent.com)
- ✔ TIAA-CREF (www.tiaa-cref.org)

If your employer uses annuities in its retirement plan and you'd like to see a socially responsible option, ask your human resources department if one can be added. Because many annuity companies contract with outside mutual fund companies for their investment options, you may find that the annuity vendor in place offers such a plan.

Managing fixed annuities

Fixed annuities are managed by the insurance company, and they rarely come in socially responsible versions. That's because the insurance company is taking all the risk of payment, and it usually wants the flexibility to invest anywhere to offset the risk.

Managing variable annuities

With a variable annuity, your payment changes with market conditions. Because you take on the risk of the amount to be received, the insurance company offers a wide range of options. With many annuity contracts, the funds are invested in affiliated mutual funds (which you can read more about in Chapter 13). And because you get to choose the fund, many variable annuity companies offer a socially responsible fund for your investing pleasure.

Variable annuities and whole life insurance policies (discussed later in the chapter) pay big commissions to the agents who sell them, and some unethical agents have been known to push them on people for whom they're not appropriate. Make sure you understand the expenses involved and the benefits to you before you sign on the dotted line. Most investors should maximize the contributions to their IRA and employer retirement plans before considering an annuity or whole life policy.

Using annuities for charity

Many investors want to get a tax deduction for a donation they make now to charity, but they also want to receive some income. For example, maybe you sell your house right before you retire in order to move to a smaller place, and you have a taxable gain on the sale. Because you're nearing retirement, you want to generate a little bit of income. If you make a donation to a nonprofit in the form of a *charitable remainder annuity trust,* also called a *charitable gift annuity,* you can get both the tax deduction and the income.

Here's how it works: The charity takes the money today. In exchange, it gives you an annuity that pays a regular amount of money each year until you die, with the rate based on your age and current market rates. You can deduct most of your contribution, but not all of it; you'll pay taxes on some of your annual payment, but not all of it, either. If you contribute $250,000 and the interest rate is 3 percent, then you'll receive $7,500 per year. Meanwhile, your favorite organization can use the money now.

Many universities and larger charitable organizations offer these annuities as a service to their donors, as a way to meet everyone's needs. If you're interested in owning one of these annuities, call the development office at the charity of your choice. If it doesn't have a charitable gift annuity offering, you may be able to set one up with the help of your insurance agent.

Whether a charitable gift annuity makes sense for you depends on your tax situation and how much savings you already have. For many people, it's a nice way to combine a donation with retirement income.

Investigating Insurance Policies

One reason people save money is to have protection in case something goes wrong in the future. Another way to get protection is through insurance, whether it be on your house, car, or other property, your health, or even your life. Insurance isn't an investment, but it is an important part of your total financial plan.

Insurance companies are, at heart, investment companies, and they're enormous. The Insurance Working Group of the United Nations' Environment Programme Finance Initiative reports that insurance is the largest single industry in the world, collecting $3.4 trillion in premiums each year and managing $16.6 trillion in assets. Those assets form the greatest issue for social investors: Just where does all of that money go?

But there are other issues too, including how insurance companies work with customers to manage risk and how they treat folks who make claims. I cover these topics in the following sections.

Following the money: How insurance companies invest

The insurance company starts its investment process by trying to figure out just how many claims it's likely to have in a given year, and it compares that to expected revenue.

For example, Allstate Insurance reports that its customers average one accident every ten years (you can blame the other, not-so-skilled drivers for these crashes). In effect, an auto insurance policy is a kind of forced savings account that takes into consideration the likelihood of an accident and the value of your car. The annual premium is more or less one-tenth of the expected cost of the accident you're probably going to have. If you buy a more expensive car, the cost of an accident goes up; if you have a bad driving record, the insurance company expects you to get into accidents a little more frequently. In both situations, you pay more for your premium.

Because the insurance company knows it will probably have to pay out on each driver that it insures once every ten years or so, it puts the money in relatively safe, short-term securities, most likely U.S. government notes and corporate notes that mature within the next ten years. This way, the insurance company can match the time frame of its claims with the time frame of its investments to get a good return while reducing its risk.

Other types of insurance companies have other types of time horizons:

- ✔ People with health insurance tend to file claims almost constantly, so the money from premiums is probably invested mostly in cash and money market securities.

- ✔ A homeowner may have very few claims over the course of owning a house, and these can range from relatively small, like the loss of several bicycles during a garage break-in, to the really large, such as a total loss of the house and contents due to fire.

- ✔ Life insurance will pay off just once, if it doesn't expire before you die; the insurance company has a pretty good idea of how long you're going to live.

With homeowners and life insurance policies, the insurance companies often assume that many of the policies won't pay out for decades, so the companies feel comfortable investing a portion of assets in riskier and long-term investments, including real estate, timber, and hedge funds.

Measuring an insurance company's social responsibility

It may be difficult or impossible to find out what an insurance company invests in, but that's only one measure of social responsibility. Other measures include how the company treats people who make claims and how it helps customers manage risks.

Satisfactory customer service

For many people, the ethics of insurance companies isn't related to how the assets are invested; it's in how people are treated when they file a claim. The customer is paying for coverage when the accident inevitably happens, but the insurance company doesn't want to see its profit go away. There's some constant tension there.

One way to get a sense of how insurance companies handle claims is to check out their ratings at J.D. Power & Associates, a customer research firm: www.jdpower.com/insurance.

Responsible risk reduction

Insurance companies have three ways to reduce risk. From most responsible to least, they can

- ✔ Work with their customers to reduce risks
- ✔ Refuse to cover people who are likely to make claims
- ✔ Refuse to pay claims

It's illegal for insurance companies to refuse to pay a legitimate claim, but that doesn't mean they don't try. After Hurricane Katrina, many homeowners' insurance companies tried to argue that the damage to their customers' homes was due to flooding, which is generally not covered under homeowners policies, instead of due to wind damage or looting, which is. A quick search of news stories can tell you how companies that you're thinking of investing in or doing business with approach these disasters.

Helping customers reduce risk and make responsible decisions often has the biggest payoff for the customer, the insurance company, and society as a whole. This can be as simple as offering discounts for drivers of cars with side airbags, because those reduce the risk of death in an accident.

On a broader scale, insurance companies can help big corporations reduce their current risks and long-term liabilities by helping them offset carbon emissions, protect their employees if they are operating near a war zone, and develop products that are safer for customers to use. After all, they provide liability insurance to corporations against problems like these.

The Insurance Working Group of the United Nations' Environment Programme Finance Initiative brings together major global insurance companies that are trying to identify future risks in order to start preventing or reversing them before they become big problems. It's a responsible approach that should pay off in a better world for everyone, including the shareholders of the forward-thinking insurance companies.

If you want to find out who's involved in these initiatives, you can look at the working group's Web site, www.unepfi.org; companies that are trying to do the right thing now tend to talk about it a lot on their corporate Web sites and in marketing materials.

Aligning your insurance policies with your social beliefs

When insurance companies talk about *personal lines,* they're referring to the types of insurance that individuals purchase most often:

- ✔ The property-casualty lines of auto and homeowners insurance
- ✔ Health insurance
- ✔ Life insurance

The social issues vary with type, and I describe those in the following sections.

You can use a backdoor way to check out the social responsibility of a company that you're interested in, and that's to see if it's owned by a mutual fund that matches your investing style or if it's included in an index that looks at the performance of companies that meet certain social criteria. If it makes the cut of people who are paid good money to check out the social standards, it may be a firm you want to do business with.

Property and casualty insurance (auto and home)

The social issues for these companies relate to how they treat claimants (see the earlier section "Satisfactory customer service"). Some may invest more responsibly than others, but it will be close to impossible to get that information.

Health insurance

The United States is one of the few nations on earth that doesn't provide government-sponsored health insurance. Or rather, it doesn't provide health insurance to people under the age of 65. Whether the government should provide health insurance is a different debate for a different book, but if you want or need health insurance, you may be wondering if you can buy a socially responsible policy.

The short answer is no: Many healthcare benefits are mandated by state law. For example, you may not want to deal with a health insurer that covers contraceptives. You can probably get a policy for yourself that doesn't (many Roman Catholic dioceses have health plans that don't cover contraceptives for their employees and family members), but you won't find an insurance company that won't cover them for anyone everywhere.

Likewise, you may not believe that blood transfusions, in vitro fertilization, or psychiatric medications are moral, but you won't find an insurance company that tailors all of its plans to your desires.

Health insurance companies can be responsible in other ways, mainly by how they treat healthcare providers and patients after they file claims.

For example, some insurance companies have had policies of dropping people who file claims in the first few months of coverage. That's why you should do a little due diligence and Internet searching before signing for a new policy.

Life insurance

Life insurance is coverage in case you die. Naturally, we're all going to die someday, but the real question (for insurance purposes) is when. Dying young is unlikely, but someone who does may leave behind a partner or children who need to be provided for. It's more likely that you'll die when you're old and have no one who depends on you for income, although plenty of older people have ongoing financial obligations to others.

Many life insurance plans have savings and tax-deferral features that may be attractive to some investors, especially those with a lot of assets.

Life insurance comes in two main types:

- **Term life** provides coverage against death for a specific time period, and then it expires if the insured person doesn't die or renew the policy. It doesn't include any savings component.

- **Whole life** provides a payoff when you die, but it also includes a savings component. Part of your premium is invested and accumulates at a guaranteed rate of return. You can then borrow against that amount; if you don't repay it by the time you die, the payout to your beneficiaries is reduced.

In general, you have no say in how your premium payment is invested. Some insurance companies affiliated with religious organizations follow social investing principles, but not all do. Baptist Life (www.baptistlife.org) won't invest in companies that support abortion, alcohol, tobacco, gambling, or pornography. Thrivent (www.thrivent.com), which sells to Lutherans, has no social screen on its investments.

Borrowing: Can It Be Done Responsibly?

This is a book about investing, but as long as we're talking about banking here, why not talk about borrowing, too? For many people, borrowing is a way to finance an investment, especially for residential real estate or education. If you're trying to be socially responsible in your choices of investment, you may be tempted to find ways to borrow along the same lines. Unfortunately, it's really hard to do that because it's hard to know exactly where your lenders receive their funds.

If your concern is that the source of the funds being loaned to you is some repressive dictator in a far-off land who cuts down trees and condones sweatshop labor, well, there's not much you can do. Those people are allowed to make bank deposits, and the bank won't tell you who its depositors are unless you happen to be bearing a subpoena.

If your concern is that the profits from your loan support the causes you care about, then you may prefer to work with the lending officers at a CDFI or community development credit union, which I cover earlier in this chapter. These organizations generally lend only to members or to people in their neighborhoods, however.

Several mortgage and loan companies tout themselves as socially responsible. In reality, these firms agree to donate a percentage of their profits or fees to nonprofit organizations. You may prefer to deal with a company like this, but there's nothing special about the loans or the sources of funds for them.

With all that being said about the limits of socially responsible lending, a different type of borrowing captures the interest of social investors, no pun intended. That type involves margin loans, which appeal to the investor side.

Many social investors, like other investors, want to take on additional risk, and one way to do that is to *trade on margin*. This involves using borrowed money to buy more shares, more contracts, or more bonds.

Margin is the money in your account that you borrow against, and almost all brokers will be happy to arrange a margin loan for you. It's great for them because it means that you'll use the money to make more trades and generate more commissions for the brokerage firm. If you ever hear traders talk about "other people's money," well, that's using margin.

With a margin loan, your own account is collateral. The funds themselves come from the broker's deposits and credit sources, so you don't know who is lending you the money.

If the security goes up in price, you'll make an even greater profit than you would have otherwise, but it if goes down, you'll lose even more because you'll have to pay back the loan — with interest — no matter what happens.

Taking the credit: Charitable affinity credit cards

A popular socially responsible personal financial tool is the *affinity credit card*. These are issued by banks under license to a charity, college, or other group. The group receives a licensing fee and a cut of the money charged to the cards.

The banks offer these cards because they get a warm, fuzzy feeling from helping out the community, right? No. The banks promote affinity cards because the folks who hold these cards are less likely to change their credit cards and are less likely to complain about fees because the cardholders get a warm, fuzzy feeling from using them. Typically, the investors who like these do so because they don't realize how small the donation is.

Warmth and fuzziness are pretty much the only attractions to affinity cards, because they aren't fundraising machines. The donation ranges by card but is often between 0.5 and 1 percent of the amount charged. That works out to between $0.50 and $1.00 for every $100 you spend — not exactly big bucks for your favorite cause. These cards often come with higher fees and annual percentage rates of interest than ordinary credit cards, too. And who gets the tax deduction for that little charitable contribution? The big issuing bank, not you.

You and your cause may be better off if you keep your current credit card, which I hope has no annual fee and that you pay off in full each month. Then send the organization a tax-deductible contribution for the amount of the annual fee on its credit card offering.

Because the contribution to the cause is small, don't charge up charitable credit cards with more than you can pay off in full and on time. Interest and late fees go to the credit card company, not the charity.

If you want to get an affinity card anyway, some of the many issuers include:

✔ Bank of America (www.bankofamerica.com/creditcards)

✔ Chase (www.chase.com/PFSCredit CardHome.html)

✔ Working Assets (www.workingassets.com)

You can also check with your favorite charity or your alma mater, because it may offer a card through another bank.

Chapter 15

The Responsible Side
of Real Estate

. . . .

In This Chapter

▶ Brushing up on real estate 101

▶ Investing where people live

▶ Counting on commercial real estate

▶ Understanding real estate securities

. . . .

*E*veryone needs a place to live, and most people need a place to work, too. As long as we have to choose one place in which to live our lives, these buildings and the land that they sit on are going to have value. Value attracts investors. And sometimes, real estate attracts questionable investors, like the stereotypical slumlord wanna-be billionaire with a bad toupee and worse taste in architecture.

Still, you can invest in real estate within a socially responsible context. This type of investing can rebuild communities, improve the environment, and provide housing to people who need it — even people with low incomes — and all without becoming a slumlord.

This chapter is primarily about investment opportunities rather than the purchase of a primary residence. It covers issues surrounding residential development and commercial development, as well as real estate investment trusts, bonds, and other securities that people can use to pick up real estate exposure. However, if your own house is or will be your largest investment, you may get a few ideas from this chapter on how to think about social responsibilities as well as the number of bathrooms and age of the furnace.

Regarding the Real Estate Realities

You may think you know a lot about real estate because if you're like most American adults, you own the place where you live. Buying residential real estate to live in isn't the same as buying real estate for an investment return. (No matter what your real estate agent may have told you, residential real estate isn't always a great investment, but if you own your own house, you can paint the walls any color you want. What's that worth to you?)

A real estate return comes in two forms, land and buildings. Beyond the two basic forms of real estate return are four categories of real estate for investors:

- ✔ **Raw land:** The land itself, aside from any development or structures
- ✔ **Core real estate:** Low-risk property that needs very little or no development, changes, or buildings
- ✔ **Value-added real estate:** Higher risk property that requires major changes or development
- ✔ **New development:** Highest risk property that requires a complete development overhaul

You need to know some basics about these categories before diving into the market. In the following sections, I tell you what to look for and how these different types of real estate can affect your investment decisions.

Like you didn't know this: Location, location, location!

It's the oldest cliché in real estate: The three most important factors are location, location, location. Like most clichés, everyone says it because it's true. The demand for people to be in a particular geographic location combined with the supply of places in that location is the primary driver of prices and investment returns. There's a reason that houses cost more in San Francisco, for example, than in Canton, Ohio.

Real estate projects, funded by investors, can change the dynamics of a location. That change may be for the better, or it may be for worse. Most social investors want to consider how a project works with the land and its current neighbors when they're making decisions about where to put their money. Whether a project is good or bad can depend entirely on where it's located.

Commercial shopping strips can add life to neighborhoods where people lack a good grocery store or a coffee shop at which to congregate, or developers can pave over open space and require people to drive for miles to shop at the same stores they can find anywhere. For the responsible investor, there's no one answer; it's about the fit between the project and the place.

The neighbors, by the way, aren't limited to the people who live and work near the project. They can include the plants and animals in the area, the people who drink water that may pass through the site, and the people who breathe the air that goes over it. Hence, an industrial project will have a much wider effect than a residential one, but that doesn't mean that an industrial project is inherently bad and a residential one good.

Landing on land deals

In general, land is a *store of value,* which is a type of asset that tends to vary in price only with inflation. (Precious metals are also stores of value.) But in some cases, the value of land can change, sometimes dramatically, up or down. If the parcel happens to be located somewhere that becomes more desirable to live or work, the demand for the property will go up, no matter what kind of structure is on it. Buildings can be torn down, but the land stays. Likewise, if the land becomes uninhabitable due to pollution or a lack of water, or if people can't make a living in the place where the land happens to be, then it will fall in value.

One of the basic categories of real estate investment involves *raw land.* Raw land is the dirt and rock that sits underneath the buildings. It may be productive if it's suitable for agriculture, timber, or mining, or it may simply be the underpinning for someone's house, office, church, or store. You should always investigate the different possible uses before deciding to invest in land.

In most cases, land doesn't generate revenue. Most investment returns will come from the change in value between when the land is bought and when it's sold.

Mineral rights are sometimes sold separately from the land. If you're considering purchasing land to open a (environmentally sensitive, worker-friendly) mine, make sure you're getting what you want!

Although Americans are used to owning land, that's not possible everywhere in the world. In some countries, people view land as something that can't be owned, like the air around us. In other places, much or all of the land is under the control of ancient landholding families; people who buy buildings enter into a long-term lease (say, for 99 years) for the land underneath them. And in some countries, only citizens can own land; investors from other countries cannot. If you're thinking of buying real estate overseas, whether for personal use or investment purposes, make sure you know the local laws before signing any contracts.

Determining the potential of developments, buildings, and structures

The building that sits on the land is almost always a depreciating asset; it will go down in value unless it receives constant maintenance. Water heaters need to be replaced, carpet wears out, and someone knocks a chair into a wall and cracks the plaster. Even with ongoing maintenance, a building can be damaged beyond repair by flood or fire, or become hopelessly out of style.

But unlike land, buildings can generate an ongoing stream of income in the form of rent. What you lose on depreciation, you may be able to pick up in the form of a regular payment. You need to take into consideration three investment categories when evaluating structural real estate for investment potential:

- **Core real estate:** This is how real estate investors describe holdings that are geographically diverse, have low risk, and require little rehab work. It may include residential buildings; institutional facilities, such as hospitals; shopping centers; and offices. Investors expect to receive most of their returns from rental income with less profit from price appreciation.

- **Value-added real estate:** This category includes investment properties that have higher risk. Usually, the properties in this group require big changes before they can be considered to be core. The building may need to be rebuilt or undergo a major overhaul. These properties may be located in places prone to natural disasters or in a neighborhood that's undergoing big changes. Investors generally expect to get capital gains from value-added real estate with some return from rents as well.

- **New development:** In a new development, the investors buy raw land or raze a defunct building, and then put something completely new in its place. It's high risk: A lot can go wrong during the construction process, and when it's done, maybe no one will want to live in the new housing development or move their operations to the new office. But high risk carries the potential for high returns. Investors expect to earn almost all of their return from price appreciation.

Who does the construction work?

When a real estate investment project involves construction, one concern socially responsible investors may have is who will do the work. Construction jobs tend to be physically demanding, but they also pay well — especially if a responsible contractor is in charge of the project.

In many places around the country, a commercial construction project will be done with union labor or with nonunion labor that's paid close to union wage rates. Construction work can be dangerous, so a responsible site will follow safe practices and mandate the use of safety equipment by the workers. Hardhats, gloves, work boots, and safety goggles should be the norm, no matter what the local laws require.

In the United States, the Davis-Bacon Act of 1931 requires that any contractors and subcontractors working on federal contracts worth more than $2,000 pay their workers at least the prevailing wage rate for the area, which is usually keyed off of union wage rates. Because many commercial and multifamily residential projects include some federal funding or tax benefits, many construction workers receive union wages regardless of whether they are union members.

Construction jobs pay so well because they are highly seasonal; in many places in the country, a construction worker will only have work for part of the year. If no new projects are underway, the worker won't have any work at all.

What materials go into the project?

A building is an enclosure of space. Hence, the responsible investor cares not only about where that space is, but also about what materials are used to contain it.

Most communities have zoning rules and building codes that govern the type and style of materials used. (Do I even have to say that a responsible real estate investment should follow local requirements or receive variances through proper channels? And that a bag of cash handed off to the alderman's campaign manager is probably not a proper channel?) In many cases, meeting the code isn't enough to satisfy a social investor. An investor who cares about the environment wants to ensure that the project uses more-efficient materials than are probably specified. An investor who cares about community development wants to see the use of local suppliers and local labor on a project that makes a neighborhood better.

The choices influence how the building will be used, too. Reusing materials may seem to be a more environmental choice, but not if they lead to inefficient operations and greater energy consumption for the building's occupants than using new materials. A floor plan that allows space to be reconfigured as a tenant's needs change may allow for a building to have a longer life than one that has less flexibility.

About a quarter of all the material dumped into U.S. landfills is construction debris: stuff thrown out when a building is razed and left over when construction is completed. Reducing the amount of debris by using buildings longer and constructing them efficiently creates big savings in landfill space.

Raising Responsible Profits in Residential Projects

Because everyone needs a place to live, housing is in constant demand. If the population is growing, the number of housing units needed grows, too.

Hence, residential real estate is a popular market for investors, and not just those who are looking to buy their own house to live in.

Residential real estate falls into three main categories:

- ✔ **Single family:** Single-family houses represent what most people think of when they think of housing. Although generally targeted at middle- and upper-income buyers, some single-family projects are aimed at lower-income and rental residents as well.

- ✔ **Multifamily:** Multifamily housing can fall into several subcategories, including rental housing, condominiums, and senior housing. The scale can vary significantly; a two-flat is multifamily housing, as is a high-rise condominium building with hundreds of units.

- ✔ **Second/vacation houses:** Second houses are built in resort areas. Almost by definition, the people who buy them are rich; they may be looking for a place to go on vacation, to rent on the side for some extra income, or to turn into a primary residence upon retirement.

Within these basic categories are several favorable opportunities for the socially responsible investor interested in real estate. I cover those opportunities in the following sections, starting with "Supporting Section 8 properties."

Supporting Section 8 properties

Section 8 is a voucher program operated by the federal government that helps low-income people pay for rental housing. Some Section 8 buildings are for senior citizens, and others are for families. Most Section 8 vouchers cover the difference between 30 percent of the family's income and 80 to 100 percent of the fair-market monthly rent. Not all buildings accept Section 8 vouchers, so there's a steady demand for developers and landlords to create more units that accept them.

Many Section 8 apartments are in *mixed-income buildings,* which have some subsidized tenants and some tenants who pay full rate. Some landlords agree to accept Section 8 tenants only when they have vacancies. Because the demand for these units is so great and the rent is paid on time, those landlords who do participate usually find that it creates steady business.

If you're looking for a socially responsible investment in real estate, Section 8 properties may be one way to go. You can buy them outright or participate through real estate investment trusts or partnerships, described later in the chapter. The rental income is usually good, and the property will provide a lot of families with an affordable place to live.

Participating in the public housing conversion

In many cities, the government built apartments for the poorest people. These projects were often high-rise buildings set away from the rest of the community. It seemed like a good idea at the time, but it turned out not to be. The isolation made it hard for the tenants to stay engaged in their communities, and thugs often took over the elevators, making residents' lives miserable.

Hence, many cities are rethinking their public housing projects. In many cases, they're being torn down. The land is often sold to a developer at a reduced rate in exchange for a commitment to build new housing that would accommodate low-income and higher-income families, the better to create a community.

This conversion of public housing often creates investment opportunities because it requires a mix of public and private funding to be successful. Done right, it creates a path for you as a social investor to improve a community. Done incorrectly, it removes places for poor people to live and forces them to leave the community. Many banks and real estate partnerships are involved in these projects and are looking for investors.

Generating responsible gentrification

Many cities have older neighborhoods that fell out of fashion years ago. At some point, though, a bright person looked around and saw interesting and well-constructed buildings, maybe close to downtown or public transit, with a lot of possibilities for a makeover that would attract wealthier residents.

This process of turning a poor neighborhood into one that draws folks with money is known as *gentrification.* Done well, it adds life to a neighborhood, creates jobs, and strengthens commerce. Done poorly, rafts of ugly McMansions attract people who don't want to mix with the current residents, draw generic chain stores that raise rents and force out local businesses, and cause property taxes to go up so much that longtime homeowners are forced to sell and move.

Gentrification can be done right, and as a social investor, that's what you want to see:

✔ First, the new developments and rehabilitation of existing buildings should be done with different types of people in mind. Units should be targeted to a mix of income levels with different-sized residences to appeal to different types of families. A longtime senior citizen in the neighborhood should not feel left out because only young families are moving in.

✔ A second key to good gentrification is gradual change. Every community changes over time as people's preferences in housing change and as the local economy evolves. Gentrification may speed that up a bit, but there will be fewer clashes between the current neighbors and the new ones if the changes happen slowly. That way, for example, existing businesses can make changes to cater to the new clientele rather than feel forced out.

✔ Finally, good gentrification shows respect for the existing flair of the neighborhood. If the block consists of old, small wood-frame houses, it's more respectful to build a new, medium-sized wood-frame house than an enormous brick mansion that stretches from lot line to lot line.

Supplying suitable workforce housing

In many expensive communities, the people who work there can't afford to live there. Some places are so expensive that teachers, firefighters, nurses, and even government officials can't find housing that suits their budget. If these people have to live too far out, they'll simply find jobs elsewhere.

That's why many places are looking to add housing that allows people who are already part of the community to afford to live there. This is called *workforce housing*, sometimes known as *affordable housing*, and it often creates new opportunities for responsible real estate investors. You can find out more about this in Chapter 6.

Cashing In on Commercial Projects

Commercial real estate includes office buildings, retail shops, and light industrial facilities (think screening designs on T-shirts, not steel mills). As a social investor, you may want to encourage certain types of development over others, or you may care about the environmental impact of different projects.

In some ways, commercial real estate is simple: You identify the need, build or remodel the building, find the tenants, and collect the rent. They write the checks, and you cash them. Hurray! But given that the building has to be constructed, costs money to operate, and may be more attractive to some types of tenants than others, there are some concerns that social investors may want to consider.

This section covers some of those key issues. These include environmental impact, space for nonprofit organizations, and access to public transit. Because commercial real estate is tied closely to community economic development, you should read this section along with Chapter 6.

Backing brownfield restoration

Brownfields are a hot area for socially responsible commercial development. These are old industrial sites that are no longer in use. Maybe the site once had a factory or a gas station or a meatpacking facility sitting on it. Redeveloping these sites is a good idea from both an economic and an environmental perspective. It cleans up the contamination and creates new opportunities in an existing community. But as good as brownfield restoration and development can be, it's not easy. However, government incentives and good profits await the investor who does it right.

The good news? Brownfields tend to be located in urban areas where the infrastructures of transportation, utilities, and workers are already in place. Further, redeveloping existing sites takes development pressure off undeveloped sites (known as *greenfields*) and reduces urban sprawl. But wait, there's a catch. Many of these older sites have possible environmental contamination that can complicate matters. Developing a brownfield site may involve environmental investigation, cleanup, and closure costs, not to mention an ongoing liability. There is risk, but risk leads to return.

Evaluating restoration risks

How real are these risks? It depends. (You knew I was going to say that, right?) Many sites have contamination problems that are easy to identify and straightforward to address, such as lead paint, asbestos-covered pipes, and underground storage tanks that aren't leaking. These types of cleanups are relatively cheap and easy, so some developers have made a tidy profit by finding properties that cost less to clean up than the purchase discount given for the potential problems.

Besides the opportunity to make money by doing an effective cleanup, the U.S. Environmental Protection Agency (EPA) offers brownfield developers money to encourage them to do the work. This can be as much as to $200,000 to assess the property's damage, with another $200,000 to go toward the cleanup of petroleum spills. Many state and local governments offer additional grants and subsidies to developers because they want these vacant lots turned into viable, tax-producing projects.

Insuring against ongoing issues

After the property is cleaned up, there are still some ongoing liabilities. New contamination may be found, or new regulations may have to be met. Maybe 15 years from now, for example, scientists discover a new cancer-causing compound, and it's found on the site, but today no one knows that the substance is a problem.

That's why investors in brownfields need to look for insurance. After all, insurance companies are in the business of transferring risk, and coverage for potential environmental liabilities is one that many insurers are happy to take on. This protects investors in two ways: First, it limits the ongoing expenses that may be associated with operating a brownfield project, and it provides some assurance that the project cleanup was done correctly. Insurance companies take on risks, not certainties!

Although the potential liabilities for contamination aren't known, costs of insurance are spelled out upfront and allow brownfield developers to shield themselves from costs.

Because of the potential for problems with unknown contaminants, brownfields are rarely appropriate for residential use, especially if the homes will have yards where children may play.

If you're investing in a brownfield, before plunking down your money, check to see

- ✔ How much research went into potential problems
- ✔ How well the cleanup costs are quantified
- ✔ How many unknown liabilities are covered by insurance

Setting aside nonprofit office space

One challenge many nonprofit organizations face is finding space for their operations. Community organizations, arts groups, and charitable service providers often have no place to operate. Because many social investors do care about nonprofits, there's an opportunity.

In some big community redevelopment projects, real estate investors who agree to create space for nonprofit organizations may benefit from subsidies or tax benefits. That's one way to do well by doing good. If the landlord allows a nonprofit to use space for no rent or for reduced rent, tax benefits may accrue from the in-kind donation.

Encouraging public transportation

Cars are expensive. They use up a dwindling natural resource, they emit pollution, and they kill lots of people every year. Hence, responsible development often includes elements designed to reduce the need for people to use cars to get between where they live and where they work, shop, and have appointments.

The easy way to do this is to locate a new project near existing public transit routes. The problems are that suitable space may not be available and many communities don't have much public transit anyway. Another option, extending existing public transit routes, is effective but can be extremely expensive.

Another alternative is for the developer to provide its own transit. For example, an office building may run a shuttle between the site and an existing train stop a few miles away. A suburban development featuring a mall, an apartment complex, and an office park separated by major highways can operate its own bus service so people don't need to get in their cars to go shopping on their lunch hour.

Saving in Real Estate Securities

Yes, real estate securities (such as mortgage-backed bonds) have a bad name because of some of the problems that took place with loans in 2007 and 2008, especially those based on speculative housing projects and made to borrowers with poor credit. But many real estate securities are fine investments, and some even meet different responsible investing criteria. Want to know more? Read on!

Making sense of mortgage-backed securities

A *mortgage-backed security* is similar to a bond in that it pays regular interest, but it's not exactly the same. Instead, the organizer pools together mortgage loans from thousands of people into one contract. People who buy shares of the pool (known as *certificates*) then receive a proportionate share of the principal and interest repaid every month.

The catch is that the cash flow isn't predictable; if someone moves or refinances his loan, the certificate holder receives the entire principal but loses out on the future interest payments. Thus, mortgage-backed securities have tremendous interest rate risk, even if they have little repayment risk. This could hurt someone who depends on the regular interest to cover expenses. The principal is returned, but that income goes away.

Why sell the mortgages in the first place? Well, it lets the bank remove the long-term exposure from its balance sheet while bringing in money that it can lend to new borrowers, thus keeping more liquidity in the mortgage market.

Mortgage-backed securities are of two main types:

✔ **Agency-backed securities:** Agency-backed securities are issued on mortgages that meet the credit standards set by Ginnie Mae, Fannie Mae, and Freddie Mac. (All of those firms once had stately names such as Government National Mortgage Association, but the acronyms quickly were smooshed into completely unrelated names such as Ginnie Mae.) These organizations guarantee that investors will receive the principal and interest due to them if the underlying borrowers default on their mortgages. All three receive funding from the federal government.

Fannie Mae and Freddie Mac were spun out from the federal government in 1968. They performed well for 40 years, providing capital to banks and creating good markets for mortgage-backed securities. But in the last few years, it seems that banks became sloppy about risk, and both Fannie Mae and Freddie Mac became overextended. In September 2008, the government resumed control, guaranteeing their securities and propping up the mortgage market.

✔ **Collateralized Mortgage Obligations (CMOs):** A collateralized mortgage obligation includes mortgages that don't meet the standards of the three agencies. This may be because they are big, cover 100 percent or more of the property value, or were made to borrowers with less-than-perfect credit. CMOs may also be issued on commercial or multifamily properties. A CMO carries some risk because it doesn't come with a guarantee of principal repayment. In exchange, the pool generally pays a higher rate of interest.

Because mortgage-backed securities are used to finance real estate, they are an option for investors looking to pick up exposure to the dynamics of the market. If your style of social investing includes support for homeownership, they may be of interest to you.

Relying on REITs

REIT (pronounced *reet*) is the acronym for *Real Estate Investment Trust.* It's almost like a mutual fund for real estate. Most REITs are publicly traded companies that invest in a group of real estate properties. Some specialize in just one type of property, such as hotels, while others invest in a diverse array of projects. Some REITs don't even invest in the properties themselves. Known as *mortgage REITs,* they buy mortgage-backed securities (see the preceding section for more on these).

Very few REITs follow an explicit social agenda when they select their hold-ings, but that doesn't mean you can't find some that fit your preferences. You can find out about the investment style and holdings by reading the REIT's annual report and then deciding if it works for you financially and ethically.

Selecting special assessment municipal bonds

A *municipal bond* is a bond issued by a state or local government. They can be issued for any purpose, but one category, the *special assessment munici-pal bond,* is often issued to finance commercial and residential construction projects. It works like this: The local government wants to attract new devel-opment to improve the community's economy. The government arranges to issue municipal bonds to offer developers low-cost capital or to build the infrastructure that the project needs.

For example, a city may build new roads, extend sewer lines, and expand a school to support a new residential development. It issues bonds to cover the cost, and then repays the bonds from property taxes paid by the residents in the new subdivision. You can find out more about bonds in Chapter 12.

These bonds might appeal to you if you're looking for socially responsible real estate exposure. They support community development, which is of interest to a lot of people.

Banking on the banks

Real estate investing is closely tied to banking. Land and buildings are expensive, so most purchasers need some help. Many real estate developers borrow money during the life of the projects. The need for funds not only cre-ates opportunities for people who want to invest in real estate directly, but it also creates appreciation potential for those lenders.

One way to add real estate exposure to your investment portfolio is to buy shares in commercial banks that specialize in lending to responsible develop-ers. In most cases, these will be *community development financial institutions (CDFIs),* which I describe in detail in Chapter 14. Some of these banks are publicly traded, so you can buy shares in them through your stock broker. For those banks that don't have public shares, you can profit from the growth of their responsible community development by opening a savings account or CD with them.

Choosing limited partnerships

Many real estate projects are structured as *limited partnerships*. The developer, who is the general partner, makes the decisions; the general partner brings in a group of investors who put up the money for the project and share in the rewards. On a larger development, one or more of the limited partners may be a REIT (see the "Relying on REITs" section earlier in the chapter).

Although limited partnerships are popular forms of real estate investments, they're not publicly traded and are usually only available to high-net-worth individuals. You can read more about limited partnerships in Chapter 16.

TECHNICAL STUFF

Calculating the taxable equivalent yield

The big advantage of most municipal bonds is that they're exempt from federal taxes and may be exempt from state taxes, too, depending on where you live. That makes it easy for state and local governments to raise money because investors will accept a lower interest rate if they don't have to pay taxes on the income.

Because of the lower rates, many investors are better off buying bonds that are not tax deductible.

To figure out whether a municipal bond is right for you, you need to calculate the *taxable equivalent yield* so you can compare returns on municipal bonds to returns on others.

Your taxable equivalent yield is found by using the equation

$$R(tf)/(1-t)$$

where R(tf) is the interest rate on the tax-free investment and $(1-t)$ is 1 less your top tax rate.

For example, if you're considering a tax-free bond that pays 3 percent interest and you are in the 28 percent tax bracket, then your taxable equivalent yield is 3/(1-0.28) or 4.17 percent. If you can find a taxable bond offering an interest rate of 4.17 percent or more, you're better off buying it and paying the taxes. Otherwise, you'll make more money with the tax-free security.

Because different people are in different tax brackets, what makes sense for you may not for someone else. Do the math first!

By the way, retirement accounts such as IRAs and 401(k)s already have plenty of tax advantages, so municipal bonds aren't appropriate for them.

Chapter 16

Getting into High Finance: Private Partnerships

*I*n the New Testament, Paul wrote that the love of money is the root of all evil (1 Timothy 6:10). Money itself isn't evil; just the misuse of it is. A rich social investor isn't an oxymoron, and social investing isn't just for the thoughtful middle class. Anyone can be a social investor, whether through a $25 microloan or a multimillion dollar commitment to a hedge fund.

Not only can rich people invest socially, but some of the most conscientious shareholders can be found among the largest pensions, foundations, and endowments. These investors are usually interested in investment vehicles that aren't appropriate for smaller investors, such as hedge funds, private equity funds, and venture capital funds. Collectively, these funds are called private partnerships.

If you are rich, hope to be rich, or are working with a rich institution, you may care about these investment options and how they can work in a social context. Because these investment pools can wield a lot of influence on the projects and companies they invest in, you may also want to know more about them so you can make better decisions about more ordinary investments, too. This chapter covers the basics of these high-end investment vehicles.

Deciphering the Structures of High Finance

When you enter the world of high finance, you'll find that the rules are different from other levels of investing. Hedge funds, private equity funds, and venture capital funds aren't merely mutual funds on steroids; they're completely different ways of investing (and with a lot less regulation than a mutual fund has).

In high finance, the funds are set up as private partnerships. Investment opportunities aren't widely promoted, and buyers have to meet strict requirements because the fund managers have to ensure that they aren't marketing an unregulated investment to people who would be inappropriate for it. These funds also have higher fees than many other types of investments. If you're considering putting money into these funds, you'll want to know more about them. I go into details about the various types of funds later in the chapter. Here I give you the basics on how to invest in these funds.

Putting up with partnerships

The three main types of private partnerships — hedge funds, private equity funds, and venture capital funds — are legally structured as stand-alone businesses. The fund's investors become partners in the business, although some types of partners are more equal than others. The arrangement is governed by a partnership agreement that lays out how the fund will be managed, what the fees will be, how often the investor will be called for funds, how often the investor can withdraw funds, and other factors.

Partnership agreements can sometimes be negotiated, giving some investors different rights than others. One area of interest to social investors is a *side pocket,* which is a part of the fund that is made available to some partners but not others. That means a fund could hold investments that would be objectionable to some of the partners without forcing them to own it. (Of course, a side pocket could also be used to give some partners better opportunities than others.)

The partnership doesn't pay any taxes itself. Instead, each year it sends the partners a report on IRS Form 1065 (also called Schedule K1) that breaks down the partner's share of the fund's income and expenses. The partner then pays taxes, or not, depending on his own situation.

General partners

The *general partners* are the people who organize the fund. They are the founders and key employees of the fund management company who put some of their own money into the investment. They are responsible for making the day-to-day investment decisions that govern the fund, and they have liability for their decisions. The general partners have to report their performance to the limited partners, but they don't have to take any input from the limiteds on the investment strategy. They receive a fee for their services and, in many cases, a performance bonus for beating certain targets.

Limited partners

The *limited partners* put up most of the money for the fund. They turn their investment over to the general partners, paying them a fee out of those funds for the management expertise and related expenses. The limited partners have little liability beyond the amount of money invested. If the investments don't work out and the fund declares bankruptcy, creditors can't go after the limited partners (but they may be able to go after the general partners).

Limited partners have little say in how the fund operates. They may receive regular reports on performance, but not much else.

Who can buy?

These funds are not for everyone. They are designed for really wealthy people and institutional investors who can afford to invest a few million dollars and still have plenty of money left over for near-term needs. If you happen to be in one of these categories, you can certainly invest in a hedge fund or other private partnership responsibly. Prince Charles, the heir to the British throne, fits the definition. He established a fund in 2008 to invest in sustainable real estate development projects in English cities. His charities will hold a third of the $2 billion fund, known as Tellesma, and other investors will contribute the rest.

Even if you're not royalty, you may want to know more about who invests and how. Limited investment partnerships aren't required to register with the U.S. Securities and Exchange Commission (SEC), so they can buy and sell securities and businesses without reporting most of their activities. They receive that exemption as long as they deal with investors who are considered to be sophisticated, and no one else.

Sophistication, under SEC regulations, is a function of how much money a person has. Pick up any gossip magazine and look at the pictures of pop stars running around without underwear, and it's pretty clear that money has no relationship to sophistication. (Come to think of it, Britney Spears lost money in a hedge fund investment that turned out to be fraudulent many years ago.) But go tell that to the SEC. Under its regulations, unregistered investments such as hedge funds, private equity, and venture capital can be sold to investors who meet the financial requirements of either accreditation or qualification (I explain these terms in the upcoming sections).

Although the SEC doesn't regulate limited investment partnerships such as hedge funds or venture capital funds, that doesn't mean these funds are operating in a state of anarchy. They're subject to contract laws regulating partnerships and fraud, tax laws, securities exchange regulations, and other regulations.

Accredited investors

To the SEC, an *accredited investor* is one who meets any of the following standards:

- ✔ Has a net worth of more than $1 million, owned alone or jointly with a spouse
- ✔ Has earned $200,000 in each of the past two years, if single
- ✔ Has earned $300,000 in each of the past two years when combined with a spouse, if married
- ✔ Has a reasonable expectation of making the same amount in the future

The thought is that a person who meets these standards can afford to lose money on a bad investment and probably knows more about investments than someone with less money to invest. Sure, that's debatable, but it's also the law.

Although a limited partnership has the right, and possibly the obligation, to ask investors for proof of their accredited status, many funds simply set their minimum investment high enough that just about anyone who invests in them would have to meet the standards. If the minimum investment is $10 million, it's safe to assume that any participating investors meet the requirements.

Qualified purchasers

The *qualified purchaser* standard is higher than the accredited investor standard, and it applies mostly to pensions, endowments, trust funds, and other institutional investors. It's simple: Those types of investors must have at least $5 million in assets in order to participate in unregistered investment partnerships.

Some funds of funds (see the section "The combo platter: Funds of funds" for details on this type of investment) allow unaccredited or unqualified investors to purchase hedge funds, private equity funds, or venture capital funds.

Carrying the carry and other charges

Private investment partnerships aren't cheap. In theory, they offer wealthy investors access to better-than-average money managers, and these managers expect to be paid for their performance. Private partnerships are also expensive to operate. The managers have to do extensive research on the companies they invest in.

A private equity investment, for example, involves a thorough investigation of the company; accountants and lawyers assist in assigning a valuation; and a proxy voting service helps track down the shareholders who need to approve the transaction. Many of these expenses are incurred regardless of whether the deal goes through.

The fund's profit is often known as the *carry,* and it can be divided among the partners in different ways. It's only one of the fees involved in these funds; the other major fee is the management fee.

Management fees

The *management fee* is charged by the fund's general partners to compensate them for running the fund. The fee is usually somewhere between 1 and 3 percent of the fund's assets, but some funds may have higher or lower fees for star managers or complex investment strategies. Most of the money goes to the fund's operations, such as hiring staff members, renting office space, and paying for research services.

Some of the fund's operating expenses may be included in the management fee, but other expenses may be charged separately. For example, legal and auditing fees are usually handled apart from the management fee. The partnership documents should spell out what fees are paid by which group of partners.

Performance bonuses

Hedge fund commentators often talk about *the 2 and 20,* which is shorthand for the typical fee arrangement on many of those funds: a management fee of 2 percent (sometimes more, sometimes less) along with a cut of performance — the carry — of 20 percent (sometimes more, sometimes less). That performance bonus is the share of the profits that accrue to the general partners, even if the general partners own a much smaller share of the total fund.

The idea behind the performance bonus is to get the managers working for the investors because they only make money if their investment choices work out. In Wall Street slang, the managers have to eat their own cooking. But there's a drawback: If the fund has a down year and the manager loses the bonus, he may shut down the fund and start a new one, rather than lose out on the cash. It doesn't happen often, but it does happen.

After all the fees are paid, many private partnership investors find that they're no better off than if they had been in a more ordinary investment, such as a mutual fund.

Exploring the Types of High-Finance Funds

As I explain earlier in this chapter, the world of high finance is defined by private investment partnerships that are closed to all but a handful of investors. Unless you have millions — note the use of the plural — these funds probably aren't suitable for you. But if you do have really big bucks, or if you are monitoring the investments of a pension or foundation that does, then you'll need to know more. Most partnerships fall into three categories:

- ✔ Hedge funds
- ✔ Private equity
- ✔ Venture capital

(Real estate investments are also structured as private partnerships. You can read more about those in Chapter 15.)

These partnerships aren't marketed to the public; investors often have to know someone to get into them. These funds are also not regulated by the U.S. Securities and Exchange Commission; that's one reason they're closed to most investors. (I cover the specifics of the structure earlier in the chapter.)

Because they have high minimum investments (often in the millions), hedge funds, private equity, and venture capital funds usually take big bets. This doesn't necessarily mean that they're risky. Some of these private partnerships take on enormous risk, but others are specifically designed to reduce it.

The lines between hedge funds, private equity, and venture capital funds are blurry. Just like clothing, investment funds go in and out of style. For that matter, a hedge fund looking for investment opportunities may make a private equity or venture capital investment, just as a private equity fund may invest by using hedge fund techniques until it finds a company that it wants to control. No matter the name, as long as there are investment opportunities, there will be private partnerships that go after them.

Hedge funds

A *hedge fund* is a lightly regulated investment partnership that's designed to get a high return for the amount of risk taken. An *absolute return* fund usually takes very little risk and has the objective of generating a steady return year in and year out.

A *directional* fund's objective is to get the highest possible return for the amount of risk taken, which means that performance can vary a great deal from year to year. Hedge fund managers like to talk about *alpha,* which is the incremental return that their investment strategy adds to the investment risk taken.

The existence of alpha is hotly debated in the investment world. Some managers do manage to add value consistently, but these folks are few and far between. They also charge high fees for their services, which can eat into that excess return.

For an in-depth look at hedge funds, I recommend picking up a copy of *Hedge Funds For Dummies,* by yours truly (Wiley). For the purposes of this chapter, though, here are the basics.

Tricks and techniques of the hedge fund

To earn a greater-than-expected return for the amount of risk taken, hedge fund managers often turn to exotic investment techniques and securities. Among these are

- ✓ **Short selling,** which involves borrowing a security, selling it, and then hoping that the price falls in order to buy it back and repay the loan at a lower price. The short seller keeps the difference between the sales price and the repurchase price.

- ✓ **Leverage,** or trading on borrowed money. This magnifies return, but it also magnifies risk because the loan has to be repaid no matter what happens to the investment.

- ✓ **Options** and **futures contracts,** which change in value based on the value of an underlying security. These can be used to reduce risk or add it, depending on the hedge fund manager's strategy.

An option gives the holder the right, but not the obligation, to buy or sell the underlying security at some time in the future. A futures contract carries an obligation to buy or sell in the future. Both types of contracts are usually settled with cash payments rather than the actual underlying security, much to the relief of people buying and selling hog futures.

Not all hedge funds pursue unusual strategies. Some simply buy and sell securities the same way that a more accessible investment, such as a mutual fund, does.

How hedge funds are responsible

Hedge funds are characterized by their investment flexibility, so they have the option to be socially responsible. Many are designed to meet the restrictions of pension funds or endowments associated with religious organizations, such as of a Catholic hospital or a Baptist college. These funds use aggressive investing strategies but avoid buying stock in industries that the fund owners object to. Other hedge funds target Muslim investors who may want a steady return without exposure to bonds or other interest-bearing securities.

One type of hedge fund, known as a *shareholder activist fund,* is of special interest to investors who care about corporate governance (covered in Chapter 7). These funds identify companies that aren't performing well relative to their industry and that have a board or management group that isn't paying attention. Of special interest to these hedge funds are boards made up of friends of the CEO, those that receive very high rates of pay, or those that lack a long-term plan.

The funds buy up shares in the company, and then use their large position to demand such changes as new managers or the sale of part or all of the company. The fund manager hopes to see strong investment returns as the changes are made.

Private equity funds

Private equity funds take stakes in operating companies. They often do this in the form of a *leveraged buyout (LBO),* borrowing large amounts of money against the assets of a publicly traded company, and then using those funds to buy out all the current shareholders. The firm then takes a breather from the public markets and those pesky shareholders with performance expectations.

Sometimes the firm is sold or broken apart; other times it returns to the public markets in a newer, stronger form.

Private equity in practice

Private equity comes in a few different varieties, some of which carry different implications than others for social investors.

✔ **Management buyouts** involve the company's senior managers and often other employees. The management group works with the private equity firm to buy a division that the parent company may have been trying to sell or shut down.

✔ **Hostile takeovers** are made by private equity firms that believe that a public company's stock price is undervalued in part because of serious mistakes made by the managers, including excessive compensation and chummy relationships. The private equity investors take a stake in the company's stock and notify the board and managers that they expect to use their power as shareholders to drive changes in the company. They then band with other shareholders or raise the money to buy them out.

The hostility of a takeover is in the eye of the beholder. Because takeovers usually happen after a string of problems with the company, they may prove to be better for the employees and community in the long run by forcing the company to improve its operations. In other words, a hostile takeover can look a lot like the corporate governance investing strategy discussed in Chapter 7. Other hostile takeovers have the explicit goal of shutting down the operations and selling the company's assets, which would be harmful to the people who depend on the company for their livelihoods.

✔ **Friendly takeovers** are private equity transactions that take place with the permission of the acquired company. The company's board may know that the business needs new sources of capital or that the stock price is so low that the company is vulnerable to a hostile takeover. The board would then find private equity firms that offered an appropriate amount of money to the existing shareholders and a suitable plan for improvement to benefit current employees, customers, and other stakeholders.

How private equity is responsible

Private equity funds can meet a range of different social investing standards. Some may avoid certain industries, others may concentrate on helping smaller companies grow, and still others may be able to structure acquisitions without the use of interest-bearing debt. Private equity can be a valuable component of employee ownership, community development, and responsible management.

Because many corporate buyouts involve employees at all levels of the firm, a private equity fund may lead to a more democratic and employee-friendly corporate culture. It may be able to create wealth throughout the organization, instead of concentrating it in the hands of a few executives. And because the private equity fund will probably want to sell the business at some point, it may encourage management to follow sustainable business practices that will create more long-term value.

Venture capital funds

Venture capital is money dedicated to fund new companies. It's often offered by funds that pool money from wealthy investors and then deploy it into start-ups that have promise and will benefit from an influx of capital.

Venture capital is risky, because so many new businesses fail and take their investors down with them. In 2006, 3.2 percent of all businesses in the United States filed for bankruptcy, according to the U.S. Small Business Association. The number is higher for newer companies, although precise data is hard to come by. And yet, a few of those small businesses succeed; some go on to create thousands of jobs and make enormous amounts of money. Microsoft, founded in a dorm room, now has a market value of $258 billion and generates almost $60 billion in annual sales.

The venture capitalist is willing to accept the trade-off of several failures in exchange for a few very successful companies, because the gains on the winners can more than offset the losses on the losers.

How venture capital works

Some venture investments are casual: The entrepreneur raises money from friends and family. As the business gets bigger, though, she may need other investors to help the business afford more employees, more research, more inventory, or whatever is necessary to get that company growing.

Venture capital firms organize funds and collect commitments from investors to fund start-up companies. Then the firm's staffers go out and evaluate companies that may make good potential investments. They talk to the management, research the products, and find information about the market potential.

If the firm likes what it sees, it will make an offer to take a stake in the company. It will prepare a *term sheet* showing how much of the company it would like to buy, how it would like to buy it, and any other conditions, such as seats on the board of directors for members of the venture capital firm or changes in management.

If the firm accepts the deal, the venture capital firm calls on the people who are investing in the fund and asks them to contribute their investment now. The investors write the checks, the money gets transferred to the start-up company, and the business gets to work on growing.

Venture capital firms don't look to invest with the company forever. As the portfolio company matures, the venture capital firm will look for an *exit strategy,* which may be an initial public offering of stock or an acquisition. That lets the venture investors take their profit, often to invest in other start-up companies.

How venture capital is responsible

Venture capital is often of interest to investors who want community development because it is intimately tied to the growth and development of new businesses. Some venture capital firms specialize in specific industries, such as healthcare or alternative fuels. And some venture capital firms avoid companies in certain industries, such as gambling or alcohol, which some investors may find objectionable.

The combo platter: Funds of funds

Hedge funds, private equity funds, and venture capital funds are designed for investors who have lots of money to put to work. The problem is that the minimum investments can be so high that even those who can afford to buy the funds may not have enough money to afford a diversified portfolio of them, or they may not have enough cash to get into their preferred funds.

A *fund of funds* is an investment pool that invests in several different hedge funds, private equity funds, and venture capital funds, and it can solve some problems for the less-rich rich person or the smaller pension or endowment fund. The minimum investment is often less than a million dollars.

How funds of funds operate

Most fund of funds managers choose one type of fund and style, and then research different funds to find ones that meet their criteria.

For example, a fund of funds organizer may be interested in hedge funds that aim for absolute return by using *macro strategies* (that is, looking for investments all over the world to play changes in global financial trends). She will raise money from investors who also are interested in this strategy but who want some diversification to reduce the risk. Then the fund of funds manager will invest the money in 10 or 15 (or more) hedge funds that meet the style criteria and that offer good return prospects.

Funds of funds are most common for hedge funds, but they can be found in private equity and venture capital, too. Very few funds of funds cross boundaries among the three types of partnerships, but it's not unheard of.

How funds of funds are responsible

If a fund of funds invests in several funds that meet the investor's criteria, then it's as socially responsible as the funds it invests in. It's that simple.

Traps and Pitfalls of Investing in High Finance

Investors like hedge funds, private equity, and venture capital because the potential returns are huge. But with that potential comes risk and limitations for investors.

Private partnerships aren't newfangled mutual funds that anyone can buy into, anyone can sell, and that report their results to the U.S. Securities and Exchange Commission every quarter. A few of the limitations involve all the fund types and may prove especially difficult for certain types of activist investors. I explain those traps first in this section. However, some of risks are related to the structure of the specific funds, and I cover those last.

Looking at transparency issues

Private investment partnerships are just that: private. They may not want to talk too much about what they're doing. The managers of a venture capital firm may be thrilled to make a big announcement after a deal closes, but they won't utter a word before the contracts are signed so as not to bid up the price. Private equity firms have to disclose to the SEC as soon as they own 5 percent of a public company's stock, but they don't have to say anything until the moment that happens. They don't want to say anything either, because a private equity firm's involvement can affect the value of a company's stock price.

Many hedge funds use proprietary trading strategies that they hope no one else has figured out yet. For these funds, with their high fees and high performance bonuses, it's important to keep an edge, and that often means keeping information about investments private.

That's all well and good unless you're a social investor who needs to know what the fund is investing in. Many investors are monitored by others who also want to know what's happening. A state employee pension plan may be forbidden to invest in companies that do business in certain world trouble spots. If that fund has investments in private partnerships that won't disclose their holdings, then it is unable to certify that it's in compliance with its requirements. A university endowment manager may be beholden to donors, students, and faculty who want to know where the fund is investing, and private partnership investments can interfere with those stakeholders' interests.

Some private partnerships will sign contractual agreements to concentrate in or avoid certain types of investments. Others will agree to disclose holdings information to an authorized person who may not be able to disclose the information to anyone else but who can at least certify that the investments meet the necessary criteria. This may be acceptable to some types of social investors.

Considering the liquidity, or lack thereof

Private investment partnerships aren't always easy to invest in. A prospective investor has to find a suitable fund, navigate the partnership agreement, and cough up a lot of money for the investment. Once in, the investor may well be stuck.

It's not easy to make a withdrawal from these funds because many of them have long-term investment strategies. A venture capital firm may have to wait three or four years between making the investment and realizing a profit on it. Until then, the limited partners had better hope that they have other sources of cash to spend.

That lack of liquidity can cause a problem for investors who change their investment strategy. Some social investors change their investment criteria frequently, especially if they try to respond to different international crises (see Chapter 9 for more information about that). A hedge fund, private equity fund, or venture capital fund may not have the flexibility that some of these investors want.

Monitoring governance in a limited partnership structure

Many investors care a lot about corporate governance. It's a key activist investing strategy (covered in detail in Chapter 7) and often a driver for private equity investments. Unfortunately, many limited partnerships have sloppy governance practices. Investors can be so happy to get into the next big thing that they don't ask questions, and the fund managers can be so greedy that they cut corners. Most of these types of fund are fine, but not all are.

So what can you do? The first is to check to make sure that the partnership agreement includes some oversight in the form of annual performance audits, an outside custodian to hold the securities, and the use of bona fide brokerage firms for trading. The second is to do background checks and other due diligence on the fund's key staffers before making an investment to make sure they don't have a history of problems that will follow them.

Pinpointing problems with each fund type

As I explain in the previous sections, just as private partnerships have a great deal in common in their investment strategies, so, too, do they have a lot in common in terms of potential problems for investors. However, each type of partnership also has its own problems that you need to understand before relying too heavily on one particular type of fund. Here I give you an overview of those problems.

Hedge fund pitfalls

Because hedge funds follow so many different types of investment strategies, some can serve the needs of social investors quite well. But not all of them can, and you need to know the risks before you invest:

- Hedge funds charge high fees, and it's not clear whether most of them generate investment returns that are high enough to offset those fees.

- Hedge funds don't have to disclose their investments publicly, and many will not, which can cause problems for investors who want some assurance about where, exactly, their money is invested (see the earlier section "Looking at transparency issues" for more on this point).

- Some stakeholders hear "hedge fund" and panic; they associate it with ugly trading tactics, high risk, and obscene profits. These people should be given a copy of *Hedge Funds For Dummies* (Wiley) forthwith.

Private equity pitfalls

Not all private equity funds will fit your definition of responsibility. Many of them intend to make over companies, which may lead to massive layoffs, renegotiations of pensions and other employee benefits, relocation of operations to low-cost locations, or even shutting down the business and selling all the assets. This can cause enormous disruption to employees and communities.

Most private equity funds are upfront with investors about what types of businesses they plan to pursue and how they'll change the operations. Investors can also investigate where fund employees worked before and what they did; a private equity fund organized by people who specialized in hostile takeovers at an investment bank will probably have a different perspective than one organized by people who have experience turning around troubled companies.

Venture capitalism pitfalls

One of the biggest problems with venture capital is that sometimes there just aren't a lot of good ideas out there. A venture capital fund can be formed to fund new green technologies, for example, but if no entrepreneurs have good ideas, the money won't be invested. Many a venture capital investor has been disappointed to find that the money committed is never invested, although that's better than having the money put toward worthless ideas.

Venture capital firms, in their zeal to put money to work, have been known to give start-ups too much money. It's a problem most entrepreneurs would love to have, but it is a problem: Companies that have money to spend will sometimes spend it foolishly. Instead of spending money to attend trade shows, they'll buy an ad during the Super Bowl broadcast!

Finally, the biggest risk of venture investing goes to the very heart of what it is: taking a chance on small businesses, knowing that most will fail but a few will succeed beyond the founders' wildest dreams. Returns on investment can vary from year to year, and they can often be negative.

It's not always sweetness and light in the venture capital world, because the fund's goal is to make money. Venture capital firms have been known to come in and fire all the employees, make radical changes in a company's direction, or even shut down a portfolio company if the venture capitalists believe it's worth more dead than alive. "Responsible" is not a synonym for "nice."

Funds of funds pitfalls

Funds of funds solve some problems inherent in the other types of private partnerships, but it will cost you. The first expense is that of management fees. Each of the underlying funds will have its own management fees and expenses (which are covered in more detail in the "Carrying the carry and other charges" section earlier in this chapter), and then the fund of funds manager will charge additional fees for his services. Those fees can eat into investment returns right quick.

Another pitfall of special concern to a social investor is the loss of oversight. The more people involved, the harder it can be to ensure that all the funds are managing money exactly the way they're supposed to.

Chapter 17

Making a Difference with Microfinance

Much of this book is about medium and high finance: using socially responsible investment techniques to pick mutual funds, sort out bank loans, or make venture capital investments. To play, you need thousands of dollars or more.

One of the most interesting areas of social investing doesn't require thousands or even hundreds of dollars. You can play for tens. It's *microfinance* (also called *microcredit* or *microlending*), which involves lending small amounts of money to people who need the smallest of boosts to get out of poverty. Maybe the investment goes to a few chickens to launch a business selling eggs, a bicycle to help a lunch stand launch a delivery service, or a cellphone to help a fisherman find the best market for the day's catch.

These are simple needs that fill enormous gaps in the global economy. In this chapter, I tell you about ways you can combine investing and philanthropy for your own microfinancing, whether it's for profit or pure charity. The financial returns may be small, but they are real, and the social returns are infinite.

Looking at How Microfinance Works

In economic development circles, microfinance is defined as the supply of loans, savings, and other basic financial services to the poor. It includes low-balance checking accounts, cellphone money transfer services, and simplified paperwork to accommodate people with low literacy.

Without microfinance, poor people are stuck. They can't get the money they need to grow businesses or receive an education. Banks won't lend to them; local thugs might, but such loans can carry a cost that's a lot higher than the high stated interest.

Impoverished people often have to keep what money they do have in the form of jewelry or livestock. Unfortunately, jewelry can be stolen, and livestock can sicken, die, or wander off. These items are hard to sell to raise funds; you really can't sell half of a goat unless you're ready to butcher it. Livestock can be productive, but jewelry doesn't do any work for you. People living in these conditions end up making small amounts of money and putting whatever they do have in bangle bracelets or bullocks rather than making a return the way people in developed countries do: lending or investing unneeded money to those who want to improve their lives or start new businesses.

In the following sections, I explain who benefits from these small loans and how banks make sure they're lending money to responsible borrowers.

Included in this chapter is a list of some microfinance funds and related programs that accept investments from individual investors. Some allow investors to get started for $25 and encourage people to open accounts as gifts for that hard-to-shop-for relative. (I started my career as a microlender with a gift certificate to a microfinance company that I received from my family for Mother's Day; I loaned it to a dressmaker in Nigeria who needed a new sewing machine. We'll see in a year if she repays me.)

Inspiring people to help themselves

A key tenet of microfinance is that poor people don't want to be poor; they are smart people who are willing to work hard and who want better lives for themselves and their families. They don't need handouts; they simply need access to the same financial services that wealthier people have, scaled down for their smaller resources. Just as the owner of a clothing boutique in the United States might need a line of credit to afford new inventory, so would the operator of a clothing kiosk in Ghana. The difference is that one is selling $250 designer jeans and the other is selling used clothing (possibly last year's designer jeans from the same boutique where the owner tired of and donated them to a charity that sold them to an international distributor to raise funds).

Much of the success of microfinance has been in providing economic opportunities for women, who often have been shut out of traditional financial services no matter how good their investment ideas. Many of these women want home-based businesses because they retain primary responsibility for the care of their families and houses. Microfinance has allowed women to sell homemade tortillas to local restaurants, open a beauty salon in their front room, or make traditional jewelry that can be sold at gift shops in tourist areas. These ventures allow them to improve their families' lives and increase their social and political power.

Microfinance isn't just for international development. Many entrepreneurs in developed countries need just a little bit of money for their business, maybe to buy supplies to start a nail salon or computers to get a secretarial service up and running. These people probably don't want enough money to qualify for a standard small-business loan from a bank; if they use their credit cards, they'll pay higher interest than they might otherwise need to pay.

Setting up and funding microfinance institutions

With most microfinance arrangements, investors place their money in an investment fund (called a *microfinance fund*) managed in their home country. The fund managers then form partnerships with organizations in the community that will receive the money, known as *microfinance institutions (MFIs),* which have a better sense of the economy in a developing country than the investors do.

The microfinance fund is used to capitalize microfinance loans. The funds can be loaned directly with the help of an MFI, or they can be used as a *loan guarantee fund* that the MFI can use as a reserve. If the MFI uses the money as a reserve, it can loan out a larger percentage of its deposits than might otherwise be practical. Some microfinance funds buy interests in the loans, giving the MFI capital to lend more money before the current loans are repaid.

MFIs are responsible for identifying borrowers with worthy projects, approving the loans, and collecting the payments. In some cases, the MFI eventually takes in enough bank deposits from its customers that it can operate without outside investors. Most MFIs also provide additional services to their communities, ranging from business training to healthcare and preschools. Some MFIs are set up as nonprofit institutions and accept charitable donations to help them fund their nonlending support programs.

Researching small-business people

Loans of all sizes involve a lot of upfront research. Think of any loan application you may have filled out over the years. You have to give your name and address and Social Security number. For a house, you have to include an appraisal verifying that the purchase price is in line with its actual value. For a car loan, you have to show your driver's license and proof of insurance. For a student loan, you need to show proof of registration. Before cutting you a check, the lender needs to know that you're likely to repay the money because you're a responsible person and the money will be put to good use.

Microfinance involves similar amounts of upfront work. Applications are made, often by folks with limited literacy. Someone needs to verify who these people are, investigate their reputation for financial responsibility, and check on the project to ensure that it's viable. That's why MFIs have staff in the communities to meet the borrowers. Grameen Bank, the original MFI that started in Bangladesh, refers to its loan officers as "bicycle bankers" who ride around and get to know their customers wherever they are.

Creating and counting on collateral

Lenders want to know that a borrower will be able to repay his loan, so they look at the *collateral* that backs it up. This may be a bank account with funds that could be used to make the payment, or it may be the asset that is going to be bought with the loan. For example, if you don't make your car payments, the friendly neighborhood repo man will come to take your car — the collateral — away.

Really poor people don't have capital assets. That's a defining part of poverty. They don't have a car that can be taken away or a bank account that can be seized. An MFI may be a socially conscious institution, but it still works with investors who are looking for a return. Microfinance only works if the loans are repaid.

One way that many MFIs help their poor customers create collateral and start building their way out of poverty is through *compulsory savings accounts.* Borrowers have to take a set percentage of their loan proceeds and put the money into a savings account. The money can't be touched until the entire loan is repaid. So the borrower ends up with some new collateral to use toward the next loan or has savings that he can apply to whatever goals he has. Because the savings earns some interest, it helps subsidize the loan payments, too.

Another way MFIs manage the lack of collateral on a microloan is through a *prompt payment incentive.* This is additional interest charged on the loan, but it's returned to the borrower if the loan is repaid on time. Like the compulsory savings account, it also helps the borrower generate a little bit of surplus capital that can be spent personally or reinvested in the business.

Some MFIs require *personal guarantees,* especially if the MFI is well established in the community and has a network of customers who can vouch for new borrowers. With a personal guarantee, a third party co-signs for the loan and becomes liable if the borrower is unable to pay.

Joining with other entrepreneurs

Many MFIs require that their borrowers join groups of other borrowers. The relationships between borrowers give the new entrepreneurs organized support similar to the networks that businesspeople in developed nations rely on. The businesspeople work together to make their communities better, to share business ideas, and to help ensure that the loans get repaid. Part of Grameen Bank's success resulted from the communities of entrepreneurs that were created in little towns all over Bangladesh.

Businesspeople the world over form networks to help them advance their own careers and promote their business and profession. I have memberships in the CFA Institute, which represents financial analysts, and Chicago Women in Publishing, which helps advance the careers of people working with words in my windy city. I get together for lunch with other writers and financial people whom I know, so we can share ideas, celebrate successes, and commiserate when things aren't going well. Thanks to MFIs, people in developing countries can establish the same types of connections.

Some MFIs issue loans to the group rather than to the individuals in it. Others issue loans to the individuals but ask the group to guarantee the loan. No member of the group receives additional money until all the loans are repaid. This creates a network of people willing to vouch for the borrower's responsibility. Think of it as a low-tech version of a credit score from one of the big American credit-rating agencies. It also generates some peer pressure to help ensure that the loan gets repaid. A borrower may be willing to stiff a nongovernmental organization backed by rich investors in Europe, but not if it means losing the neighbors' respect. Even worse, if default means that the neighbors have to cover the loan, the borrower won't exactly be welcome at block parties.

In addition to making loans and establishing entrepreneur networks, MFIs often provide training to groups of borrowers on such topics as writing business plans, setting prices, doing competitive research, and managing employees.

Peer-to-peer lending

Some MFIs become so large that they no longer need the support of outside investors. That's bad news for the socially responsible investor like you who wants to make money helping small-business people break out of poverty, but it's great news for the MFI because it means the mission has been fulfilled. An MFI that no longer needs outside investor partners is one that has generated enough growth in a community that it can now fund its own loans. As the entrepreneurs become successful, they have enough surplus funds that they can save some of them. The MFI can then lend those funds, generating a return for the local savers rather than for you, the socially responsible investor in a far-off land.

"But wait," you may be thinking. "If people borrowed money and then repaid it, where did the community find enough extra money so it no longer needs investors' help?" The money was created in the banking system. Here's how it works: Say you put $100 in the bank. The bank is required to keep 10 percent on reserve, but it can loan out the other $90. You have your $100 deposit, and the borrower has her $90, so the total amount of money in the system is now $190. Voilá! That's how savings can help an economy grow, in Boston and Bolivia alike.

To keep the focus on community development and individual empowerment, a large MFI will turn to *peer-to-peer lending.* Under this, the current borrowers and depositors decide if a project is worth funding. They help direct where their investments go. This gives the savers a bigger stake in the growth of their communities and ties the borrowers more closely to the source of the funds. In some cases, a successful group will have enough funds to make its own loans, and it can help the MFI by evaluating applications to determine who the new members should be.

This was the original model for savings and loans in the United States. These institutions collected deposits from local savers, made loans to local homeowners and businesses, and had boards of directors made up of prominent community businesspeople.

Bracing Yourself for Microfinance Risks and Ethical Bumps

Microfinance is often promoted as the ideal solution to the problems of the poor. It builds financial institutions to meet the needs of ordinary people, creates new businesses that lead to economic growth, and it does it all with a taxable return to the investors.

It's a powerful method for making the world a better place, but microfinance isn't perfect. If you're going to invest in microfinance, you should think about the risks and issues involved to make sure they don't bump heads with your values.

Because microfinance involves making loans to people who are at the lowest levels of wealth and income, the risk is great that the lender takes advantage of the borrower. That's why some social investors are leery of microfinance.

The biggest concern is the relatively high fees and interest rates that lenders sometimes charge. Another big concern is that repayment of the loan is sometimes more important than whether the borrower received anything of long-term economic value from it. (Plenty of people use their credit cards to buy rounds of drinks in bars on Friday night; they may pay off the credit card in full and on time, but it's hard to say that any real economic development took place with that loan.) I cover these and other concerns in the following sections.

Poverty is a complex problem with no one solution. Microcredit can make a difference to some people, but not to everyone. It's just one tool used to fight poverty, and it's just one tactic that socially responsible investors and philanthropically minded individuals can use.

Dealing with high interest rates and fees

One of the biggest concerns about microfinance is that the interest and fees charged to borrowers are big relative to the size of the loans. A $10 application fee, for example, represents just 1 percent of a $1,000 loan but 10 percent of a $100 loan. These rates can cause a lot of consternation to borrowers, who don't have much money to begin with, and to lenders, who don't want to be seen as taking advantage of already disadvantaged people.

MFIs look at a couple of factors when they set interest rates and fees. Here, I explain those components so you can figure out if a microfinance institution that you want to invest in is handling loans fairly.

> ✔ **The cost of money:** No matter how likely someone is to pay you back, when you lend money, you give up the use of it. For that, you want compensation, and that comes as a basic interest charge. (In financial terms, it's the *risk-free rate of interest,* the percentage rate you'll charge even if you know you'll be paid back.)
>
> Think of it this way: You may lend your best buddy $5 tonight that he'll return tomorrow, but if you end up walking home in the rain because you don't have bus fare, then he's going to owe you big time. You gave up the use of that money, and it had a cost to you. The *cost of money* is a percentage of the amount borrowed; the longer it takes until the loan is repaid, the higher the cost of the loan will be.

✔ **Default risk:** Lending to your best buddy aside, there's almost always some risk that you won't get your money back. That's the *default rate,* and it's added to the risk-free rate of interest to come up with the quoted rate that the borrower pays. If 10 percent of a certain type of borrower always defaults, then the lender will charge 10 percent additional interest to offset that. All borrowers in that category will be charged that amount, too.

Microfinance loans can have high default rates because the borrowers aren't always savvy about business. To increase the chances of success, many microfinance lenders operate educational and training programs for their borrowers.

✔ **Transaction costs:** No matter where in the world the lender is or how much money is being loaned out, a loan involves a lot of paperwork. There are applications to verify, forms to copy, meetings to arrange, and appraisals to conduct. And all of that costs money. Some lenders roll those expenses into a higher interest rate on the loan, while others charge a flat fee that has to be repaid in addition to the principal borrowed. But because the amount of work involved is more or less the same regardless of how much money is being borrowed, the transaction costs can look huge relative to the typical microfinance loan.

The problem with transaction costs is that some lenders — macro- and microfinance alike — have been known to tack on fees for costs that may not be real as a way to boost their return. (If you've ever taken out a home loan, you're probably familiar with all the mysterious closing costs that have to be covered before you get your money, and it's entirely possible that you were able to get a few of them waived.)

Responsible microfinance involves charges that are proportional to the length of the loan. The charges may be high as a percentage of money borrowed, but they should be justifiable. Here are some examples:

✔ Grameen Bank charges rates ranging from 20 percent for loans to entrepreneurs to 0 percent for members of its beggars program.

✔ Accion's MFI partners charge rates as high as 85 percent in Mexico and as low as 10.62 percent in Chicago; in both countries, that's lower than what similar borrowers can obtain from competing institutions.

✔ The government of Bangladesh has a loan program that competes with Grameen; it charges 22 percent interest.

Of course, if you follow an investing style that forbids paying or charging interest, a typical microfinance arrangement won't work. But even a micro-lease or micro-equity investment will involve fees; check to make sure they're proportional to the services that the small business receives. Ask the lender for information before you make your microfinance investment.

Some well-intentioned MFIs have run up against local laws against *usury* (the charging of outrageous interest rates) because of their rates and fees. In the West African Economic and Monetary Union (WAEMU, made up of Benin, Burkina Faso, Ivory Coast, Guinea-Bissau, Mali, Niger, Senegal, and Togo), financial institutions are prohibited from charging interest rates more than twice the discount rate (the rate charged by the union's central bank), set at a ceiling of 7 percent in 1996.

MFIs have successfully lobbied the central banks in WAEMU member countries to grant an exemption to the usury law for microcredit, so they can now charge up to 27 percent annual interest. The central banks recognized that microfinance is an important way to improve the economies in those countries and decided it was better to allow a high rate on microfinance than to lose the MFIs.

TIP

Think 27 percent is a high rate of interest? Check the fine print on any department store credit cards you have — the rate may be awfully close.

The pain of repayment

Microfinance only works if the borrowers repay the loans. Otherwise, there won't be money to lend to other deserving folks, nor will the investors receive the return they expect. Sometimes repayment becomes a bigger focus than spending the loan productively. That means that the money loaned may not contribute to economic growth, and it can have worse repercussions in the community.

As anyone who has ever attended junior high knows, peer pressure can be downright ugly. A group that starts out supportive and helpful can sometimes turn mean and spiteful; the people who once were friends are now enemies.

Most microfinance programs rely on groups of entrepreneurs who share common business goals (see the "Joining with other entrepreneurs" section earlier in this chapter for more information). This is usually great because all the members can support each other and even share business leads. But sometimes the members can turn on each other.

The annals of microfinance are filled with stories of group members behaving badly toward each other, especially if one member is in danger of defaulting. If a member dies, there are rumors that others in the group will put social pressure on his surviving family to repay the loan, making a bad time in their lives even worse.

Navigating the obstacles of government and social status

Because the amounts involved with microfinance are pitifully small relative to the wealth of the people making the loans, some have argued that it's almost immoral to demand repayment of $25 or so, money that means almost nothing to the lender and the whole world to the borrower.

There's some evidence that the people who benefit the most from microfinance aren't the very poorest. They are the people who are a little higher in status and resources, who have a small but viable business that has the potential to become larger and take on employees. These people make great borrowers, but lending to them doesn't alleviate the worst poverty. That's why some people have argued that microfinance is simply taking attention and funds away from efforts that would help the world's poorest people.

Other critics point out that people in some countries wouldn't be so poor if their national leaders served them better. They believe that microfinance places responsibility for economic development on the citizens rather than the rulers who got them into their fix. Sometimes people are poor because they live under a government that is completely dysfunctional.

In 1998 Amartya Sen of India won the Nobel Prize in economics for his work on poverty. His key finding was that famines are failures of distribution, not of agriculture. If there are no roads (a government's responsibility to provide) to get crops to the people who need them, for example, the people may starve. In any newspaper on any day, you and I can read stories about how foreign aid is being diverted, economies have shut down while dictators consolidate power, and senseless wars keep people hungry.

If this situation bothers you, then microfinance may not be right for you.

Running out of opportunities

Although there's a lot of demand for microfinance in the world, it's entirely possible that the supply of funds will outstrip it. When it's so easy for relatively rich people to put small amounts to work, the market can be flooded with money, and that's not good. The money may be used for bad loans that don't get repaid, and then the lenders lose their investment. (On a grand scale, this is exactly what happened in U.S. financial markets to create the crash in 2008.)

Not every small business is based on a good idea and run by a capable manager, and that has nothing to do with where it operates. MFIs with access to excess funds may be tempted to make bad loans to put the money to work. And if the MFIs don't put the money to use, more investors may see low rates of return on an investment for which they already have low expectations. That may put an end to microfinance.

Locating Microfinance Opportunities

Microfinance loans may be small, but make enough of them and the total quickly gets big. It's unclear just how big, but Accion International, one major microfinance funder, has a loan portfolio of $2 billion. Grameen Bank alone has more than $500 million in outstanding loans. Although microfinance is hardly the largest sector in the investment universe, it's big enough to accommodate most investors, and it will only get larger as the concept expands to other parts of the world. After all, this planet is home to billions of poor people, and most of them don't want to be poor.

Even though returns on microfinance may be low, or even negative, the Internal Revenue Service still considers it to be an investment. You won't get a tax deduction for your microfinance activities, and you may not make any money, either, for the worst of both worlds. If you choose to invest in microfinance, it should probably be with excess capital after you have provided for your big savings goals, such as retirement or a college fund.

If you're researching microfinance on behalf of a pension, foundation, or endowment account, you'll find that many of these funds accept institutional contributions.

Because of the fees involved, the percentage returns to investors from microfinance are small. There are potential returns, though, and it doesn't take a lot of money to try it out. In the following sections, I tell you about companies that allow small investors to make small investments with folks nearby and faraway.

Taking action through Accion

Accion Investments (www.accion.org) is the money management arm of Accion, a nonprofit microfinance organization that helps match borrowers and lenders. At first, it concentrated on Brazil, but now it works with small entrepreneurs all over the world, including in the United States.

You can participate in Accion's projects in two ways. The first is with its Bridge Funds, which are lines of credit that can be tapped by Accion's local microfinance partners. The second is through Accion USA, its loan fund for American borrowers, who are typically recent immigrants who have no credit history here. Both investment options have a minimum investment of $2,000 and an 18-month time commitment. The interest varies between 0 percent and $5^1/_2$ percent, depending on market conditions. Interested investors should call or e-mail Accion for more information, using the contacts listed on the Web site.

Contributing capital to Kiva

Registered users on Kiva's Web site (`www.kiva.org`) can search for entrepreneurs in developing countries who are looking to raise money for small projects. Kiva works with existing microfinance companies in areas that need capital to lend. Those companies screen the applicants; typical clients include a street vendor in Ukraine who wants to expand his inventory of sneakers, a man in Mexico who wants to launch an advertising campaign for his painting company, and a small grocer in Tajikistan who wants to add a meat counter to her shop. You can search the list, find a project that interests you, and contribute funds toward the total loan value.

Kiva is structured as a nonprofit organization, so it can't pay interest. Instead, it offers investors the likely return of their investment, usually within a year, which they can withdraw or reloan to another entrepreneur. Because almost all investors get their money back, this is not a charitable contribution, even though Kiva doesn't pay interest. The minimum investment is $25.

Making a little money with MicroPlace

Pierre Omidyar, the founder of online auction giant eBay, invests much of his personal fortune in microfinance, and he gave a $100 million donation to his alma mater, Tufts University, with the provision that it, too, be committed to microfinance. Then he wanted to find a way to let people with much smaller fortunes play in the market, so eBay acquired MicroPlace (`www.microplace.com`) in 2006.

MicroPlace is a registered broker-dealer, so it can pay interest and dividends to investors. You can't choose specific borrowers; instead, you choose a region that interests you and direct you funds to a microfinance company operating there. The minimum investment is $100.

Investing endowments with Oikocredit

Founded in 1975 by the World Council of Churches, Oikocredit (www.oiko
credit.org) was originally designed to help congregations invest parts
of their endowments into microcredit, helping the churches grow their
long-term capital while doing good in the world. You can buy notes from
Oikocredit for a minimum of $1,000 for one-, three-, or five-year terms; the
interest paid is generally below market rates.

Oikocredit also works with MicroPlace (see the preceding section) to help
smaller investors put their money to work.

Funding small businesses through Prosper

Prosper (www.prosper.com) brings the concept of microfinance home. It's
an online lending site, working with a federally regulated bank, that allows
individuals to lend money to others. (Legally, it's structured as the purchase
of a loan rather than direct borrowing.)

Prosper's borrowers state their case, including their credit rating. Some are
looking for personal funds, but many are small businesses looking for help
financing new facilities, inventory, or equipment. You then state how much
you're willing to lend and at what rate, bidding on the loan as with any
other auction. You can commit as little as $50 and can earn interest on your
investment.

Given the cross between microfinance and lending, it should be no surprise
that one of Prosper's venture capital investors is Omidyar Network, the venture fund of eBay founder Pierre Omidyar.

Get a little, give a little with Zopa

Want to help people close to home? Help someone refinance credit card
debt, buy textbooks, or cover the costs of a divorce? Maybe Zopa.com (us.
zopa.com) is the microfinance company for you. It brings together borrowers and investors in the United States who work through established credit
unions.

As an investor, you purchase certificates of deposit with a minimum balance
of $500. The borrowers receive personal loans. Then you look through the
list of borrowers on the Web site and choose some to receive a cut of the

interest from the CD, which reduces the total amount that the borrower has to pay. Borrowers who get enough investors to support their causes could end up owing nothing. In the meantime, you receive interest income from your CD.

The company's name comes from *zone of personal agreement,* a negotiating term that represents the spread between the minimum that one side will accept and the maximum that the other side is willing to pay. (Zopa is based in the United States, but it also has affiliates in the U.K. and Italy.)

Part IV
The Part of Tens

The 5th Wave   By Rich Tennant

"I read about investing in a company called Unihandle Ohio, but I'm uneasy about a stock that's listed on the NASDAQ as UhOh."

In this part . . .

In this For Dummies-only part, you get to enjoy some top-ten lists. I present ten tips for social investors and ten traps that can derail your performance. And then there's my favorite chapter: ten success stories that reveal how social investing affects company performance for the better, changes business practices, and even leads to the development of new products to meet specialized needs.

I also include an appendix full of references so you can get more information to help you find out more about investing, social and otherwise.

Chapter 18

Ten Tips for Social and Activist Investors

. . . .

In This Chapter

▶ Keeping in mind the power of diversification

▶ Performing research, now and forever, alone and with a group

▶ Fitting investing into your financial and personal life

▶ Creating a legacy

. . . .

*W*ant to be more successful in your social investing program? Then take it seriously! Investing in general isn't terribly difficult, but it does require some attention. Social investing involves a bit more attention to ensure that all of your social and financial goals are met. But it's not impossible.

In this chapter, I've compiled ten important tips to help you become more successful in meeting the goals that are important to you. Some cover basic investment advice worth remembering, such as diversification and research. But others, like keeping your perspective and making investing just part of your social goals, can help you find the balance you seek when you embark on a social investing program.

Diversify! Diversify! Diversify!

Problems can beset any company, no matter how it operates or who it sells to. The best way to protect your portfolio is through diversification. If you own a variety of investments in different industries, you can still work toward your financial goals even if one of them is having an off year. All the investments can be socially responsible; Part III has a long list of different investments that can meet your nonfinancial goals, too.

Do Your Research

Companies change in response to market conditions, customer preferences, and investor demands. Rely on a rumor from years ago, and you may shut yourself off from a really good investment opportunity. Do your homework. Take the time to find out about different investments and how they fit your social criteria. Read company reports, keep an eye out for company news in newspapers and on news programs, and talk to people familiar with the company (the next three sections cover these points). You may discover that today's opportunities are a little different than you once believed.

Monitor Your Investments

Because companies change all the time, an investment that once fit your style may not anymore. Traditional investors are often content being passive, putting their money into a mix of stocks and bonds, and then riding out market conditions. By definition, a social investor can't be passive. A social investor is an activist! That means you need to pay attention to the news (see the next section), read company reports and mutual fund shareholder letters, and ask questions when you can. Pay attention to what's happening to your investments in terms of both financial performance and corporate performance. You may want to get out of an investment that makes money but no longer suits your style.

Follow the News

As you look for new investments that fit your investment strategy, pay attention to the business news. Many companies that you may have ruled out at one time may now meet your standards because of a change in management or the political climate. And new issues can crop up, ranging from product problems at home to wars and upheaval overseas. The more you know about current business and political events, the more you can identify good investments and refine your criteria to reflect the world as it is now. You may just find that keeping up with the news becomes the most interesting part of being a social investor!

Join Forces with Others

Although we're told that it's not polite to discuss money, it makes a lot of sense to discuss investments with others. If you can find others who share your social goals, you may find that your research is easier and more fun.

You can look for a financial planner who respects your vision, a newsletter service that tracks investments by using your criteria, or a group of investors trying to get a company to commit to significant change (Chapter 5 contains information about this). Just don't get into some cocktail party bragging game that keeps you from sticking to your investment plan.

A great resource for starting and managing an investment club is the National Association of Investors Corporation, www.better-investing.org.

Vote Your Proxies

For many investments, you receive a proxy statement each year. This tells you who the members of the board are, what the executive compensation package is, and what other key issues may be facing the company. Then you're asked to vote. The process isn't quite as simple as in a government election, and your vote will probably be small relative to all the other people who hold shares. But your vote is important. Part of being an activist investor is taking action and letting the company management know that you're paying attention. (Chapter 5 covers proxies in more detail.)

Consider Your Spending

If you want to support businesses that do right by the world at large, you can do better than investing in them — you can buy their goods and services. The hardest thing for any company to do is to come up with something to sell that people are willing the pay for. The second hardest thing is to come up with something that people are willing to pay enough for to let the business cover its costs and make a profit. You can support different social values by the ways you spend your money, not just by how you invest. And, of course, the money you save by not buying things you don't support can help fund your investment program!

Keep Your Perspective

Confusing money with values can cause all kinds of problems. Some social investors seem happiest if their investments lose money, because that makes them feel like they're better than someone who has profitable investments. Others stick with bad investments, believing that any company that supports their way of thinking has to become a great investment eventually. If they just stick with it long enough, they know their commitment and good virtue will be rewarded.

The stock doesn't know you own it, traders like to say. Just because you've found a company that matches your values perfectly doesn't mean it's going to perform well. And just because you've found a company that makes tons of money doesn't mean it's run by bad people doing bad things. Successful investors can detach their emotions from the market. That may be harder if you've invested in a company because of its alignment with your values, but you need to.

Make Investing Just Part of Your Life

Social investing is no substitute for voting, making charitable donations, doing volunteer work, and otherwise being part of a community of people who care about the world. Investing is one of many ways to do the right thing. Putting your money in a bank that specializes in community redevelopment or buying shares in a mutual fund that doesn't invest in tobacco companies can help you influence the world, but you may find that you can have a bigger impact in other ways. Social investing isn't a form of indulgence. You have to lead your life first, in whatever way is important to you. Your investments are an extension of that, not a replacement.

Consider Your Estate Plan

If you care enough to determine where your money goes now, you should care where it goes after you're gone. You need an estate plan. Besides making allowances for the people whom you care about, you can also leave funds for the causes that are important to you. You can do this through your will or by adding the organization as a beneficiary to your account. (In most cases, an account that is co-owned or has a named beneficiary will be handled outside of your estate.) Or you can find investments that support you now and the charity upon your death, through charitable remainder trusts and insurance contracts. You can find out more about those in Chapter 14.

Talk to a lawyer about your estate plan. In some jurisdictions, you may be required to leave a certain percentage of your assets to your spouse or to your minor children. If you decide to avoid all the headaches by dying without a will, then the headaches go to your presumed heirs, and the courts decide how your assets should be distributed — a total waste of all the effort you put into your investing program.

Chapter 19

Ten Investment Traps and How to Avoid Them

In This Chapter

▶ Keeping perspective on your investment policy

▶ Using current research

▶ Monitoring fees and performance

▶ Understanding the limits of investment activism

A ll sorts of investors make all sorts of mistakes. Legendary investor Warren Buffett has made them; so have well-paid traders and average guys taking a chance in the market. Social investors are especially likely to make mistakes because they can let emotion take over, and emotion is the bane of every investor of every stripe. It leads to cloudy thinking and panicky decision making.

An easy way to improve investment returns is to make fewer mistakes. Doing careful research, staying up-to-date on your investments' performance, and getting out when an investment is no longer working out can help prevent mistakes that drag down your investment performance. In this chapter, I point out common mistakes and give you tips for avoiding them.

Defining Investments Narrowly

To many investors, "social investing" means buying a socially responsible stock mutual fund, and then not worrying about it anymore. Other investors feel that they can't invest socially because they don't want exposure to the stock market. Although in the long run most investors are best off with at least some money in stocks, you have plenty of other social investment options. In fact, diversifying assets across several different types of investments usually leads to better returns for a given level of risk. Chapters 14 through 17 have information on how bank accounts, real estate, hedge funds, and other investments can meet socially responsible criteria.

Expecting Perfection in an Imperfect World

The perfect boyfriend, perfect job, and perfect life don't exist. Neither does the perfect investment. You may have to make trade-offs between investment performance, social criteria, and time spent on managing your investments. If your standards are too high, then nothing will meet them.

Because the goal of social investing is to do well by doing good, you may get frustrated if your expectations are too high. Not only do very few pure investment opportunities exist, but you may have to sacrifice performance to find investments that meet your criteria. (The evidence of performance versus social responsibility is mixed; one issue, of course, is that each social investor defines the suitable investment universe a bit differently from the others.)

One way to meet your social objectives is to maximize investment performance, and then contribute a share of the profits to the charities of your choice.

Not Accepting Neutrality

Most businesses and investments are neither good nor bad. They just are. They may neither add to nor detract from your social goals, so they're considered *socially neutral*. And some investors have a really hard time with that. They want to sort the world into good and bad: Good company! Bad company. Good bank! Bad bank. And so on. But just as perfection is nonexistent (see the preceding section), investing also comes with a huge amount of gray area.

Although socially responsible versions of most finance and investment products are available, you may not always be able to find one when you need it. That's okay. You won't be a bad person for going with a socially neutral vendor. Just keep an eye on changes with your neutral investment to make sure it doesn't go from neutral to worse.

Falling in Love with the Company

You found a company that makes all of its products from reused and recycled materials, that has the smallest carbon footprint in the market, that has the most generous employee benefits, that makes all of its products in unionized manufacturing plants, and that is a model of corporate governance. So why's the stock so lousy? Maybe no one wants to buy its products at a price that covers all of its costs. As a social investor, you can get so caught up in all the good things that a company is doing that you can completely lose sight of your goal, which is to make money.

Furthermore, no company is going to do well just because you own it, but you *really* hope that the business will turn around, and you know that management will come through for you because you are *such* a nice person who is *so* committed to the social mission. You just *know* things will work out!

Unbridled optimism doesn't work with relationships, and it doesn't work in investing. You can't wish and hope for good performance. Sometimes your best choice is to sell the stock and move on to the next investment opportunity.

Relying on Old Research

Companies change. A new management team comes in, a big acquisition takes place, and a strategy is adapted to new market realities. But the rumors persist: "Do you know what the company did in the Vietnam War?" "I remember protesting their sweatshops when I was in college." "The nuns at my grade school led a big boycott of their products because of how they marketed infant formula in developing countries." All of these stories may be true, but they may have no bearing on what the companies involved do today. The past has passed, and during the period in question, the company may have been directed by people who are no longer coming into the office, let alone still alive.

On the other hand, a company that has a responsible reputation can backslide so it no longer fits your criteria. An automaker may quietly abandon an alternative fuels program that it once promoted to customers and investors; a bank may cut back on lending to underserved communities when the credit markets get tight; or a model international manufacturing facility gets sold to a subcontractor offering a different pay-and-benefits package.

To be a successful social investor, you have to pay attention to the changing financial and operating climate. A company that once met your definition of responsibility may not now. A stock that you once would have avoided and a product that you once would have boycotted may now be something you should support. Research is ongoing; it doesn't end when you make your buy or sell decision. (See Chapters 4 and 5 for more tips about researching companies and applying that information.)

Paying Excessive Fees

Some brokers, financial planners, and investment companies love social investing, not because they want to change the world, but because it gives them an excuse to charge higher fees. They sometimes reason that a socially responsible portfolio is so important to the customers that they'll pay more than an investor who doesn't care about the ethics behind the investments.

Some social investment styles require more research than others, and research can be expensive. If a mutual fund company sends its analysts to far-off countries to check on the conditions workers face, then the trip's costs will show up in the fund expenses. That form of research isn't cheap. On the other hand, a governance investment style that tracks such matters as CEO compensation and board members' meeting attendance is relatively less expensive; all of that information is public and can be checked by anyone with Internet access or a library card.

Fees come out of performance. A financial advisor or research consultant who adds value and helps you make decisions deserves to be compensated, but not all are helpful. First decide if you need assistance before you pay for it.

Sacrificing Performance

The knock on socially responsible investing is that it leads to poor investment performance. That's not true if you invest carefully, screening for both financial and social criteria. (You can find out more about screening in Chapter 4.) Many social factors can lead to better performance: Good corporate governance practices help management work for shareholders, sustainable manufacturing practices can reduce costs, and clean business practices around the world can help a company keep a good reputation with customers.

You shouldn't sacrifice performance because you don't have to. If an investment offers below-average returns for its type, then don't buy it just because it's socially responsible. Keep looking, and you may find a stock, mutual fund, or real estate investment trust that has both good performance prospects and a social commitment. Or you can find a socially neutral one that meets your performance needs.

Forgetting that Everyone's Preferences Cancel Out

Some social investors want nothing to do with defense contractors because they want their investing to support peace. Others like defense contractors because many of the companies treat their employees well, contribute to their communities, and are committed to transparency and responsible corporate governance. With so many varied preferences out there, company management doesn't know how to make changes.

And that's one of the key limitations to social investing. Unless investment activism is carefully coordinated and publicized, it often slips into a feel-good exercise. Traders refer to social investing as a *noise factor* — a buzz in the background that doesn't change anything. Investors' different preferences, whether they stem from environmental policies or how cute the CEO is, cancel out and leave pure risk and pure return.

The fact that people's preferences cancel each other out is no reason not to invest in support of your values; that's exactly what you should be doing. Just keep in mind that your investment choices may not change the world.

Letting Your Investments Do Your Activism

Your investments are just one part of your life — an important part, but just one. While you're saving for the down payment on a house, college tuition, and retirement, you also have to work and play and contribute to your community. If you care about something, it should be reflected in your entire life. A socially responsible investment isn't an indulgence that offsets what else you're doing.

Most activist investing success stories use shareholder activism as just one of the tools in an overall protest. South African divestment, for example, was based on institutions refusing to invest in companies that did business with the former regime there, but it included product boycotts, student protests, and extensive publicity about the evils of apartheid and the treatment of people who opposed it. It proved to be successful, but not just because of the behavior of investors. (I like to think that the red armband I wore during the spring quarter of 1986 had something to do with it, too, but it probably didn't.)

Expecting Companies to Do the Work of Government

Many investors put pressure on companies to do things that government should be doing. They want companies to make better financial disclosures, even though those disclosures aren't required. They want companies to meet certain fuel-efficiency standards that aren't called for by law. They want companies to stop hiring child labor, even though it may be allowed in some places.

Financial disclosure and fuel efficiency are good things, and child labor is a bad thing, and pretty much anyone you talk to will be in general agreement. But it's misplaced activism to give companies the burdens of government. It may not be fair to a company, either, in a ruthlessly competitive market. If you're dissatisfied with your government's policies, then the best route is political activism, not investment activism.

Chapter 20

Ten Socially Responsible Investing Success Stories

*B*eing a responsible investor might make you feel good, but it's even better if it allows you to *do* good. Does it? Yes! Activist investing strategies have often forced companies to change their business practices, improve conditions for employees, and create new investment products to meet different people's needs. To inspire you on your quest to do well while doing good, here's a list of some of the many activist and social investing success stories.

Disney and Corporate Governance

The California Public Employees Retirement System, known as CalPERS, is the largest pension plan in the world. The fund's managers are committed to investing some of its assets in California companies, but they won't stand by when they see mismanagement. Another part of CalPERS's strategy is to press companies for management and governance changes when it sees a record of problems that lead to poor stock price performance.

In 2004, CalPERS added Disney (NYSE: DIS) to its focus list, arguing that the company underperformed the S&P 500 index even while its senior executives were collecting enormous bonuses. Given that the pension fund owned more than nine million shares, this was leading to real losses for the plan beneficiaries. CalPERS organized a group of other institutional investors to add more independent directors to the board, develop a succession plan to replace the CEO and chairman of the board, and tie employee compensation to performance. Disney's management acquiesced, and the company's stock beat the market in 2006.

DeQingYuan

The chicken business is messy, even in the United States. It's a *commodity business,* which means that most customers care about price more than any other factor. Human and animal rights activists and environmentalists have long been concerned about cramped cages for the chickens, poor working conditions for employees, and solid waste streams that seem to go along with chickens no matter who is raising them or where.

DeQingYuan (www.dqy.com.cn) is a Chinese chicken processing company. Its founder, Zhong Kaimin, has the company produce eggs stamped with the date they were laid to show how fresh they are. Chickens are raised in roomy cages and fed well. Chicken waste is turned into high quality organic fertilizer that's sold to local farmers to grow corn for the company's chicken feed. The local farmers make more money by growing corn than they could by growing chickens, so DeQingYuan's chickens are protected from contagious diseases, allowing the company to use fewer antibiotics and lose fewer chickens to disease. DeQingYuan provides workers with healthcare; it also uses high-tech equipment to tackle ammonia and dust problems on its farms to minimize employee health problems.

DeQingYuan's socially and environmentally conscious management are attracting the interest of foreign investors, including the International Finance Corporation, the industrial lending arm of the World Bank. Availability of foreign capital has allowed the company to contemplate a public offering in 2009 to give it access to capital it will need to further expand operations nationally.

South African Divestment

For decades, the Republic of South Africa was ruled by the white descendants of the original Dutch and English colonists, despite the fact that the majority of the people in the country were African natives. This was a system known as *apartheid,* from the Afrikaans (Dutch) word for "separateness." No surprise, the majority resented this and rebelled, causing the minority government to crack down on the people. Among other atrocities, Nelson Mandela, the leader of the African National Congress, was imprisoned, and another activist, Stephen Biko, was killed in prison.

South Africa also had what few other African nations did: a developed consumer economy that was attractive to international companies. By the early 1980s, people looking for a way to force the apartheid rulers to accept democratic rule shifted their attention to the companies that were doing business in South Africa. They pushed major institutional investors, including university pension funds and charitable endowments, to sell their holdings in companies that did business in South Africa.

Although not everyone sold, the issue came up enough that it put companies on the defensive. Managers had to justify why they were still in South Africa even though their stock prices were being dragged down because of it. The executives started putting pressure on the South African government to make changes that would make it easier for companies to stay in South Africa and even expand their businesses there.

By 1990, Mandela was released from prison after 27 years, and the government began a peaceful transition to democracy. In 1993, Mandela shared the Nobel Peace Prize with Frederik Willem de Klerk, the last apartheid president of South Africa. Investor pressure helped hasten nonviolent change in South Africa, and many activists see that as a model for motivating other investors for change.

Shell and Nigeria

Royal Dutch Shell (NYSE: RD) is a major oil company with operations all over the world. In 1957, oil was discovered in Nigeria's Niger Delta. The problem is that the Nigerian government hasn't always behaved responsibly toward its citizens, and because of Shell's business interests in the country, many have accused the company of siding with the government. The people who lived in the Niger Delta lost their land to government appropriation and were compensated based on the value of the crops grown on it, not the oil and gas reserves underneath. Then Shell hired very few local workers. Environmental contamination from drilling operations affected farmlands and fisheries, and displaced many local residents.

Because of Shell's questionable environmental and human rights actions in the Niger Delta, local groups formed to oppose Shell's practices, and they were soon joined by socially conscious activists in a boycott of Shell products. Actions brought oil production in the region to a halt in 1992. In 1995, opposition leader Ken Saro-Wiwa and eight other people were killed, prompting condemnation by such world leaders as U.S. President Bill Clinton, South African President Nelson Mandela, England's Queen Elizabeth II, and British Prime Minister John Major. Several environmental groups, including Friends of the Earth and Greenpeace, bought shares in Shell stock and began filing shareholder resolutions to bring their priorities before the shareholders. Eventually, Shell committed to spending $100 million per year for five years on social development and oil spill cleanup projects in the Niger Delta. This led to peaceful relations for a while, although tensions between Shell and different Nigerian groups seem to be reigniting as of press time.

AXA and Land Mines

AXA (NYSE: AXA) is a global insurance company headquartered in the Netherlands. In 2005, it attracted the attention of activists because the company invested some of its money in weapons manufacturers that made antipersonnel land mines. The problem with land mines is that they can remain viable long after a war is over, essentially making swaths of land uninhabitable for decades and killing or maiming children who, unaware of the danger, wander out to play. Because of the long-term effects on civilians, many people think land mines are an especially heinous form of weaponry.

AXA initially rejected calls that it divest its holdings in these companies, but by 2006, it realized that not only were the investments affecting its customer retention, but it was also the wrong thing to do. The company announced it would accept the terms of the Ottawa Convention, an international treaty that prohibits the production and sale of antipersonnel land mines, and that it would no longer invest in companies that made them.

Pepsico and Myanmar

Myanmar, formerly known as Burma, has been the scene for much political unrest. In 1988, the military cracked down on people protesting for democracy, including the arrest of Aung San Suu Kyi, who would win the Nobel Peace Prize in 1991. In 1990, elections were held, and the democracy side won 82 percent of the popular vote, but the military regime didn't relinquish power. Despite the political turmoil and human rights violations, Pepsico (NYSE: PEP) entered into a joint venture with Thein Tun, who had ties to the military junta, and opened a bottling plant near Rangoon in 1991.

To get its profits out of Myanmar and into the U.S., Pepsico purchased Myanmarian agricultural goods for export, despite the common use of forced labor in the country's agricultural sector. The company argued that international trade would open the country up for international development and lead to an end of repression. Democracy activists and protesters countered that Pepsico's presence and willingness to do business with the junta gave hard currency and legitimacy to the repressive military regime.

Activists in the United States and Europe responded. Along with boycotts and campus protests, the Interfaith Center on Corporate Responsibility organized institutional and individual shareholders to argue that Pepsico should divest from Myanmar. They introduced shareholder resolutions to force the issue. Forced to choose between unhappy shareholders and questionable business opportunities abroad, Pepsico withdrew from Myanmar, and the shareholder resolutions were dropped.

Nike and Sweatshops

Many companies contract with others to do manufacturing, figuring that marketing and design are very different skills than managing an assembly operation. These contracts often go to low bidders who then have an incentive to run the operation as cheaply as possible, treating workers terribly in the process. Because there are so many contract manufacturers out there, it's hard to police them all. Many consumers look the other way when they're paying bargain prices, but if they're paying top dollar, they expect some of that money to go to the workers.

Nike (NYSE: NKE) is known for making high performance sneakers sold at high prices. Hence, labor activists were especially outraged to discover that the people who made the shoes were often paid low wages and worked in dangerous conditions. Although Nike wasn't operating the factories, it was paying people to do its manufacturing and thus had the ability to force accountability. The company resisted at first, leading many socially responsible pension, endowment, and mutual funds to sell the shares. Eventually, though, the company changed its contracting practices and began audits of all of its suppliers, and it's now owned by many of the investment funds that sold it.

ShoreBank

Founded as South Shore National Bank in Chicago, ShoreBank (www.shore bankcorp.com) was a community development financial institution long before the government created that banking category. (You can read more about community development financial institutions in Chapter 14.) The bank was acquired by a group of community activists in 1973; they were disturbed by the economic decline that affected much of Chicago's South Side and believed the downturn was being hastened by the lack of financial institutions in the neighborhood. The bank was committed to making loans to homeowners, small businesses, and nonprofit institutions in the area. Within two years, the bank was profitable; it became proof to skeptics that a responsible financial institution could make money by helping its community grow.

ShoreBank now has banks in Chicago, Cleveland, Detroit, Portland, and Seattle. It continues to concentrate on community lending in disadvantaged areas, more recently emphasizing environmentally responsible development. And it's been a model for other banks all over the country.

Grameen Bank

In 2006, Mohammad Yunus won the Nobel Peace Prize, which was unusual because he's an economist who founded a bank, not a politician or protestor. However, the bank he founded in Bangladesh is unusual. Called Grameen Bank (*grameen* meaning "village" in the Bangla language), its mission is to provide financial services to very poor people, including making small loans to really small businesses to help people who want to work hard to get out of desperate poverty. Grameen Bank provides services to help borrowers succeed, such as training in how to create a business plan. The bank now has 2,504 branches in Bangladesh and has loaned out $6.9 billion U.S. Unlike almost any bank anywhere in the world, 98 percent of its borrowers repay. Grameen Bank's success has led to similar projects in other places, backed by the capital of social investors. (You can read Chapter 17 for ideas on how you can participate.)

Shariah Mortgages at Fannie Mae and Freddie Mac

Islamic law, known as Shariah, forbids Muslims from paying or receiving interest (you can read more in Chapter 10). However, Muslims still want to buy things that are difficult to pay for in one lump sum, especially a family house. Several U.S. financial institutions have developed home finance products, including rent-to-own and joint purchase agreements, that allow Muslims to have the American dream while still honoring the precepts of their faith. However, these banks couldn't offer terms comparable to those on traditional mortgages because they couldn't *securitize* them through Ginnie Mae, Fannie Mae (NYSE: FNM), or Freddie Mac (NYSE: FRE). The three agencies arrange for federal guarantees of mortgage payments, which make it possible to sell the mortgages to investors; this reduces risks for issuing banks so they can then charge lower interest rates to qualified borrowers.

Seeing a market opportunity, Fannie Mae and Freddie Mac developed standards that would allow certain Islamic home-finance contracts to be guaranteed and available for sale to investors, thus expanding opportunities for Muslim homeowners and the banks that serve them. Fannie Mae and Freddie Mac have had their problems, but these financing arrangements weren't the cause.

Appendix

Resources for Socially Responsible Investors

. . . .

Social investing combines social issues and investing issues, and there's more information on both than can be easily contained in any one book! Here's a list of some great resources that you can turn to for more information on the topics that matter to you.

Books for Building Social Investment Savvy

Because social investing means different things to different people, you may want more information on the topics that matter to you than this book contains. You're in luck — your local bookshop and library have a lot of great titles that can help you build your investment savvy.

- ✔ *Angel Investing: Matching Startup Funds with Startup Companies — A Guide for Entrepreneurs, Individual Investors, and Venture Capitalists,* by Mark Van Osnabrugge and Robert J. Robinson (Jossey-Bass)

- ✔ *Banker to the Poor: Micro-Lending and the Battle Against World Poverty,* by Muhammad Yunus (PublicAffairs)

- ✔ *Bond Investing For Dummies,* by Russell Wild (Wiley)

- ✔ *A Christian's Guide to Investing: Managing Your Money, Planning for the Future and Leaving a Legacy,* by Danny Fontana (Revell)

- ✔ *Community Economic Development Handbook: Strategies and Tools to Revitalize Your Neighborhood,* by Mihailo Temali (Fieldstone Alliance)

- ✔ *Compelling Returns: A Practical Guide to Socially Responsible Investing,* by Scott J. Budde (Wiley)

- ✔ *Corporate Governance,* 3rd Edition, by Robert A.G. Monks and Nell Minow (Wiley)

- ✔ *Dictionary of Accounting Terms,* 4th Edition, by Joel G. Siegel and Jae K. Shim (Barron's Educational Series)

- ✔ *Dictionary of Finance and Investment Terms,* 7th Edition, by John Downes and Jordan Elliot Goodman (Barron's Educational Series)

- ✔ *Exchange-Traded Funds For Dummies,* by Russell Wild (Wiley)

- ✔ *Green Investing: A Guide to Making Money through Environment Friendly Stocks,* by Jack Uldrich (Adams Media)

- ✔ *Green to Gold: How Smart Companies Use Environmental Strategy to Innovate, Create Value, and Build Competitive Advantage,* by Daniel C. Esty and Andrew S. Winston (Yale University Press)

- ✔ *Jews, Money and Social Responsibility: Developing a "Torah of Money" for Contemporary Life,* by Lawrence Bush and Jeffrey Dekro (B'nai B'rith Book Service)

- ✔ *Market for Virtue: The Potential and Limits of Corporate Social Responsibility,* by David Vogel (Brookings Institution Press)

- ✔ *Mutual Funds For Dummies,* 5th Edition, by Eric Tyson (Wiley)

- ✔ *One Up on Wall Street: How to Use What You Already Know to Make Money in the Market,* 2nd Edition, by Peter Lynch and John Rothchild (Simon & Schuster)

- ✔ *The Rise of the Creative Class: And How It's Transforming Work, Leisure, Community and Everyday Life,* by Richard Florida (Basic Books)

- ✔ *Socially Responsible Investing: Making a Difference and Making Money,* by Amy Domini (Kaplan Business)

- ✔ *Stock Investing For Dummies,* by Paul Mladjenovic (Wiley)

- ✔ *A Traitor to His Class: Robert A.G. Monks and the Battle to Change Corporate America,* by Hilary Rosenberg (Wiley)

- ✔ *The Triple Bottom Line: How Today's Best-Run Companies Are Achieving Economic, Social and Environmental Success — and How You Can Too,* by Andrew W. Savitz and Karl Weber (Jossey-Bass)

- ✔ *Values-Driven Business: How to Change the World, Make Money, and Have Fun,* by Ben Cohen and Mal Warwick (Berrett-Koehler Publishers)

Magazines and Newspapers for Social Investors and Their Money

Several different periodicals cover the hedge fund industry, and one covers the world economy better than any other in the world *(The Economist)*. Add these to your media diet to help you stay current on trends in the social investment world. When you're finished reading them, be sure to pass them on to someone else or put them in the recycling bin!

- *Barron's* (www.barrons.com): This weekly publication, a sister to the *Wall Street Journal,* covers the markets and financial conditions in depth. If you want a thoughtful analysis of the news and ideas for where to invest, this is the publication to check out.

- *The Christian Science Monitor* (www.csmonitor.com): This newspaper is operated by the Christian Science church with the mission of covering the world. It's politically independent with an emphasis on substantive reporting of good news. This carries through to its business and financial coverage (with a section on money and values every Monday), so it may be interesting to many social investors.

- *E: The Environmental Magazine* (www.emagazine.com): *E* is a bimonthly magazine with features on every aspect of the environment, from vegetarian recipes to news about the plastics industry. If you care about the environment, this publication can give you a heads-up on business news and emerging issues that may affect your investing.

- *The Economist* (www.economist.com): A newsweekly published out of London, *The Economist* specializes in global business and politics, and it offers in-depth analysis of what's happening in the world and why. If you have an interest in emerging markets and issues affecting multinational companies, it's a must-read.

- *Environmental Finance* (www.environmental-finance.com): This monthly magazine examines the business aspects of climate change and other key environmental issues of the global financial industry, including markets for carbon and alternative energy. This magazine is based in London and takes a European view of financial aspects of environmental issues, including green investing.

✔ *Fast Company* (www.fastcompany.com): This monthly business magazine isn't inherently dedicated to sustainable or responsible companies. Instead, it wants to cover the most innovative businesses out there; in most cases, that means sustainable, responsible companies.

✔ *World Watch Magazine* (www.worldwatch.org): A bimonthly publication of the World Watch Institute, *World Watch* is devoted to various big-picture environmental and social issues that affect the world. This magazine publishes in-depth articles about various environmental issues and includes interesting statistics and quantitative information to complement the articles.

Blogs, Web Sites, and Other Online Social Investing Sources

The Internet has seemingly unlimited information on investing, business, and the wider world (maybe that's why it's called the World Wide Web?). Here are some of the many sites that may help you discover more about socially responsible investing; new sites are added all the time.

✔ **Biblical Responsible Investing Institute** (www.briinstitute.com): The institute provides data to allow Christians to align their investments with their faith. BRI screens about 2,000 companies for involvement in alcohol, abortion, anti-family issues, bioethics, gambling, homosexuality, human rights, tobacco, and pornography.

✔ **Boston College Center for Corporate Citizenship** (www.bcccc.net): The center approaches social responsibility from both sides. It provides resources for companies that want to be better corporate citizens, and it also operates the Institute for Responsible Investment to help investors make responsible choices. The site has a wealth of resources available to all, but some items require a subscription.

✔ **Business of Green** (blogs.iht.com/tribtalk/business/green): The *International Herald Tribune,* a European publication of the *New York Times,* offers thoughts and comments on a wide range of thought-provoking topics. The site includes many good links to institutions and private entities.

✔ **CSRwire** (vcr.csrwire.com): CSRwire provides daily updates on corporate social responsibility issues in a variety of industries. On a recent day, the site featured stories about social issues affecting pulp and paper producers, cocoa companies, the hotel industry, and electronics manufacturers.

- ✓ **Environmental Leader** (www.environmentalleader.com): This site bills itself as "the executive's daily green briefing," and it's a good source for environmental news and information and how it affects business.

- ✓ *Green@Work Magazine* (www.greenatworkmag.com): This online magazine bills itself as the premier corporate sustainability publication. It's aimed at corporate managers to help make the business case for improving their environmental performance. The site includes case studies and tools to help business professionals green up their acts.

- ✓ **Icahn Report** (www.icahnreport.com): Carl Icahn is one of the better known activist investors, regularly stirring up trouble at companies where he perceives that management isn't standing up for shareholders. Some people love him, some hate him, but his blog is good reading for investors who care about good corporate governance.

- ✓ **International Corporate Governance Network** (www.icgn.org): This is a coalition of institutional investors, academics, and activists who share information about key corporate governance issues.

- ✓ **Investopedia** (www.investopedia.com): This site offers quick definitions for different business and investing terms.

- ✓ **Morningstar** (www.morningstar.com): Want to know about mutual funds and exchange-traded funds? This is the place. Much of the information is free, although many investors may find that the premium services are well worth the cost.

- ✓ **People for the Ethical Treatment of Animals** (www.peta.org): This organization maintains a listing of companies that don't test products on animals and a separate list of those that do at search.caring consumer.com. It's useful information for investors who are concerned about animal rights.

- ✓ **Point Carbon** (www.pointcarbon.com): Point Carbon is an international energy market consultant, and this site features resources about the global carbon, natural gas, and power markets. The site provides good technical information on carbon pricing and energy consumption trends, and news affecting the global carbon and power trading markets, including glossaries and primers for nonspecialists about how the markets work.

- ✓ **Triple Pundit — People, Profit, Planet** (triplepundit.com): This site offers intelligent and nuanced (and some not-so-nuanced) views on various environmental issues, as well as links for business and financial concerns on environmental issues.

Index

• C •

BUSINESS, CAREERS & PERSONAL FINANCE

Accounting For Dummies, 4th Edition*
978-0-470-24600-9

Bookkeeping Workbook For Dummies†
978-0-470-16983-4

Commodities For Dummies
978-0-470-04928-0

Doing Business in China For Dummies
978-0-470-04929-7

E-Mail Marketing For Dummies
978-0-470-19087-6

Job Interviews For Dummies, 3rd Edition*†
978-0-470-17748-8

Personal Finance Workbook For Dummies*†
978-0-470-09933-9

Real Estate License Exams For Dummies
978-0-7645-7623-2

Six Sigma For Dummies
978-0-7645-6798-8

Small Business Kit For Dummies, 2nd Edition*†
978-0-7645-5984-6

Telephone Sales For Dummies
978-0-470-16836-3

BUSINESS PRODUCTIVITY & MICROSOFT OFFICE

Access 2007 For Dummies
978-0-470-03649-5

Excel 2007 For Dummies
978-0-470-03737-9

Office 2007 For Dummies
978-0-470-00923-9

Outlook 2007 For Dummies
978-0-470-03830-7

PowerPoint 2007 For Dummies
978-0-470-04059-1

Project 2007 For Dummies
978-0-470-03651-8

QuickBooks 2008 For Dummies
978-0-470-18470-7

Quicken 2008 For Dummies
978-0-470-17473-9

Salesforce.com For Dummies, 2nd Edition
978-0-470-04893-1

Word 2007 For Dummies
978-0-470-03658-7

EDUCATION, HISTORY, REFERENCE & TEST PREPARATION

African American History For Dummies
978-0-7645-5469-8

Algebra For Dummies
978-0-7645-5325-7

Algebra Workbook For Dummies
978-0-7645-8467-1

Art History For Dummies
978-0-470-09910-0

ASVAB For Dummies, 2nd Edition
978-0-470-10671-6

British Military History For Dummies
978-0-470-03213-8

Calculus For Dummies
978-0-7645-2498-1

Canadian History For Dummies, 2nd Edition
978-0-470-83656-9

Geometry Workbook For Dummies
978-0-471-79940-5

The SAT I For Dummies, 6th Edition
978-0-7645-7193-0

Series 7 Exam For Dummies
978-0-470-09932-2

World History For Dummies
978-0-7645-5242-7

FOOD, GARDEN, HOBBIES & HOME

Bridge For Dummies, 2nd Edition
978-0-471-92426-5

Coin Collecting For Dummies, 2nd Edition
978-0-470-22275-1

Cooking Basics For Dummies, 3rd Edition
978-0-7645-7206-7

Drawing For Dummies
978-0-7645-5476-6

Etiquette For Dummies, 2nd Edition
978-0-470-10672-3

Gardening Basics For Dummies*†
978-0-470-03749-2

Knitting Patterns For Dummies
978-0-470-04556-5

Living Gluten-Free For Dummies†
978-0-471-77383-2

Painting Do-It-Yourself For Dummies
978-0-470-17533-0

HEALTH, SELF HELP, PARENTING & PETS

Anger Management For Dummies
978-0-470-03715-7

Anxiety & Depression Workbook For Dummies
978-0-7645-9793-0

Dieting For Dummies, 2nd Edition
978-0-7645-4149-0

Dog Training For Dummies, 2nd Edition
978-0-7645-8418-3

Horseback Riding For Dummies
978-0-470-09719-9

Infertility For Dummies†
978-0-470-11518-3

Meditation For Dummies with CD-ROM, 2nd Edition
978-0-471-77774-8

Post-Traumatic Stress Disorder For Dummies
978-0-470-04922-8

Puppies For Dummies, 2nd Edition
978-0-470-03717-1

Thyroid For Dummies, 2nd Edition†
978-0-471-78755-6

Type 1 Diabetes For Dummies*†
978-0-470-17811-9

Separate Canadian edition also available
Separate U.K. edition also available

Available wherever books are sold. For more information or to order direct: U.S. customers visit www.dummies.com or call 1-877-762-2974.
U.K. customers visit www.wileyeurope.com or call (0)1243 843291. Canadian customers visit www.wiley.ca or call 1-800-567-4797.

 **WILEY**

INTERNET & DIGITAL MEDIA

AdWords For Dummies
978-0-470-15252-2

Blogging For Dummies, 2nd Edition
978-0-470-23017-6

Digital Photography All-in-One Desk Reference For Dummies, 3rd Edition
978-0-470-03743-0

Digital Photography For Dummies, 5th Edition
978-0-7645-9802-9

Digital SLR Cameras & Photography For Dummies, 2nd Edition
978-0-470-14927-0

eBay Business All-in-One Desk Reference For Dummies
978-0-7645-8438-1

eBay For Dummies, 5th Edition*
978-0-470-04529-9

eBay Listings That Sell For Dummies
978-0-471-78912-3

Facebook For Dummies
978-0-470-26273-3

The Internet For Dummies, 11th Edition
978-0-470-12174-0

Investing Online For Dummies, 5th Edition
978-0-7645-8456-5

iPod & iTunes For Dummies, 5th Edition
978-0-470-17474-6

MySpace For Dummies
978-0-470-09529-4

Podcasting For Dummies
978-0-471-74898-4

Search Engine Optimization For Dummies, 2nd Edition
978-0-471-97998-2

Second Life For Dummies
978-0-470-18025-9

Starting an eBay Business For Dummies, 3rd Edition†
978-0-470-14924-9

GRAPHICS, DESIGN & WEB DEVELOPMENT

Adobe Creative Suite 3 Design Premium All-in-One Desk Reference For Dummies
978-0-470-11724-8

Adobe Web Suite CS3 All-in-One Desk Reference For Dummies
978-0-470-12099-6

AutoCAD 2008 For Dummies
978-0-470-11650-0

Building a Web Site For Dummies, 3rd Edition
978-0-470-14928-7

Creating Web Pages All-in-One Desk Reference For Dummies, 3rd Edition
978-0-470-09629-1

Creating Web Pages For Dummies, 8th Edition
978-0-470-08030-6

Dreamweaver CS3 For Dummies
978-0-470-11490-2

Flash CS3 For Dummies
978-0-470-12100-9

Google SketchUp For Dummies
978-0-470-13744-4

InDesign CS3 For Dummies
978-0-470-11865-8

Photoshop CS3 All-in-One Desk Reference For Dummies
978-0-470-11195-6

Photoshop CS3 For Dummies
978-0-470-11193-2

Photoshop Elements 5 For Dummies
978-0-470-09810-3

SolidWorks For Dummies
978-0-7645-9555-4

Visio 2007 For Dummies
978-0-470-08983-5

Web Design For Dummies, 2nd Edition
978-0-471-78117-2

Web Sites Do-It-Yourself For Dummies
978-0-470-16903-2

Web Stores Do-It-Yourself For Dummies
978-0-470-17443-2

LANGUAGES, RELIGION & SPIRITUALITY

Arabic For Dummies
978-0-471-77270-5

Chinese For Dummies, Audio Set
978-0-470-12766-7

French For Dummies
978-0-7645-5193-2

German For Dummies
978-0-7645-5195-6

Hebrew For Dummies
978-0-7645-5489-6

Ingles Para Dummies
978-0-7645-5427-8

Italian For Dummies, Audio Set
978-0-470-09586-7

Italian Verbs For Dummies
978-0-471-77389-4

Japanese For Dummies
978-0-7645-5429-2

Latin For Dummies
978-0-7645-5431-5

Portuguese For Dummies
978-0-471-78738-9

Russian For Dummies
978-0-471-78001-4

Spanish Phrases For Dummies
978-0-7645-7204-3

Spanish For Dummies
978-0-7645-5194-9

Spanish For Dummies, Audio Set
978-0-470-09585-0

The Bible For Dummies
978-0-7645-5296-0

Catholicism For Dummies
978-0-7645-5391-2

The Historical Jesus For Dummies
978-0-470-16785-4

Islam For Dummies
978-0-7645-5503-9

Spirituality For Dummies, 2nd Edition
978-0-470-19142-2

NETWORKING AND PROGRAMMING

ASP.NET 3.5 For Dummies
978-0-470-19592-5

C# 2008 For Dummies
978-0-470-19109-5

Hacking For Dummies, 2nd Edition
978-0-470-05235-8

Home Networking For Dummies, 4th Edition
978-0-470-11806-1

Java For Dummies, 4th Edition
978-0-470-08716-9

Microsoft® SQL Server™ 2008 All-in-One Desk Reference For Dummies
978-0-470-17954-3

Networking All-in-One Desk Reference For Dummies, 2nd Edition
978-0-7645-9939-2

Networking For Dummies, 8th Edition
978-0-470-05620-2

SharePoint 2007 For Dummies
978-0-470-09941-4

Wireless Home Networking For Dummies, 2nd Edition
978-0-471-74940-0

PERATING SYSTEMS & COMPUTER BASICS

ac For Dummies, 5th Edition
8-0-7645-8458-9

ptops For Dummies, 2nd Edition
8-0-470-05432-1

nux For Dummies, 8th Edition
8-0-470-11649-4

acBook For Dummies
8-0-470-04859-7

ac OS X Leopard All-in-One
esk Reference For Dummies
8-0-470-05434-5

Mac OS X Leopard For Dummies
978-0-470-05433-8

Macs For Dummies, 9th Edition
978-0-470-04849-8

PCs For Dummies, 11th Edition
978-0-470-13728-4

Windows® Home Server For Dummies
978-0-470-18592-6

Windows Server 2008 For Dummies
978-0-470-18043-3

Windows Vista All-in-One
Desk Reference For Dummies
978-0-471-74941-7

Windows Vista For Dummies
978-0-471-75421-3

Windows Vista Security For Dummies
978-0-470-11805-4

PORTS, FITNESS & MUSIC

aching Hockey For Dummies
8-0-470-83685-9

aching Soccer For Dummies
8-0-471-77381-8

tness For Dummies, 3rd Edition
8-0-7645-7851-9

otball For Dummies, 3rd Edition
8-0-470-12536-6

GarageBand For Dummies
978-0-7645-7323-1

Golf For Dummies, 3rd Edition
978-0-471-76871-5

Guitar For Dummies, 2nd Edition
978-0-7645-9904-0

Home Recording For Musicians
For Dummies, 2nd Edition
978-0-7645-8884-6

iPod & iTunes For Dummies,
5th Edition
978-0-470-17474-6

Music Theory For Dummies
978-0-7645-7838-0

Stretching For Dummies
978-0-470-06741-3

Get smart @ dummies.com®

- Find a full list of Dummies titles
- Look into loads of FREE on-site articles
- Sign up for FREE eTips e-mailed to you weekly
- See what other products carry the Dummies name
- Shop directly from the Dummies bookstore
- Enter to win new prizes every month!

Separate Canadian edition also available
Separate U.K. edition also available

vailable wherever books are sold. For more information or to order direct: U.S. customers visit www.dummies.com or call 1-877-762-2974.
.K. customers visit www.wileyeurope.com or call (0) 1243 843291. Canadian customers visit www.wiley.ca or call 1-800-567-4797.

Do More with Dummies Products for the Rest of Us!

DVDs • Music • Games • DIY
Consumer Electronics • Software • Crafts
Hobbies • Cookware • and more!

Check out the Dummies Product Shop at www.dummies.com for more information!

WILEY